Corner Flags and

Jas Bains was born in 1963 and has spent most of his professional life working in the public sector. He is also an Associate Research Fellow at the Sir Norman Chester Centre for Football Research, University of Leicester, and is author of the *Asians Can't Play Football* report. A season-ticket holder of some twenty years at Molineux, he remains a loyal supporter of his hometown club Wolverhampton Wanderers, although he now lives in Solihull.

Sanjiev Johal was born in 1972 and has completed undergraduate and postgraduate degree courses in Birmingham and Leeds, as well as having worked as a youth worker. He is presently working towards the completion of his Ph.D. at the University of Warwick, where he is researching the South Asian experience of sport in Britain. Currently living in Edgbaston, he is a lifelong Manchester United supporter, who has become well accustomed to refuting the obligatory 'glory-boy' jibes.

CORNER FLAGS AND CORNER SHOPS

The Asian Football Experience

Jas Bains and Sanjiev Johal

VICTOR GOLLANCZ

LONDON

First published in Great Britain 1998
by Victor Gollancz
An imprint of the Cassell Group
Wellington House, 125 Strand, London WC2R 0BB

© Jas Bains and Sanjiev Johal 1998

The right of Jas Bains and Sanjiev Johal to be identified as authors of
this work has been asserted by them in accordance with
the Copyright, Designs and Patents Act, 1988.

A catalogue record for this book is
available from the British Library.

ISBN 0 575 06636 9

Typeset by Rowland Phototypesetting Ltd,
Bury St Edmunds, Suffolk
Printed and bound in Guernsey by
The Guernsey Press Co. Ltd, Guernsey, Channel Isles

98 99 5 4 3 2 1

Dedications

To my family and the memory of my late parents
Pritam Bains and Gurmit Bains – Jas Bains

To my father and mother Malkiet and Harbans
Johal, my sisters and their families, and also to the
memory of my late grandparents – Sanjiev Johal

'Clubs are spending millions in the transfer market. What we need to do is to plough some of that money back through Football in the Community Schemes and target it towards developing Asian football' *Gordon Taylor*

'There are still barriers in the game; just look at why there are no Asians playing professional football' *Ian Wright*

'Very soon you'll have the next generation of Asian lads coming through. I'm sure of it; just like once Laurie Cunningham and Viv Anderson started with black players' *Peter Reid*

Contents

Foreword
by Glenn Hoddle, Head Coach – England

Football is the world game, enjoyed around the globe by millions, regardless of their background – two hundred countries are members of FIFA, the world governing body.

I am proud to be part of a rich and diverse multicultural and multifaith society, and one in which football is played by our many communities. For over twenty years Britain's players of African and Caribbean descent have made an enormous contribution to the game, at both club and national level. The fact that they have done so in the face of, at times, great antagonism and hostility only adds to my admiration and respect.

Whilst applauding the contribution of our black footballers, I must confess to being both surprised and intrigued at the lack of a breakthrough by Asian players into the professional game. Travelling extensively as I do around the country, it is hard not to notice the skills and enthusiasm of Asian youngsters playing football on car parks and wasteground around football stadia. Contrary to some popular opinion, these children are revelling in games of football, and not cricket or hockey.

As England Head Coach, it is essential that the talent which I have at my disposal is the very best available. We are facing a major period of change in the training of our young players, following the publication of Howard Wilkinson's *Charter For Quality*, and it is vital that the new structures provide equitable access to all sections of the population.

I know that a great deal of work is already being done at grassroots level, through partnerships with clubs, local authorities and community organizations, to involve Asian youngsters in organized football. We all need to ensure this work is developed to provide proper access to the ranks of professional football in the future.

I firmly believe that we are now beginning to see a change in which the old stereotypes of Asian players are being broken down, and football is realizing the tremendous potential that exists in Asian communities. I look forward to seeing Asian players coming through at the highest levels of the game, with the ultimate aim of a place in the England team.

Glenn Hoddle
July 1998

Acknowledgements

We would like to thank all those people who allowed us to share in their experiences, and are grateful for their stories, thoughts and ideas that all helped to shape the book. The contributions of Dilawar Singh, Ramon Mohammed, Jaspreet Gahia, Jimmy Khan, Tarlock Singh, Abdul Rashid, Sohan Singh Cheema, Coventry Sporting FC, Hema Chauhan, Fiaz Khan, Jas Jutla, Jim Weir, Tariq Mahmood, Tony Sanghera, Mashuq Hussain, Abdul Karim, Robert Singh, Shapal Rahman, Hasib Ashgar, Pumi Singh, Mumtaz Hussain, Mohammed Khalid and Kash Taank are greatly appreciated. We would also like to thank the following people for the advice, input and support they offered at various stages of the book's life: John Williams, Rogan Taylor, Les Back, David Davies, Piara Powar, Ben Tegg, Mick King, Rashid Mama, Sean Perkins, Tim Crabbe, Gordon Taylor, Brendon Batson and Raj Patel. Special thanks to our editor Ian Preece, who had the foresight and professionalism to ensure the book was successfully realized.

Introduction

During the summer of 1998, 20-year-old Arprit Mishra joined the throngs of hopeful overseas trialists seeking to make their mark in English professional football. But Arprit's particular circumstances had little in common with those of his fellow aspirants. Admittedly, he was beguiled by the ubiquitous World Cup hype, and was anxious to become part of the sporting riches that putatively lay in wait on English shores. Eager to exhibit his talents before a coaching fraternity keen to dip into foreign markets, Arprit was well aware that his services would be available to interested clubs at no charge. He was, however, not a by-product of the Jean Marc Bosman Ruling. Arprit's most distinguishing feature was that his route to England was not via the Continent, or even South America, but direct from Delhi, not exactly a renowned hotbed of international footballers.

Considered by the Indian national selectors as one of the country's brightest soccer talents, Arprit had decided to seek his footballing fame and fortune in the old mother country. His arrival in London signalled the beginning of a six-week exhibition period, during which Arprit paraded his talents to any club willing to hire that elusive breed: a top-class Indian footballer. Since this was his first time in England he was somewhat oblivious to the debate raging among his exiled compatriots concerning their relationship with the British game. The absence of British-Asians from professional football, and the misguided view that Asians held little regard for the game were issues that held little significance for Arprit. He could not work out what all the fuss was about; in India he had only ever really played football, and no one had tried to block his progress.

His appetite for football had been further whetted by extensive coverage of the English Premier League on satellite television in India, care of Mr Murdoch. Despite the recent efforts of certain nationalist Indian politicians to try to sever the close ties between Britain and India, association with anything British retains strong resonance in many Indian circles. For Arprit, the rigours of a long plane journey had been lessened by thoughts of stepping out at Old Trafford and Anfield, facing the likes of Ryan Giggs and Michael Owen, both of whom enjoy a strong following among India's growing number of soccer converts. Typically, it is the flair players who feature highly among the pin-ups of young Indian fans; Owen and Giggs being joined by Ronaldo, Ariel Ortega and Zinedine Zidane. Close proximity to the emerging footballing nations of Iran and Japan has added the likes of Ali Daei, the prolific goalscoring Iranian centre-forward, and Hidetoshi Nakata, the Japanese midfield dynamo, to the expanding list of new sporting heroes.

Arprit began his search for soccer stardom by surfing the Internet back home in India. He followed up those cyberspace enquiries with a few speculative phone calls to managers seeking top-class players at knockdown prices. His early intention had been to seek out those clubs with young playing squads, those who appeared to show little interest in the overinflated transfer market. So it was as a result of such reasoning that Peterborough, Plymouth, Torquay, Cardiff and Swansea were among the initial group of clubs that Arprit approached. Surely a foreign-sounding name, together with the inevitable press headlines refering to some kind of PASSAGE TO INDIA or the JEWEL IN THE CLUB'S CROWN, would do wonders for attracting additional media coverage, thus increasing match- and season-ticket sales, and possible increased corporate sponsorship. Getting through to football managers in the early part of the close season proved to be relatively straightforward, particularly when their secretaries were informed of the 'foreign interest' on the line. But within a few minutes of that first telephone call Arprit had come to terms with the reality faced by many of his fellow Asian footballers, namely that people in the game are not often convinced that Asian people play football. As Arprit's own words testify: 'The manager was genuinely very surprised when I told him we play football in India, and that we have our own national league, in which professionals play. He thought we only played cricket, hockey and tennis.'

This perceived non-association with the game is just one of the common misconceptions held of Asian people, yet nothing could be further from the truth. *Corner Flags and Corner Shops* seeks to explode these common myths by demonstrating just how central football is to the lives of Britain's diverse Asian community. This book has been written out of frustration and passion: frustration at the ignorance with which the relationship between football and British-Asian people is regarded; and the passion that the game has imbued within us and which holds us all hostage.

The truth is there is mass Asian participation in football on a variety of different levels. From playing the games in their thousands to travelling around the country supporting their favoured teams, from working as executives within professional football clubs to buying them out completely, British-Asians, be they young or old, rich or poor, male or female, have either dipped their toes or fully immersed themselves in the dynamic waters of the modern game. The journey from earnest amateurs to recognized professionals has not yet been completed by the insurgent band of British-Asian footballers. However, as *Corner Flags and Corner Shops* attempts to illustrate, we are on the threshold of new sporting times. The shackles that once proscribed Asian access to the game are no longer in place. Professional football does now have a clutch of aspiring young Asian players, each with their own history, their own aptitude, and their own ambitions. Time and fortune will tell just what kind of impact they will make on the national (and possibly international) soccer stage.

Arprit Mishra's entry into the combative climbs of English League football seems to have been timed perfectly. At the time of writing Arprit is deliberating over the choice of three professional clubs (Plymouth, Millwall and Barnet), all of which have invited him to join them for pre-season training. Whilst overjoyed at the prospect of playing professional football, Arprit will still have to contend with the issue of the work permit. Presently the rules stipulate that non-European citizens need to demonstrate that they have played in at least 75 per cent of their national team's fixtures in the preceding twelve months, a criterion which precludes Arprit's eligibility.

A similar situation involving another Indian player arose some two years ago when Coventry City offered a young Indian goalkeeper, 20-year-old Didar Sandhu, a full-time contract. Despite his outstanding potential, his shortage of international experience would deny him the required permit to work in this country. Integral to Coventry City's argument was that, as a role model, Sandhu would do much to help other Asian players make a breakthrough into the game. As City chairman Bryan Richardson confirmed: 'It's on this basis that we've pushed Sandhu's claims for a permit.'

If he finds himself similarly denied, Arprit has shown his determination to succeed by proposing to undertake his postgraduate studies in the United Kingdom. This way he may be able to combine playing football on a semi-professional basis with completing his academic pursuits. Whatever the outcome, he deserves success for his application and ingenuity. Could Arprit Mishra become the first professional footballer to have been recruited in England via the Internet? Multiculturalism and multimedia – two words and two concepts that embody the Zeitgeist of the late-twentieth century merging in the popular global arena we call football.

1 Football Through Our Ages

A Shot from the Seventies (Jas Bains)

Charlie George's brilliant winning goal, those limply flowing locks and his prostrate mock-crucifixion celebrations during Arsenal's 1971 FA Cup Final triumph over the team of the seventies, Liverpool, were to strike a chord with a whole nation (Liverpool and Tottenham supporters, excepted). In those days the FA Cup Final was still cause for special household gatherings, as the whole family cleared the dinner table in preparation for the big event. The occasion was a bit like the Queen's speech at 3 o'clock on Christmas Day. The build up to these peculiar institutions was similar, only the opening of presents was replaced by a host of celebrity interviews, footage of the two teams relaxing at their hotels, and similar pre-match tasters. As the players entered Wembley Stadium in their flared trousers and blazers, a genuine lump in the throat emerged to intensify that moment of anxious sentimentality, enabling you to momentarily pretend that it was your team taking part in the afternoon's proceedings. Thanks to wall-to-wall TV coverage, FA Cup Final day will never be the same again. On that sunny afternoon in May 1971, though, it seemed as if the only person unaware of the events at Wembley Stadium was my mum. I can't say she hated football, although she had just cause in our house, but she was always somehow seemingly oblivious to it, carrying out her daily tasks around us. That afternoon she would occasionally make passing reference to this strange-looking long-haired chap, describing him as a Hell's Angel. In those days Hell's Angels were on a par with skinheads and mass murderers when it came to choosing friends. And, with the Black Country renowned for its production and consumption of heavy metal bands (Ozzy Osbourne's Black Sabbath being at the helm) the sight of a Hell's Angel type figure on television did little to appease her anxiety. As extra time approached, those frequent, and annoying, forays into the living room began to subside as she discovered the significance of a match that had exceeded our earlier predictions of being out of the living room by 5 p.m (her appointed time for removing crisps from the corners of the settee and the sweet wrappers from wherever we had planted them). Later, as if to demonstrate her understanding of her new found conversion, whenever my younger brother Raj and I went off to play football she would inform people that we had gone to emulate Charlie George: *'Merey munde Charlie George bunnan geh'* (loosely pronounced Punjabi translation). Although I am sure she was being her usual endearing, motherly self, there was certainly more than a touch of affectionate ridiculing. You could say that we did our level best to live up to her high billing, only our football had more in common with another famous Charlie, Charlie Chaplin that is.

If George was the national icon, his soul-mate at a local level (our immediate locality being Wednesfield, near Wolverhampton) was Derek Dougan, aka, the Doog. The Doog, supporting his long dark hair, droopy moustache, Irish brogue, and not infrequent brushes with authority, was a legendary figure in the town. But above all else, he was a goalscoring hero. As a child, I was raised on a staple diet of David Wagstaffe for starters, Derek Dougan for the main course, and John Richards for my dessert. Waggy would begin the proceedings by mesmerizing the opposition full-back. Having left the poor chap completely in knots, Waggy would spit him out at the far post where in gazelle-like fashion, on those wind-tunnel legs, the Doog would leap to the stars and knock the ball down invitingly into the oncoming path of King John to smash the ball past the helpless keeper. It was vintage 1970s Wolverhampton Wanderers (how I long for a return of those days). One full England cap between them – Richards (1) and Wagstaffe (0) – was nothing short of scandalous.

We would rehearse this move for hour upon end, taking it in turns to be Waggy, Doog and King John, only it used to be a touch contrived because Waggy was exclusively left-footed (I once saw him play 'keep it up' football with a box of cigarettes. It was the greatest exhibition of football ever seen in the old Molineux car park). But then that's the beauty of the game: you can be just about anybody and anything in order to imitate your heroes.

Backing on to our long but thin rear gardens used to be this high stone-cladded wall, which was topped with barbed wiring. Beyond that boundary was an assortment of cylinders containing chemicals and mass stockpiles of steel tubing – registered trademarks of the heavily industrialized Black Country. We grew up to become well accustomed to this industrial landscape, not only because we lived next door to it, but also because the site was immediately adjacent to our football ground; an area of about 200 square feet. Pivotal to our ground were metal gates, standing about 10 feet high and 20 feet wide, known as the 'Green Gates'. The flow of football was regularly disrupted by the passing of motorists on their way to the working men's club. Given our relatively weak negotiating position we accepted, for the most part with good grace, the greater priority afforded to the club's visitors. During the summer months foundry workers, careful not to hurt us with their steel toe capped boots, came to join in our games. Occasionally we were even joined by the foundry manager who talked to us for long periods about the halcyon days of Wolverhampton Wanderers. Stories of those pioneering floodlit games involving the defeat of foreign opposition like Honved, Moscow Dynamo and Real Madrid used to send a shudder down my spine (and still do). I cannot help but attribute my near infatuation with the club, in part, to a man we only knew as the 'Big Gaffer'. Playing fantasy football down the local wasteground was one thing, the task of fulfilling those same ambitions on the school playground was an altogether different proposition. Here the rules of football fantasy engagement were determined by others, mostly the bigger white boys, and in the early days we, Asian boys, had to accept our lot as admiring observers, a bit like the girls, only our outward admiration hid our real feelings.

Wards Bridge Comprehensive, now listed among the 5000 other playing fields lost to Thatcher's sporting revolution for schools, has no particular claim to fame, although Olympic Gold Medallist Tessa Sanderson OBE was once a pupil. Actually, the very location where Tessa began her javelin-throwing career is now a housing estate; still, at least it's named after Tessa. The school's catchment area was drawn from two quite distinct residential locations. From the north tended to come those children who lived in the more upmarket suburban area, while from the south came those who lived in the older terraced houses and the big high-rise tower blocks. Needless to say, the white children, with the exception of the more deprived, who occupied the tower blocks, came from the north. On the other hand, virtually all the black and Asian children lived in the older terraced dwellings. As school closed for the day the environment resembled a sort of scene from an American 1950s high school, with the white pupils heading for waiting parents' cars at the northern exits, whilst the non-whites trudged off in the opposite direction. Of course, it was never as stark as the impression portrayed, but there were marked differences in the respective lifestyles. Over the next decade the balance between both communities began to shift quite markedly, as the economic aspirations of an ever aspiring Asian community saw them relocating to the suburban northern parts, occupying the housing left by a white community relocating to the rural outlying regions of Staffordshire. For us Asian pupils, those early schooling days had defined a clear role with regard to playground etiquette. We were made to understand our territorial claims by the older white boys. Encroachment of the said protocol was not deemed an act of great wisdom.

Assuming the dominant position in the playground had come to rest with the white pupils by virtue of strength in numbers, history and an acknowledgement on our part that it was somehow theirs by right. Clearly the legacy of the British Empire and the subcontinent's subservient sponsorship of that bygone age still remained intact in Wolverhampton in the 1970s. Typically, during break periods and lunchtimes, us Asian boys would congregate in small huddles in an attempt to portray an out-of-sight community, hoping to avoid any likely assault. In hindsight these small gatherings were a foolish way of avoiding trouble. Fortunately we managed to avoid many beatings, largely assisted by our black friends who threatened to join us against any attack by the whites. The regular sweet rations to our black friends' leadership was a small price to pay, besides which there were enough sweet-shop-owning fathers to sensibly rotate the supply. The host community's outpourings normally extended to mockery of our gatherings as war dances; at least that was an improvement on past gatherings of the Singhs, who were said to be practising for the choir. One particular benefit of the gatherings was that they enabled the young ones to enhance aspects of the Punjabi vocabulary that were not taught in Punjabi classes.

As we congregated in the far distant corners of the playground, the white boys in their obligatory flares and long hair occupied centre stage to display their footballing (and other) ambitions to the admiring female audiences. Occasionally one of us would be asked to participate, usually as the stand-in goalkeeper, but, for the most part, we remained onlookers as the white knights in Wolves scarves (no United or Liverpool scarves in those days) cast themselves as the Doog, Waggy and King John to play out our combined fantasies. Enter Surjit Singh, aka Shita.

Surjit, like most of us, lived in the blocks of crumbling

terraces. The nickname Shita originates from his mother's insistence to shout him in from the streets, only she had no idea that the shortening of her son's name would give cause to ceaseless embarrassment to her favoured offspring. To all intents and purposes he was one of us, and yet there was something wholly different about him, something that was difficult to identify. We admired him because he had this remarkable ability to fit most comfortably among all groups, regardless of race or sex. At break-times he would emerge from the bike shed smokers' group and flirt with the girls as they chatted about the sartorial merits of Led Zeppelin and Slade. He was at his most impressive when playing in the playground football matches, where he would often arrive at a point to suit him and not at the pre-ordained times set by the organizing committee. Quite simply, he had bags of self-confidence and no shortage of footballing ability. Even as a junior member of the playground XIs, he would give the older boys the run-around, prompting muted shouts of *savvash* (well done) from the watching Asian entourage. His favoured party piece was to nutmeg an opponent and then turn around to do it again. Quite how he survived regular beatings from his beleaguered opponents is something that will always baffle those who saw him.

Surjit did not realize was that his confident performances on the playground were gradually helping to shift the balance of power in our favour. Arguably, what he was doing was removing a few traditional myths held about Asians. His footballing abilities were by no means confined to the playground. He went on to have trials with a host of top clubs, including Manchester United, Wolves and Queens Park Rangers. It would be nice to say that I had the privilege of playing alongside this famous footballer. Sadly, this is not a possibility, for Surjit joined the ranks of the many hundreds of other nearly made it Asian professional footballers. I can, however, afford him another tribute, albeit less glamorous. There are many of us who owe a great deal to him for the way in which he helped to assert the

Asian identity, and with it self-respect and dignity, in what was for long periods a seemingly lost cause. It goes without saying that he was more Charlie George than Charlie Chaplin.

The Asian Pitch Invasion (Sanjiev Johal)

Whilst Jas and his Asian peers struggled to assert their right of occupation in their school playground, my schoolyard experiences of football, and those of my contemporaries, were somewhat less compromising. Having little idea as to who exactly Charlie George, Derek Dougan and Dave Wagstaffe were, the footballing icons who shaped the memories and enslaved the imaginations of this generation had their origins both on their own doorsteps and much further afield. Resisting the ritual absorption into local team support, Asian boys growing up in the late seventies and early eighties succumbed to the lure of the glamour clubs, Manchester United and Liverpool. These kids were drawn away from tradition, away from the teams supported by their older brothers, cousins, uncles and fathers (in my case, the local team being West Bromwich Albion). Whilst players such as Cyrille Regis, Brendan Batson and Laurie Cunningham promoted the growing influence of black players in the professional game, young Asians from that region were swapping items of great value just to get Panini stickers of Kenny Dalglish, Ian Rush, Graeme Souness, Frank Stapleton, Remi Moses and Bryan Robson. But even these magnificent players were subordinated by an idolization that went beyond the English game. The exotic names of Zico, Socrates, Platini and, almost ubiquitously, Diego Maradona bore the idolatry burden and privilege of my Asian peers.

Like most other kids I'd play football in the school playground, in the local park, in the side-streets and on any other patch of clear tarmac that was available. Before I started at my secondary school I was provided with another arena in which I could explore and develop my soccer talents. At that time my parents ran a retail clothing and textile business from a shop in Oldbury, which also had living quarters (well, there was a living room that doubled as a kitchen, two bedrooms and a bathroom). Earlier on in our time in these premises we had my grandfather and two of my uncles living with us – us being my parents, myself and my three elder sisters. My father worked various shifts at a local foundry in between sorting things out with the business, which my mother ran whilst raising four young children.

When I reached an age when football started to become more than just a game and increasingly a passion, I wanted to play it anywhere I could. If it was too cold or wet outside, then I would take my plastic 'flyaway' football and kick it around the shop. Our premises were shaped like a perfect pitch. There were shelves and clothing rails all around the walls with a large playing area in the middle. On one wall there was a large stand on which the loose textiles (used for Asian dress such as the salwar kameez) were displayed. This stand made for perfect goals into which I could score at will. Either one of my friends would come around to the shop and have a game, or my youngest sister Raj would stand in as a goalkeeper. My older sisters Susan and Bal would not allow themselves to indulge in such boyish activity, especially in full view of the passing trade. The shop-floor football action would only be interrupted by the sound of the bell above the front door, which signalled the arrival of a customer. The football would stop and my mum would come out from the rear living quarters, yell at us for playing with the ball in the shop and then proceed to serve the awaiting customers. This was strange business practice, but one that the local clientele became warmly accustomed to.

Whilst the shop space gave me the chance to nurture my nascent soccer skills, it was at Bristnall Hall High School that my peers and I replicated the recognized genius of players such as Zico, Platini and Maradona. We didn't want to be a Dougan, with his limp long hair and a sad droopy moustache; we wanted to be like Maradona and Zico, with tanned skin, silky skills and elusive coolness. Whatever else Derek Dougan may have been, he wasn't really cool, not in the way that Maradona or Zico were cool – they were more than football players, they were superstars.

By the early-to-mid-eighties white pupils were not the sole masters of the school playing field. Access to the football pitch no longer involved putting oneself in grave physical danger. Instead, the Asian and black schoolboys assumed one patch of the field for themselves; there they played their own game with teams made up almost entirely of black and Asian players. Some white kids would join in with this group, usually those who were already within these ethnic groups on some social level, but non-blacks and non-Asians took part in a separate match. Early on in my time at this school, the white part of the pitch was much the larger, and was watched by most of the girls. However, as the decade wore on, the greater ethnic presence amongst the lower years began to manifest itself in the classroom and in the playground. By the time I was in my final year at secondary school, the Asian boys were the first on the playing field. They were the first to get the football out and first to organize a game. It was no longer the case that we had to wait for an invitation to play alongside our white peers, or fearfully start a kick-about in a small corner of the pitch. Now we had our own team, we had our own crowd of female admirers and, most importantly, we were appreciated as amongst the best footballers in the year.

It wasn't the case that we had extended our ethnic ghetto to incorporate the playing field, the field itself was a patch of grass where kids of all colours and creeds enjoyed the game of football. In fact, teams were organized around the very difference between white kids and non-white kids. Crudely put, when we played football at break-times and lunch-times, it wasn't fourth years against fifth years, nor Form 5E against Form

5L, but Blacks v Whites. It was as simple and as clearly defined as that. If you had white skin, then you were on the Whites side, if you were anything else, if you were anything other than white, anything other than English, you became embraced by the black team. In truth, there were only two or three Afro-Caribbean players in the Blacks team. The Blacks were made up mostly of Asians. Retrospectively, there was a political statement being made here by the non-white footballers in the school. They were defining their allegiance to, and defining themselves by, the broad black struggle, and the more potent black power movement; they were expressing a solidarity that united non-white citizens in their shared struggle against systematic oppression, cultural ignorance and racial intolerance. Or maybe they were merely organizing a group of young lads into two easily discernible teams for a decent game of footie. The latter may be somewhat nearer the mark, but politics is never completely disengaged from sport.

Due to the lack of in-depth ability amongst the Whites, the better white players refrained from regularly participating in this daily fixture for fear of humiliation; this, in turn, meant that the Whites were little competition for the dominating Blacks, who had a wealth of talent to call upon. The apolitical nature of this contest was highlighted when a few of us from the Blacks made free transfers over to the Whites. One of the players who 'went over to the other side', Harjinder Malka, was a talented player who played every game as an exhibition, not allowing any consideration of the score to distract him from his Fancy-Dan swaggering on the pitch. Another defector to the Whites was Peter Panayai. Peter (also known as Chippy because his dad owned a fish and chip shop) was of a Greek-Cypriot background, a detail which, allied with the non-whiteness of his appearance, made him eligible for the Blacks. The fact that he was the most gifted player in the school only served to reiterate the Blacks' dominance over the Whites.

The third member of this treacherous triumvirate was myself.

Admittedly, I was not in the same class of a Panayai, but at the time of my switch to the Whites side, I was in the greatest footballing form of my entire life, a level of consistent perform-ance that I have never managed to reproduce. Panayai himself rated me as being in the top three players in the school at the time. During this period the three of us transformed the ailing, lifeless Whites team from obliging whipping boys into a force to be reckoned with. We were not intimidated by the Blacks, they didn't scare us with their violent tackles, threatening shrieks and numerical majority, we used to be part of all that. There were too many players on the Blacks team who wanted to do their own bit of showboating to impress the girls, and this meant that not everyone in the side got their chance to steal the limelight. Once we had swapped over to the white camp, their lack of conceit and arrogance (and ability) gave us ample licence to indulge our vain exhibitionism: taking on and beating four or five opponents at a time, attempting outrageous shots on goal, pulling off amazing flicks and tricks to leave the bullying Blacks begrudgingly bemused. Many of the Blacks players weren't best pleased at being made to look like imbeciles, especially by me. Some thought that I should have been playing for the Whites anyway since I didn't listen to bhangra music, had some white mates and had unusually pale skin that denied my ethnic origin. I experienced the strangest form of verbal racial abuse from guys who themselves were Asian, I was often accused of being a 'white Packi'. A 'white Packi', now that would confuse a Combat 18 member.

Further transitions have taken place since the late eighties involving Asian kids and schoolyard football. The story con-tinues at a multi-ethnic comprehensive school in Walsall in the West Midlands, namely, Joseph Leckie.

This last decade has seen a proportional increase in the number of young Asians in secondary schools in particular regions. In certain parts of Birmingham, Leicester, Bradford, London and other cities, Asian schoolkids outnumber their white counterparts. Asian families have established themselves in local communities, and have, naturally, sent their children to schools within those areas. This, combined with the migration away from these areas by white residents, has engendered a concentration of Asians in particular enclaves. Joseph Leckie is in a part of Walsall that fits just this kind of model. With Asian kids no longer representing the numerical minority, their presence no longer regarded with intolerant suspicion, and their cultural peculiarity no longer viewed as an exotic other, they have asserted a new order to the school playground. Whereas in the seventies Asian youngsters grouped together in small bands and were largely isolated from the white hub of the playground, in the eighties they formed larger groups, often incorporating members of other minorities as well as their white contemporaries, and moved to the active centre. The nineties have reflected a wider, almost global tendency, to strengthen the bonds between those of the same ethnic background in the face of growing pressures towards mass homogenization.

Asians at Joseph Leckie are not a unified, homogeneous group. They are made up of kids whose parents hail from Pakistan, India, Bangladesh and even east Africa. They are differentiated in terms of religion into Sikhs, Muslims, Hindus and Christians. Further points of separation are plotted along the lines of residential location, particular sections of the Asian community living in greater, more concentrated numbers in certain areas of the school's vicinity. All this has meant that these particular subgroups have tended to stick together and this ethno-specific unity is reflected in the school playground. In such a school the Blacks v Whites match would be a virtual impossibility. The predomination of a 'black' team over a 'white' team would make it a complete one-sided affair. Football games are played between different groups of kids from the various religious, social and ethnic bands. They understand that the fundamental of a good soccer match is to have two equally matched teams of roughly the same number, so they put together two teams for themselves, made up of young Asians, Afro-Caribbeans and white lads. This doesn't detract from their association with their own kin-group, they still hang around with their fellow kinsmen, but football requires of them an active participation with pupils they may otherwise regard as different, as not being of the same background as them, even as an untrustworthy 'other'. It would truly be one of the game's greatest glories if football could dispel such notions of 'otherness' and inward alienation. It must be said that the high proportion of Asian pupils at Joseph Leckie manufactures a playground football culture and politic that is not necessarily replicated in other schools in other parts of the country. With the Asian community having spread out to many other regions of Britain, this third generation of British-Asians is now located in schools away from the inner cities, away from a concentration of an Asian populace, and clearly in a minority. The politics involved in the pursuit of cultural integration and identity for pupils at these types of schools vary considerably from those in the established ethnic 'reservations'. When a school such as Joseph Leckie has to accommodate a substantial number of various ethnic minorities, it immediately establishes a need for a revised set of conditions that will ensure the existence and development of its varied school population. A look at the top club teams in Europe reflects this type of coming together of different nationalities and different ethnicities under one nominal banner to represent one unified football team. Juventus, AC Milan, Manchester United, Newcastle United, Arsenal, Barcelona, Chelsea and Real Madrid, among others, all boast a significant number of players who do not hail from the country of the club they play for, but nevertheless are invaluable members of their squads. So-called 'foreign' players adorn the bedroom walls of Joseph Leckie youngsters. Cantona, Bergkamp, Zola, Vialli, Ronaldo and Sneekes (well, maybe not the last one) are superstar players whose 'foreign-ness' has become subsumed into the football kudos: they are fantastic footballers first, and non-British

31

second. The kids at Joseph Leckie get together and pick teams by and for themselves. Players are picked on ability, popularity and hardness; with the hapless and the feeble either left on the sidelines, or made to suffer the petty indignities at the feet of the most skilful players and at the fists of the most volatile. By comparison, Blacks v Whites seemed so much more democratic and just.

2 Asians Can't Play Football

The 1980s saw a transformation of the UK's political, social and economic landscape. Where the 1970s saw local government as a key partner in the political process, the 1980s, under the Prime Ministership of Margaret Thatcher, brought about an altogether different role. This resulted in a transfer of power away from town halls over to Whitehall, and with it went the platform from which local authorities were able to develop their multifarious equality agendas. Faced with years of sustained cuts in expenditure to ever-diminishing public spending programmes, local authorities were forced to re-examine priorities. Consequently, lesser emphasis in town halls was afforded to issues such as race equality, anti-poverty and other social welfare programmes, all of which were considered to be peripheral to the core service provision. Instead, local government continued with the task of rationalization, a euphemism for cost-cutting measures. This resulted in the closure of elderly persons' homes, community centres and voluntary sector projects – many of which were working in the anti-racism field. Local government, the institution that had provided the vehicle for change to the race agenda, was now, involuntarily, too preoccupied with its own survival. There followed little actual encouragement, or for that matter interest, from the government in addressing issues of race, unless it was the introduction of more anti-immigration legislation. The race issue was fast disappearing from the horizon, and more significantly from the national consciousness. Enter football.

A culmination of events, notably the tragic disasters at Heysel, Hillsborough and Bradford, the escalation of terrace violence and the aimlessness of a game torn apart by power struggles and unhealthy balance sheets didn't exactly sound like a cue for developing a race agenda. But with the prospect of new television money looking as if it could provide much needed salvation, football's authorities were well aware of the need to clean up the image of the game. A direct effort was being made to enable football to appeal to wider television audiences, and to key new groups being targeted as new spectators of live football (i.e., women and families). Whilst the Football Association, the game's most senior and governing body, was certainly aware of the growing problem of racism in football, it had made no specific efforts to deal with the issue. In this regard the situation was helped by the coming together of two other organizations, the Commission for Racial Equality and the Professional Footballers Association, both of which shared a commitment to addressing the problem.

By 1993, with an ever-growing membership of black players (approaching 20 per cent), a black deputy (Brendan Batson) at the helm, alongside Chief Executive Gordon Taylor, and a former black player (Garth Crookes) serving as Chair before retiring, the PFA were growing increasingly concerned about the levels of racist abuse suffered by black professional footballers. Following his appointment in 1992 as the new CRE Chairman, Herman (now Sir Herman) Ouseley outlined a new approach for the Commission. Central to the Commission's revised thinking became the undertaking of campaign-orientated missions. It was thought this change in policy direction would also help to raise the profile of the Commission. Sir Herman's keen interest in football was also recognized to be a helpful factor.

At the time of writing, some encouraging progress has been made in addressing the issue of racism in the game. The subject has a firm place on the national football agenda, demonstrated by a number of measures, the most recognized and prominent vehicle being the government's Football Task Force, which has made the issue of racism its first major priority. Specifically, the Task Force was asked 'to make recommendations on appropriate measures to eliminate racism in football and encourage wider participation by ethnic minorities, both in playing and spectating'. In March 1998 the Task Force reported back on its findings; a process that had involved consultation across the country and with a wide range of supporters and organizations interested in football.

The Task Force report commented that the game's ruling bodies, clubs and players must accept responsibility to protect and promote an image of a game that 'unites the world'. Although pointing out that racism is 'not a problem of football's making', it accepted football's potential in helping to challenge racism and xenophobia – '[in football] there is no more powerful vehicle to take to young people a positive message of tolerance and respect'. In identifying a number of positive recommendations for proposed action and implementation the Task Force has not only underlined the importance that it attaches to tackling racism in the game, but has also fuelled the optimism of those who continue to look in from the outside. By outlining an ambitious programme the Task Force has made a commendable attempt to take forward this issue. However, its words of wisdom will count for little without the full backing of those it must ultimately call upon to translate the words into meaningful action. It also maintains an enduring and high profile through the national anti-racist campaign/organization – Kick It Out. Supporters everywhere continue to pursue a variety of local initiatives and sympathetic sections of the press continue to give it wide coverage. Moreover, as the nation continues to discuss the merits or otherwise of a federal European Union, it is encouraging to see the UK offering to share its anti-racist football experiences with other member states. Clearly this is an area where the UK has a great deal of knowledge and experience which could be beneficial to French, German, Dutch, Italian, Belgian and Spanish counterparts. However, perhaps the greatest service of the anti-racist footballing initiative has been to help alert the national consciousness to the threat that racism brings to a supposedly civilized society.

By the late 1970s and early 1980s, the position of the British ethnic minority population had been further undermined by the economy's entry into structural decline, which subsequently, but not solely, lead to increased unemployment. These factors combined, and were imbued with an aura of ill-informed paranoia, and engendered the inception of nationalist far-right factions. The rise and relative fall of these groups could be plotted through their territorial claims over football grounds.

Paul Thomas, a leading figure in the supporters' anti-racist movement, witnessed at first hand these developments. 'At Leeds United, my own club, National Front paper-sellers appeared regularly from the mid-1970s onwards, building up a considerable block of support. By the late 1970s, the NF's approach had become highly sophisticated, with the appearance of *Bulldog* magazine. Its key feature was 'The Racist League', where fans of various clubs were ranked according to the ferocity of their racist chants.

At Wards Bridge School the hooligan exploits of some of the older boys became enshrined in playground folklore, and as a result they were afforded a certain glamour and reverence, which exceeded even that of the school's best sportsmen. This allure was fashioned in part by a perceived toughness and in part by their roles as ambassadors. When they were out in the field doing the business, they were seen as flying the flag on the part of Wards Bridge and Wolverhampton Wanderers, both of which we could all identify with. The emerging influence of the National Front, however, saw to it that us non-whites could never really be part of the scene, as 'Paki-bashing' and 'Coon-hunting' became integral to their missions as well as the distribution of racist propaganda.

During one weekend every non-white household on our road received a NF leaflet. The road was made up of small terraced houses, with neat little boundary walls fronting on to the pavements and adjoining alleyways, which served as communal routes to half a dozen houses either side, and resulted in a strong and close community spirit. During warm summer evenings, while the kids played football on the road, our parents would exchange tales whilst inspecting over their tomatoes, carrots and coriander. That NF leaflet had the desired effect in that it brought about a panic reaction. Immediately visions were conjured of the aftermath that had spread following Enoch Powell's infamous 'Rivers of Blood' speech, some even made exaggerated forecasts of a compulsory repatriation scheme. Subsequent events at school were to reveal the source of distribution had indeed been our former 'heroes'.

The events described in this chapter begin in and indeed owe a debt to the 1980s football supporters' movement. Their emergence coincided with a period when the game appeared to be stumbling from one crisis to another. In their book *Out of Time*, Alex Fynn and Lynton Guest, when talking about this period, refer to the 'stupefying ineptitude engulfing the English game'. With hooliganism serving to undermine the safety of spectators and those living in close proximity to football grounds, allied with the government's open hostility towards the naïvely homogenized band of 'football fans', the situation was crying out for community action. In the absence of appropriate measures being forthcoming by the authorities, and the totally irrational depiction of all football fans as hooligans and racists, the football supporters' community took it upon itself to influence the course of future events. The formation of the Football Supporters' Association after Heysel (1985), the campaign against the introduction of compulsory ID cards and the football fanzine phenomenon all contributed to a new way in which football supporters were to be perceived in the future.

At certain clubs, like Leeds United, anti-racist fan-led

37

campaigns started to appear. Appalled at the racism, a small group of fans began to produce their own anti-racist literature. Backed by local politicians the Leeds Fans Against Racism were able to apply pressure on the club, and within a couple of years the presence of right-wing groups outside of Elland Road had disappeared. It would appear that for the most part the problem has been contained, however the club still manages to attract a hardcore following who persist in racist chanting, particularly at away matches. The events at Leicester City's Filbert Street in 1997 being a case in point, when Leicester City fans were taunted with the chants: 'You're just a town full of Pakis.'

More significantly, supporters' efforts had helped to encourage a new spirit of co-operation between the football authorities and the loyal band of football followers. Coupled with this was the fact that the market place of the 1980s demanded all customer service industries to apply premium value where clients were concerned. Whilst consulting supporters about matters such as kit design, match day programmes and refreshments was welcomed, the rapidly developing state of the game required consultation over more central issues affecting the future of the game.

Nineteen ninety-three saw the launch of the Let's Kick Racism Out of Football (now abbreviated to Kick It Out) campaign. During the early period of the advisory group's work the subject of Asians in football was not a prominent point of discussion. This was due to a number of reasons. Firstly, it appears that no individual or organization represented on the advisory group actually knew very much about the subject. Secondly, the Asian community, unlike the black community, had no formal representation in the game. Whilst the black community could call upon any number of former black players, the lack of playing success would deny the Asian community a similar facility. Though there was some evidence, both empirical and anecdotal, that a not insignificant number of Asian people were watching live football every week, no one from that community had yet come forward to play an active part in the supporters' movement. Another factor that served to conspire against the Asian interest was that little was actually known about the relationship between the Asian community and football. A combination of these factors had led those within the Asian community to conclude that the starting point for any constructive discourse was one of disenfranchisement. The basic premise applied was that our lot could only improve. It is against this backdrop that the story behind the *Asians Can't Play Football* project unfolds.

In the summer of 1992, I (Jas Bains) together with my close friend Raj Patel, formed the Midland Asian Sports Forum. Our initial impetus had been provided by sections of the media who were attempting to portray Pakistani Test cricketers as ball-tampering cheats, on the strength that they thought the process of reverse swing was only possible through some form of witchcraft. At that time the Shakoor Rana–Mike Gatting incident resurfaced, as did Ian Botham's comments about sending mother-in-laws to Pakistan. What made this whole episode particularly galling was that the alleged antics of the Pakistani cricket team were being remorselessly pilloried, and yet the similar tactics of Australian Test cricketers were generally accepted because they were said to be part of the 'Aussies' natural competitive character'. This interpretation was particularly telling because it implied that Asian cricketers should conform to their subservient stereotype, and that any behaviour outside this accepted norm was something the British media had real difficulty in coming to terms with. Although it was a cricket issue that initially brought the group together, football soon assumed a position of predominance within the Forum's dialogues, in particular, the absence of Asian players from professional football. Over the next couple of years it became our charge to produce a recognized piece of work in this area; but exactly how does a proposal document get translated into a commissioned piece of work? As far as the project was concerned, the answer to that particular question is as revealing as the execution of the research and the production of the report itself.

The absence of research into the area of Asians in sport raised some challenging questions, not least of which were in the academic world. The relatively poor record of Asian sporting achievement may be a contributory factor here. The British sporting experience shows how Afro-Caribbeans living in Britain have utilized sport in vastly differing and more successful ways to the Asian minorities. Given that British Afro-Caribbeans are proportionately over-represented in the national sporting domain, there is evidence to suggest that for black people in Britain sport can provide a route for advancement, be it high profile or not. One acknowledges this to be a general statement that does not consider the limitations that still operate for black people within the professional sporting arena, and the persisting restrictions and prejudice that prevent progress in other fields. Rather than indulge in our condemnation of others for failing to address this matter, we decided to view the situation as an opportunity for the promotion of enlightenment. Preliminary investigations also strengthened our belief that the best way to proceed was for the Asian community to assume ownership of this issue and to maintain a stake throughout the process – a case for empowerment. Having overcome this important hurdle, the task of securing the support of key agencies and organizations, in particular prospective sponsors, began. Using the benefit of Raj Patel's knowledge and experience of these matters, we estimated the actual cost of undertaking this project would be in the region of £20–30,000. With no funding to speak of, the prospect of raising such a sum of money seemed a million miles away.

The art of fundraising is a specialist skill. Little did we realize what we were entering into. Dealing with statutory bodies was one thing; asking for money from the private sector, quite another. Whereas sections of the public sector were known to be sympathetic to supporting anti-racism work, there was as yet little evidence of similar sympathy in the private business community. This period also coincided with the very early days of the Let's Kick Racism Out of Football campaign, when it was still unclear as to the extent the Football Association, let alone commercial sponsors, would commit funding to anti-racism projects. As those with fundraising experience will know, the psychological boost of the first payment into the account is immeasurable, almost regardless of the amount. It supports your conviction that the project will be delivered. That was precisely the effect of the first cheque – £500 that came courtesy of Leicester University. For the next four months, except for the university's money, not a further penny materialized, then things somehow began to fall into place.

During those four months it was rare for a single day to go by without receiving yet another letter of rejection. They were, for the most part, polite, but still contained those dreaded words, 'We regret to inform you . . .' Depression was occasionally broken by a piece of good news in the form of strong and encouraging letters of support from the likes of Herman Ouseley and Keith Vaz, MP. Vaz must get inundated with similar requests for assistance from other members of the Asian community in Britain, who look upon him as having real influence. Sadly, Vaz's position is a reflection of a democratic system that consistently fails to reflect the changing make-up of the British electorate. Even in parliamentary constituencies in which the make-up of the population is largely non-white, thus avoiding the scare-mongering claims of those who suggest that the adoption of non-white candidates represents a high-risk strategy among white voters, the numbers of black and Asian candidates have been pitiful. In the current Parliament Vaz is joined by only three other Asian MPs: Ashok Kumar, Marsha Singh and Mohammed Sarwar, a situation which equates to about one MP for every 450,000 Asian voters.

Vaz, to his credit, dispatched a suitably worded letter of support. In the interests of political neutrality a similar letter of support was sought from the then Conservative Sports Minister's office. Unfortunately, a reply was never received. Although the CRE were not able to allocate funding due to cuts to its budget, Herman Ouseley offered to lend his support and influence in other ways. He offered to contact Richard Faulkener to see if the Football Trust could look favourably upon our application. Herman Ouseley's role in respect of the wider anti-racist football campaign should not be underestimated. There is little doubt that Sir Herman's drive and determination to see the work through and to actively engage the footballing authorities in the process are key reasons behind its ultimate success. En route he has encountered many difficulties and obstacles, particularly from the Football Association, initially, and subsequently the Football League, but to his credit he has managed to steer the ship through these choppy waters.

The support of Keith Vaz and Herman Ouseley was a timely and significant boost to the project. One of the most commented upon aspects of the project is its title, *Asians Can't Play Football*. Indeed, in the best traditions of shameless marketing ploys, the report's title helped to raise the profile of the project. The inspiration for it came from the American basketball comedy *White Men Can't Jump*. In the film, actor Woody Harrelson plays a basketball player who sets out to disprove the theory that because of their inability to leap as high as black basketball players white players are inherently not as good as their black counterparts. Throughout the movie, the otherwise very capable basketball player (Harrelson) is shown to reinforce the stereotype as he struggles to perform the sporting art of a slam-dunk, a move where a player jumps above the hoop to ram the ball through the net. Eventually, Woody is able to perform this act and, more significantly, the stereotype is successfully dispelled.

Although, at this time, little was known about the factors

behind the absence of Asians from professional football, one of the more commonly cited reasons was the suggestion that Asian footballers were physically unsuited to the demands of the professional game. Unfortunately, the irony of the title didn't always register with people, and some individuals approached the report as a testimonial document that confirmed an eternal maxim. On one particular occasion I was made to realize the impact this project was having on a group of people that one would not normally have assumed to be the most informed and inquisitive students of the Asians-in-football issue.

At an FA Cup tie in December 1996 between Walsall and Burnley at the Bescot Stadium, my two nephews and I were making our way towards the home enclosure when we were confronted by a small group of Burnley fans. Clearly the worse for drink, one of the Burnley fans approached us to offer some racist obscenities, the sort of profanely dumb monosyllabic tirade that almost parodies itself. This verbal volley was devastatingly returned, which appeared to surprise the Burnley fans, who suspected that their victims would cower away, accepting the abuse as a duty we were expected to fulfil. Then the same drunken Burnley fan blurted with an air of assured ignorance, 'I thought that you fucking Pakis said you couldn't play football.' Whether this polite English gent was making direct reference to the *Asians Can't Play Football* report is debatable, although the report had been in circulation for several months by then. Retrospectively, the fact that the issue had common currency in popular discourse, the fact that it was negative discourse, made it all the more impressive, meant that it had transcended the minds of its progenitors and leapt from the pages of its capsule. Asians in football had become something that was talked about by different people in different settings.

This illuminating incident occurred some time after completion of the report. The process that saw its production was made idle by seemingly interminable financial problems. The most painstaking task was organizing the funding to do the research. Ultimately all the best intentions and deliberations would count for nothing if the pioneering researchers failed to secure the necessary funding. Fortunately, in the coming months, we would be well served by our boundless enthusiasm and a determination to succeed.

John Williams at Leicester University identified Paul Hughes, Sponsorship Director for Carling, as someone who could be sympathetic to the project's aims. Carling were already funding the Premier League fans' survey, undertaken by Leicester University. Following several weeks of trying to track Hughes down, the initial hope appeared to be fizzling out in the duration of one phone call as Hughes, whilst interested in the project, claimed he could not justify financial support on commercial grounds. Given that Hughes was on the verge of putting the phone down, a swift but plausible retort was urgently required. There was no time to seek empirical evidence, the case had to be instinctive and personally emotive. I informed him that contrary to popular opinion, many British-Asians did in fact enjoy the odd tipple or two. In particular, the strong drinking traditions of the Punjabi Sikh community were brought to his attention. (It did not seem a good time to introduce the teetotal Muslim community. Nor was it a particularly good time to divulge my own alcohol-free habits – having never managed to acquire the taste, I can barely distinguish between a pint of bitter and lager.) In the course of the frantic telephone conversation, I strategically (and shamelessly) placed considerable emphasis on the large quantities of alcohol consumed at some Asian weddings, and the fact that most traditional corner shops, many of them off-licences, were run by Asians. (If you can't beat the stereotype, then deploy it for as much cynical profit as you may possibly procure. It does, however, seem that white guests never cease to be amazed at the copious amounts of liquor that are wantonly guzzled at Punjabi Sikh weddings – the fact that it is free may be linked to its consumers' over-indulgence.) A week later Hughes rang to say Carling were on

44

board. In doing so they became the single largest contributor. Upon consideration, Hughes had felt that it was in Carling's interests to be seen to be supporting the project because of the high number of small Asian retailers in the alcohol-vending business. This was good PR, and therefore good business for Carling. There are times when being of an ethnic minority persuasion can be manipulated into a point of argumentative strength, rather than a point of enforced subordination.

With £8000 (Carling – £5000, Churches Commission for Racial Justice – £2500, University of Leicester – £500) already committed to the project, the prospects were looking up. However, the target figure still fell some 22,000 short of the original total. Several months had passed since an application had been made to the Football Trust. Although Trust Administrator Mary Finney was sympathetic in recognizing the unfairness of the long waiting period, the matter was outside her control. The postponement on two occasions of the meeting scheduled to discuss the application added to the tension. Finally the call came. The Football Association, Professional Footballers Association and the Football Trust had agreed to award £4000 each towards the project. Subsequently, we were informed that PFA Chief Gordon Taylor had taken the initiative by pledging £4000 if the FA and Football Trust would make similar commitments. The early identification of Taylor as a likely sympathizer and ally had been vindicated. The news was greeted with a mixed response. On the one hand the £12,000 was seen as an enormous boost to the project, but it still left a £10,000 shortfall. More importantly, the football authorities were the last remaining hope of securing the outstanding monies. It was now crunch time for the project; a decision had to be made as to whether or not to proceed. In truth there was no real option. Too much time and effort had already been expended to abandon the proposal. It was as though the obsessive spirit of Victor Frankenstein had become infused within the minds, bodies and souls of the united members of the Midland Asian Sports Forum.

We had become subsumed by our own creation, a creation that only existed in our informed collective psyche, a disparate idea that required the vital injection of funds to bring it to life. If it meant cutting costs to the bone then so be it, and that's exactly what happened, it became Operation Shoestring. But who cared? The cause was what really mattered.

Almost twelve months on from the project start date (July 1996) the exercise was completed. So, what was the verdict? Was there a charge for the game to answer? And if so, in what way was the game culpable? The report's authors were mindful that the absence of any examples of overt racism in the publication could be cited as a means of vindication for those claiming that there was no discrimination against Asians. During the last twenty years a combination of factors (i.e., a general improvement in awareness of ethnic minorities, and legislative measures), have helped to reduce acts of outward racial prejudice. That is not to suggest that this type of behaviour has been completely eliminated, far from it. Instead, those with racist intentions are forced to display less crude methods of undermining their victims. Arguably, this is a more insidious form of racism because it is both more difficult to detect and prove. The *Asians Can't Play Football* report argued: 'Advocates of the "colour blind" school of thought propose that discrimination is impossible if "race" is not considered to be an issue and if everybody is "treated the same". Given this view it is unnecessary to amend practices and structures which have served host communities well but which now, in fact, provide barriers to minorities. A more productive and realistic approach, however, recognizes everybody is not the same, and if people are to be given equal opportunities to achieve then consideration must be given to the variety of social and cultural backgrounds people are drawn from.'

Unsurprisingly, those in the game considered Asian footballers to be physically inferior, less interested and less talented than their white and black counterparts. Given the club representatives' lack of contact with Asian people generally, and footballers specifically, on what basis were they formulating such opinions? The report went on to assert: 'How can the skills of an Asian footballer be judged fairly if those with responsibility for recruitment into the professional game hold such ill-conceived notions? It is fortunate that some of these prejudices have not been applied to professional footballers drawn from other racial groups, particularly those that apply to size and strength. If they had, would we have been denied the opportunity of seeing the talents of such outstanding young white players as Barmby, Fowler, McManaman and Anderton, to name but a few? The notion that British-Asians are uniformly smaller and weaker than other groups in Britain is, in any case, simply wrong, as any visit to watch Asian "parks" football will confirm. Also, the fact that Middlesbrough have spent £4m on a 5ft 6in Brazilian who is hailed as a major new international talent in the sport might be expected to put down, once and for all in this country, the notion that size and strength are everything in the British game.'

Nowadays the road to becoming a professional footballer is fairly clearly defined. Although some continue to gatecrash through the semi-professional circuit, the overwhelming majority will gain their entry via the established route. This begins with the school team and progresses through representative football. Playing junior boys' club football is also considered to be an advantage. At this point a potential professional footballer is spotted by a scout and is invited to join a club's centre of excellence, where he may be offered associate schoolboy forms. On reaching school-leaving age a boy is offered an apprenticeship, and if he is considered to be good enough, within a year or two he enters the world of professional football. The report's research showed that while Asian boys were playing football in comparable numbers to all other groups, for the most part that participation was taking place outside the recognized system. Consequently, this was a key factor in why Asian boys were being overlooked by clubs' 'scouting' operations. The report also highlighted that the Asian community were less aware of the recruitment system than other groups. Asian children were generally found to have been less likely than their white and black counterparts to receive the practical and moral support of parents. In the absence of parental encouragement, the role of physical education teachers can be very important. However, there was some worrying evidence discovered during the course of the research about some PE teachers: 'At secondary school there was an even balance between Asian and white pupils. In my time only two Asians ever made the City boys' representative team. It was as if the PE teacher thought we (Asians) were OK to play for the school's team but not the City boys' team. Every year our school's nominations for the City boys' team only ever seemed to be the white boys. The whole thing always seemed just too much of a coincidence to me.' (Asian respondent).

The next test for the *Asians Can't Play Football* report was in ascertaining the footballing authorities' response to its findings. These were, after all, the findings and observations of a small independent group of people with no formal links to football, a self-generated and self-sustained ensemble who, it could be argued, had an axe to grind with the footballing establishment. Uppermost in our minds was this feeling that our efforts would be undermined because of our lack of a concrete connection to the world of professional football. There was also concern about the reputation football has of not being particularly receptive to the opinions of outsiders (i.e., non-footballing people). However, the Forum's worst suspicions never materialised. In a most welcome outcome the FA, PFA and others associated with the game made very encouraging noises about the report's findings and future significance for the game.

But even then the group were left seemingly less than satisfied. More than two years on from publication many of those misgivings are retained.

With respect to the report, although being a thorough and competent piece of research, it must be said that the findings were not of earth-shattering proportions. As far as we were concerned, the report had produced a relatively predictable set of results. Yes, there was evidence of institutionalized racism. No, the Asian communities were not disinterested observers of our national game. Yes, cultural factors had been identified as a barrier within the Asian community. And the disproportionate levels of interest shown in our report could, in part, be attributed to the novelty factor. It may also have something to do with an admission of guilt and responsibility, albeit not openly admitted to, by those in the game.

Whilst *Asians Can't Play Football* may have helped to act as the catalyst for action, its impact would be somewhat limited were it not for those actively working within the field, people like Rashid Mama. Mama, as he is affectionately known in local football circles, has for over ten years trudged the streets of inner city Leicester in pursuit of the cause. In that time he has run several hundred (probably a few thousand) coaching sessions for Asian youngsters, often without payment, but never without enthusiasm. It is only recently that Mama's work has begun to be properly appreciated by Leicester City Football Club, and he has been appointed as a member of the club's centre of excellence team. In 1995 Leicester City Council instigated the Leicester Asian Soccer Initiative (LASI), a scheme designed to increase the participation of Asian youngsters in football. There is nothing complicated about LASI, indeed its strength lies in simplicity. It involves targeting coaching sessions in areas of high Asian concentration, using local Asian coaches. If, in future years, Leicester provides a rich supply of Asian professional footballers, football will owe a huge debt to the likes of Mama, Mick King, and their team of dedicated officers. For Mama, read any one of hundreds of others working away without recognition and reward, but without whom the dream can never be attained. In the meantime there is a confident

49

prediction that a small number of Asian players will make that elusive breakthrough and finally put to rest the misguided notion that Asians can't play football.

3 Asian Games

For more than thirty years, sport has been used by Britain's Asian communities as a means of maintaining social and cultural cohesion. Other events and occasions held similar significance, such as weddings and religious festivals. For the British Sikh community this situation has been achieved via the Asian Games, or tournaments as they are more commonly known. Those responsible for the development of the tournaments saw them as a method of fulfilling two main objectives. The first was to provide opportunities to participate in sport in an organized and friendly but competitive environment. Back in the sixties access to sports clubs and facilities was particularly difficult for a community who were encountering problems of social, cultural and linguistic exclusion. Those insecurities made the task of approaching a local football club very difficult. They were also handicapped by an uninformed, common perception among the indigenous population that Asian people did not play football. After all, unlike their Afro-Caribbean counterparts, there was no evidence of Asian role models, no players of international repute whom white British people could identify with. Whilst Afro-Caribbean immigrants also encountered problems when playing in white football teams, they were undoubtedly assisted by their ability to converse in the same language, the wearing of similar clothes, and the worshipping of the same nominal God. Above all else there was no doubt in the minds of white footballers that the black British community could play football. Watching the likes of Pelé,

Garrincha and Eusebio on their television screens, and live during the 1966 World Cup, had ensured that.

The second task that the Asian Games purportedly undertook was to serve as a means of maintaining links between the distanced descendants from the Indian state of Punjab. In times of social, cultural and economic isolation, the need to develop strong community networks was seen to be important in consolidating fragile confidences and restoring morale. The opportunity to meet and empathize with fellow exiled compatriots was a valuable early stepping stone in the establishment of Asian communities in Britain. Subsequently, community networks were also to play an important part in the development of Asian businesses. According to Sohan Singh Cheema, a founding member of the tournaments, the latter objective was even more important than the former. 'We were very new to this country and were unsure of ourselves in this foreign country. In some of the towns, like Coventry, by the early 1960s there were a few hundred Asian families, so we began to feel a bit more confident, but in some of the other towns our [Sikh] community was still small, and maybe they didn't have the same confidence. By getting together we could share our thoughts about "home" and what was going on back there. I think that people sometimes forget how difficult it was for us to adjust to this country.'

It would be reasonable to suggest that the founders of the tournaments were ahead of the times. They identified sport to be an important vehicle to channel the energies and ambitions of an Asian youth being nakedly exposed to a nation where sport was an integral part of the cultural fabric. Let us not forget the majority of Asian immigrants were from rural rather than urban communities, where sport was seen to be a leisurely pastime for small children. Beyond the cities and colleges, organized sports, like football, cricket, hockey and athletics, were only accessible to the privileged few. Also, with the exception of hockey, none of the subcontinent nations had made its mark on international sport. The success of the Indian and Pakistan national cricket teams was to come much later. To understand the background and ethos to the first Asian tournaments one has to trace the events back to India, 1919.

On 13 April 1919, an incident occurred that was to shake the foundation of Indian faith in the bona fides of the British Government. British rule in India had been determined by the Defence Act of India. However, the Act was only intended to last until the end of the First World War. Once the war had ended there was a degree of optimism among many Indians that the British would relinquish part, if not whole, control of India. As subsequent events would unfold, this confidence was sadly misplaced. The legislation that was to supersede the Defence Act – the Rowlatt Bills, as they came to be known – provided no encouragement for independence-seeking Indians. Instead they recommended the most extraordinary powers for dealing with sedition, as is evidenced in the following statement: 'It is not desirable at present time to allow trials of these revolutionaries or other seditious mongols to be protracted by the ingenuity of counsel and drawn out to inordinate lengths by committees and appeal procedures.'

The prejudicial spirit of the Rowlatt Bills legislation is aptly summed up in the popular statement of those days: 'No *dalil* (no argument), no *vakil* (no lawyer), no *apil* (no appeal).' Not surprisingly the legislation led to mass scale protest and demonstration. Earlier in 1919 Sir Michael O'Dwyer had been appointed Governor of the north India state of the Punjab. On April 13 Brigadier General Dyer, instructed by Sir Michael, policed a gathering of around two thousand people at Jallianwala Bagh, in the Sikh holy city of Amritsar, who were attending a non-violent public meeting. The meeting was being held on Vaisakhi, an important day of cultural and religious festival, a celebration in the Sikh calendar commemorating the annual harvest period. Without warning Dyer blocked the only exit of an area enclosed by high-house walls and ordered his troops to uniformly open fire. Within minutes, approximately five hundred people were ruthlessly killed or grotesquely wounded. Innocent, unsuspecting men, women and children were slaughtered without mercy or reason. These events were to have a particularly profound effect on a young man named Udham Singh. Singh was shot in the arm while rescuing a friend. He vowed to inflict his personal revenge, and a greater moral justice on O'Dwyer. Following a meticulous and rather painstaking process, Singh eventually infiltrated the then closed ranks of English society, and seized the opportunity to assassinate O'Dwyer at Caxton Halls, London, in 1940. Although it had taken him twenty-one years to complete his mission, in doing so he had subjectively avenged a national, indeed universal, travesty. Three months later Udham Singh was convicted of murder and subsequently hanged. The name and deeds of Udham Singh would be forever etched in the hearts and minds of Indians, particularly Punjabi Sikhs. Upon his martyrdom, he was posthumously assigned the honour of having his name prefixed by the Punjabi word for martyr. He had become Shaheed S. Udham Singh. Along with other Indian Sikh nationals who also gave their life to the Indian independence cause, particularly Shaheed Bhagat Singh and Shaheed Kartar Singh Sarabha.

The idea of bringing together Asian sporting teams from other towns to play in sports competitions was first established by the Sikh temple in Smethwick (one of Birmingham's, indeed Britain's, first Sikh temples). In 1965 Smethwick Temple organized a small tournament at nearby Victoria Park involving kabbadi (Asian tag sport, seen today on Channel 4) and volleyball. The original participants were teams from Coventry, Wolverhampton, as well as the host team. Thereupon was established a format that has continued to play an important part in the British-Asian sporting calendar to this day. As a mark of respect for the late Punjabi freedom fighters, the title Shaheedi was conferred upon the Games. During the relatively brief history and lifetime of the Games significant changes have taken place to the tournaments, and in some respects they are a microcosm of the wider changes that have affected sport. The original spirit of the Games – friendship, fraternity and participation – is less in evidence today, as over the years the idea of winning has become of overriding importance. Nowhere is this better exemplified than in the professionalism debate. The two major attractions at the Games are the sports of kabbadi and football. In the case of kabbadi, for more than twenty years various teams have engaged top players from India to come and play in the tournaments. During their stay in England, in return for playing in the tournaments, these kabbadi players will be provided with free accommodation, meals and pocket expenses. Although football teams have not been recruited from India, it is common knowledge that incentives are provided for some of the best players. To give but one example, during the early days of the tournaments a football team would select its players from the local town, whereas these days it is not in any way peculiar to see players from as far afield as Bradford or Leeds playing for Birmingham, Leicester or Wolverhampton teams. The underpinning influence here has been sponsorship, particularly in regard to football.

Arguably, sponsorship has always played its part in the tournaments. Many participating teams have benefited from donations to help purchase kit or even assist with travelling expenses. Given that the tournaments are held far and wide across England, teams have been very grateful for such support. In the past the donations came from one primary source – the local gurdwara (Sikh temple). However, in more recent times, the bulk of sponsorship has come from the Asian business community. In financial terms the quite significant contribution of Asian business bears no comparison with the occasional donation of a few hundred pounds from the local gurdwaras. The role of Asian business in football is discussed in more detail elsewhere in this book, although it is worth making the point here that the actual contribution is probably much greater than we may realize. There is no doubt that sponsorship has been beneficial in improving standards and organization, but it has caused divisions between the traditionalists, who do not like the increasing influence of the business community, and the non-traditionalists, who argue the Asian Games would be a distant memory were it not for the intervention of Asian businesses. Currently each of the eleven national tournaments are held over a weekend between late May and late July, featuring five separate football competitions, in order of rank: 'A', 'B' and 'C' bands, under-14s and under-16s. The tournaments are held in locations with a significant Asian population, namely Leamington Spa, Gravesend, Derby, Slough, Barking, Coventry, Reading, Leicester, Wolverhampton, Bedford and Birmingham. The absence of a major tournament in northern England reflects the concentrated location of the Sikh community in the Midlands and the South. In total, anything up to a thousand adult and youth footballers can be involved during a single event. Yet despite this vast array of footballing talent on display, the tournaments have been notorious for failing to attract the attention of professional football club representatives. This situation may be attributed to three main reasons. Firstly, the tournaments outside of local Asian communities tend not to be particularly well advertised. Secondly, club scouts have argued that it is difficult to assess the relative abilities of a tournament player in a playing environment where it is difficult to gauge the overall standards. They also argue that most of the better players are too old to be seriously considered by professional clubs. And, thirdly, generally speaking, British-Asians continue to be perceived as an insular community – and in many ways the idea of Asian tournaments tends to reinforce this view. Asian footballers are therefore regarded as being happier and more comfortable when playing in their 'own' company. Some people argue that the principle of the Asian Games 'legitimizes' the views of those professional football club representatives who allege that the object of recruiting Asian players is partly, if not wholly, futile, because 'they prefer to play in their own company'. Sadly, such a position overlooks the specific history and social and cultural context of these tournaments. What it also does is to ignore the obvious enthusiasm of the players who play in mainstream football as well as the Asian Games. Indeed, it speaks volumes for these players' love of the game that they are prepared to play all year round, year after year. It's an enthusiasm for football that one would struggle to find in other communities. Another important development has been the appointment of qualified match officials to all 'A' band matches. In the past too many games have been marred by violent incidents, a situation attributed to a lack of firm handling by match officials who, up until recently, were mainly non-qualified volunteers from the tournament organizing committee. Participation in the Asian Games is not solely restricted to fit, active and energetic sporting 'players', but these players do, however, provide the spectacle for the greater mass of lesser-committed sports fans to engage with.

Tournaments encompassed, and continue to encompass, varying degrees of importance and participation for the different age groups of Asian males (this is discussed in greater detail in Chapter 9). Since female participation in the tournaments was tacitly outlawed on all fronts, any variety in the crowd was in the ages of its constituents. The Punjabi-Sikh bias was substantial enough to allow non Punjabi-Sikhs (Hindus, Pakistanis, Bengalis) to become subsumed into their jovial collective. Sport was the homogenizing agent in this masculinized arena. However, the way that older Asian men enjoyed the tournaments was quite different to a young Asian child's appreciation of the Games which, in turn, was rather different to the manner in which Asian adolescents and young men partook of the sporting festivities.

Back in the sixties and seventies the enigmatic tournament weekend was a time when normal conditions of everyday life were turned on their head and a revised rule of subversive excess assumed governance. Whilst toddlers and younger children were left at home under the supervision of mothers, grandmothers, aunts and sisters, young boys (from the age of around 5 or 6 upwards) were allowed to accompany the other menfolk to the Games. Here they found themselves set adrift in a bustling world of littered grass, male-bonding and strange vocal noises emanating from large speakers above Portakabins. Upon entering this new dimension, fathers rapidly relinquished any physical or chastising grip that they may have held over their sons. Fathers and male guardians were faced with the moral quandary of watching grown men in tight shorts, covered in oil, slapping each other, and getting rapidly drunk on a variety of alcoholic beverages, or, spending the day conscientiously watching out for and tending to little terrors persistently enquiring as to exactly why those large men were chasing each other vigorously across a field. Basically, getting drunk whilst watching a good game of kabbadi, or looking after the little lad?

So the sons ran around unsupervised, screaming and shouting with other young boys, and getting up to as much mischief as they could possibly cram into an anarchic few hours. Without any disciplined or often sober paternal guidance, tournaments represented an opportunity for young lads to indulge in the kind of behaviour that would ordinarily be strictly prohibited or at least met with a stern word or two. Many kids would have dressed up in their Sunday best to attend the Games. It wasn't the Games *per se* that warranted such formality, but it was often the case that you would be visiting relatives if the tournament was being staged away from your city. However, fine clothes and new shoes did not prevent youngsters from wrestling in the mud, climbing trees, playing football and gener-ally ending up resembling a bunch of Dickensian street urchins. Whilst the organized sporting events such as football, volleyball, tug-o-war and kabbadi took place around them, young boys 'organized' their own sports matches. Official football tournaments for young boys (under-16s, under-14s and under-12s) are a relatively recent phenomenon and are restricted to players affiliated to recognized teams who are registered in the tournament. Wherever and whenever any volleyball match was waiting to be played, or had just been played, you could guarantee that a small group of boys would be trying in vain to hit the ball over the comparatively sky-high net. On realizing that they did not possess the power or prowess to effectively play the game, they could be seen resorting to wildly kicking the soft volleyball around the court and over the now tamed net. This lasted only until an official, a player or any other adult came along. No matter, for there were balls that were purposely designed to cope with the stresses of being kicked about to be found in abundance. Although there were often two, three or even four football matches being played at any one time during a tournament, the odd spare pitch could always be found somewhere. It was on these temporarily vacant pitches that small groups of young boys would play their own mini-football tournament. Full-size goals (no jumpers and T-shirts here, these were goals with posts, a bar, nets and everything) were used; well, actually, one full-size goal was used because the other one was way too far down the other end of the pitch. Indeed the size of the goals themselves (in comparison to the less than mature frames of the youngsters) meant that scoring goals was quite a simple task, involving merely evading the minuscule figure in between the uprights. This was the beautiful game played with beautiful abandon and brutish wanton.

With the onset of the late teen years in young men comes the inevitable upsurge in hormonal activity, apathetic cynicism and the irresistible drive to prove one's manliness, or rather, to disprove one's unmanliness. In locations like Birmingham and Southall, tournaments provided the venue for young Asian men to parade their particular gang membership and united strength. From the late seventies through to the mid-eighties such places accommodated separate gangs from within the Asian male community, gangs that were often engaged in petty 'disputes', occasionally spilling over into violent confrontations. But violence was not the main objective for most groups. Membership of these gangs signalled your allegiance to a certain kin-group from a particular part of a city, and symbols and 'badges' were worn that set you apart from the others. Many young Asians associated with such groups simply because they were from the same area and it was the 'done thing'. For those who fell under the fashionable spell of a false gang ideology, being part of the gang was just as important as not being white, or not being old, or not being employed. Many were foolish rebels with due cause. If you told someone that you were from Smethwick, you would be asked whether or not you were in the Smethwick Mob (the local gang), or if you knew such and such a person from the Smethwick Mob. This was a way of identifying the region in which you lived, but antagonism began to surface when two or more gangs would exist and operate within the same region. So, at tournaments, the different gangs would attend the event to display their dominance of a given area, showing themselves to have a greater and more dynamic following than the others. By comparison, playing tag in the mud and running around screaming doesn't seem quite as childish as it did before. Much of this adolescent exhibitionism was contained to the collective flexing of muscle, and did not cause any major disruption to the spectacle or competitive participation of the event.

For the many Asian adolescent males who did not attend the tournaments as symbols of gang cohesion, there were also fleeting moments of freedom from parental jurisdiction. It was now OK to have a can of lager because your uncle, or your dad's friend had said, '*Leh ah peelah*' (loosely translated as, 'Go on, drink it'). With your father somewhere else in the grounds, and most probably quite inebriated, this represented a chance to drink copious amounts of free alcohol, only for your father to get the blame once you had managed to find your way back home. Your mother would interrogate him as to how he could be so damned irresponsible and careless to allow you to get in such a state, yet you knew that your mum just couldn't understand the liberating ethos of the tournaments. You were drunk, your old man was drunk, you had watched some footie and kabbadi, had a few laughs with the lads, belched, burped, farted and celebrated the pathetic contrived pretences of modern manhood. Of course, wives and mothers were never impressed.

Apart from the free beer, tournaments were a place where you could meet your friends, watch friends play football, or even play in games yourself. Local teams are often accompanied by a loyal entourage that follows the team around the country during the tournament season. When the team plays at home, there is the added expectation of success, which is visibly apparent in the hordes of supporters: in addition to the regular stalwarts, many other friends, relatives, neighbours and friends of neighbours venture down to the tournament at such times. For visiting opposing teams this is often quite daunting, facing a crowd of predominantly middle-aged Asian men keen to vicariously indulge their sporting fancies in a display of kabbadi expertise, and, of course, eat, drink and be merry before the Sunday evening sunset and normal, work-oriented order would remorselessly resume.

Gone are the days when people brought their own home-cooked pots, chapattis and dahl with them to the tournaments. Sitting down on blankets and having a picnic used to be an integral part of the events. Typically, mothers and daughters would slave over the oven whilst fathers and sons prepared themselves for the abundant pleasures that lay ahead. As many spectators came from outside the town, local families were expected to ensure that their food containers carried enough to serve the masses. Local gurdwaras, recognizing the long distances many had travelled, also served up free refreshments. The spirit was communal, convivial and served to confirm the best traditions of Punjabi hospitality. Today, people's taste buds are more likely to be gratified by the fast food brigade, as sizzling samosas are served up with hot dogs and burgers. It may well be more efficient and hygienic, and no doubt more profitable, but somewhere along the line tournaments seem to have lost the old romance created by the chaotic clean-up operations involving half-eaten chapattis and spilt dahl everywhere.

Such occasions tended to be as much a festival as a football tournament, as great numbers turned up in order to meet up with out-of-town relatives as well as to watch the sports events. The earlier lack of interest and knowledge of football among some spectators became both a source of legendary amusement and frustration for footballers. It was not uncommon when watching a match to hear spectators greet the kicking of the ball at great height and distance as a highly commendable feat, shouting '*Savasheh – eh munda budhiah player heh.*' (Well done! That boy's a good player.') In contrast, a clever pass, interception, or piece of exciting dribbling would often pass unnoticed. Modern footballing audiences are, however, altogether more enlightened as to the esoteric complexities of the game. Their ability to appreciate the finer points of football very much reflects the changing make-up of tournament followers. Whereas in the past spectators had a greater tendency to move between the kabbadi arena and the football environment, people are now much more inclined to stick to their preferred sport. For thirty years a handful of teams have dominated the tournament scene, most notably Southall, Smethwick Rangers, Wonder Vaults, Mahal Warriors, Punjab United, Punjab Rovers and Supna. Each of the above clubs has made a special contribution to the tournaments and to local Asian communities. Their individual histories contain many memorable situations, events, stories and characters.

Punjab Rovers

One of the first major areas of re-settlement for Asian immigrants in Britain was Wolverhampton, a town renowned for its heavy manufacturing industry. The work environment was often dirty, hot and polluted, but these immigrant workers were a grateful and compliant people willing to work under almost any conditions. Until the late 1950s relatively few Asian-born children had migrated to England. For most children the social isolation and disadvantage brought about by their late arrival into the formal state education system meant that school was often a matter of compulsory attendance and little else.

By the early 1960s the numbers of Asian children in local schools had begun to grow appreciably. Given the popularity of football in schools and in the streets, it didn't take long for young Asian boys to become infused by football fever. Wolverhampton's Asian community had settled in two main locations in the region. To the north of the town they had first settled in the Whitmore Reans district, immediately adjacent to Molineaux, home of Wolverhampton Wanderers. To the south they congregated mainly in Wednesfield, a small town containing a number of districts, including Park Village. Both locations provided a springboard for the launch of two of the country's first Asian football clubs. In subsequent years both Punjab United (north) and Punjab Rovers (south) were to become fierce local rivals and join the élite band of Asian football clubs in the country. The footballing Asian community of this locality had replicated the soccer rivalry that had festered for generations in many other parts of the country. Manchester had United and City, Merseyside had Liverpool and Everton, Birmingham had City and Villa; now Wolverhampton had Rovers and United. For many of the Asian boys whose families had settled in Park Village, playing football in the nearby Fowlers Park quickly became part of their daily routine. On pleasant evenings upwards of thirty Asian youngsters would put down makeshift goals and play into the dark hours. Because many of the team were 14 years old when they first became involved (this was 1966), the team were able to play together for a number of years in the Wolverhampton Youth Service Under-18s League. Those early days provided many uncomfortable experiences, but a strong sense of camaraderie and unity kept them together and consolidated their collective spirit. Many of the problems were as a result of white footballers not having come across Asian people before. The racism was altogether more overt than it would be today, but after four years in the Youth Service League the club were in a position to run junior and adult teams. So they entered an open-age team in Division 5 of the Wolverhampton Amateur League, as well as continuing with a youth team.

In 1971 Tarlock Singh joined the club as a 20-year-old football fanatic. Although Tarlock was from the other side of Wednesfield, he had heard through the grapevine that a progressive and dynamic Asian football club existed in the town: 'I suppose I went to Rovers because I felt it would be safe to play in an Asian team.' Tarlock was to go on to have a major influence on the development of Punjab Rovers for the next twenty-five years. His story typifies that of hundreds of other junior football clubs where the entire club has been hugely indebted to the goodwill and commitment of one individual: the sort of person who willingly marks the pitch, collects the subs, attends league committee meetings, runs the side and, in Tarlock's case, also influences proceedings on the pitch. During the thirty-two years of its existence the club has undergone many trials and tribulations. Anyone visiting the Rovers Sports social club cannot help but be impressed by the huge respect Tarlock still commands. Every visitor entering the club makes a point of approaching him and either shaking him by the hand or embracing him. Within Tarlock's first season he had become player-manager. In five seasons the club had progressed from the bottom division to the premier division of the Wolverhampton District League. Following another three seasons of continued success they moved up to a higher standard of football in the West Midlands Metro League. That was followed by five seasons in a yet higher grade of football in the Staffordshire County League. Along the way there have been many triumphs, various league championships and cups. According to Tarlock the most satisfying achievement came in 1985: 'The Aston Villa Cup was open to all clubs. It was a prestigious trophy because it had been going since the nineteenth century. The feeling I had that night was the most satisfying I've ever had in football.'

As well as enjoying considerable success in domestic competitions, Rovers became a major force in the Asian tournaments. Although having recorded only four actual successes in the 'A' band tournaments, they have contested countless Finals and semi-finals. A case of the bridesmaid and rarely the bride, according to Tarlock. He cites two specific reasons: 'If you think about teams like Supna and Punjab United, who dominated the tournaments in the 1970s, and other teams who have been successful, like Smethwick Rangers and Southall, all of them were physically very strong and intimidating sides, particularly Supna. Whereas Rovers were always regarded as a very attractive passing side. You could always guarantee us to play in the most attractive matches, you know, those that would end up 5–3, 6–2 or 4–3. Our games would also attract the most spectators because people knew we would be entertaining. Although I think we underachieved, because we should have gone on to win more Finals, I still take great pride in the way we played the game.'

Leicester-based Supna (Supna's literal Hindi translation is 'dream', although their opponents would regard playing this surly outfit as more like a nightmare) endeavoured to live up to their hard, uncompromising and intimidating image. To reinforce this image some Supna players used to arrive at matches wearing donkey jackets and Doc Martens boots.

Although having an unfavourable reputation, Supna could also perform with the best of footballing sides. Whether or not it was deliberate, they certainly succeeded in intimidating teams and even supporters. The number of stories of touchline brawls involving Supna players and opposition supporters has become the stuff of folklore. Their antics, coming as they did in the 1970s, often saw people comparing them with the hatchet Italian club sides, and one or two of Supna's players were re-named Benetti and Fachetti after those great Italian hard men.

Another reason for Rovers' relative under-achievement can be put down to a similar principle to the former UEFA ruling about the inclusion of a restricted number of 'foreign' players in club teams for European competitions. Participating teams are permitted, by the rules of the tournament competitions, to play no more than two non-Asian players, a situation that was intended to preserve the Asianness of the Games. This arrangement has enabled ambitious (well-resourced) teams to recruit two outstanding players to add to existing squads. More often than not these two non-Asian players are recruited specifically for the period of the tournaments. Some have argued that this approach is very mercenary, others have called it backdoor professionalism. What is not in doubt is that those teams who have recruited non-Asian players have tended to fare better than those who have not. Rovers have never been a particularly well-financed club, but according to Tarlock they would not have recruited 'outsiders', as a matter of principle. 'Why should we have given up places to a couple of mercenaries who would have disrupted our excellent team spirit?'

On the subject of good Asian players, Tarlock is privileged to have played against so many over the years. Near the top of the list is Shinda Singh, who played for local rivals Punjab United. At 16 Singh was offered an apprenticeship with Wolverhampton Wanderers. He went on to appear in the losing FA Youth Cup Final team in 1976, playing alongside the likes of Steve Daley and Alan Sunderland. After being released by

Wolves at the age of 18, Singh drifted back into junior football with Punjab United. At the time he must have been one of the first Asian professional apprentices, and it's depressing to think that since then no Asian player of any note has managed to make the elusive breakthrough. Among the finest, Tarlock recalls three former Rovers players, all of whom could have gone on to play a good standard of professional football. Ghulam Labhani was an exceptionally talented footballer. He captained Wolverhampton schoolboys in the late 1960s, and attracted the attention of many big clubs, including Manchester United, Tottenham Hotspur and Wolves. Ghulam's failure to break into the professional game baffles all who knew him. The brothers Jassell, Vijay and Satish were also highly talented individuals. Older brother Vijay was a big strong centre-forward, good in the air, with a great touch, described by opposition players as twinkle-toes, and the scorer of spectacular thirty-yard pile-drivers. Satish was an old-styled inside-forward. Like his older brother he possessed a great touch and clinical finishing skills that made him devastating in front of goal. Those fortunate enough to have played with or against him will know that only a chronic asthmatic condition prevented him from making the grade. It is highly significant that in citing these very players, Tarlock highlights the club's most laudable virtue – non-sectarian selection policies. Unlike some of their rivals Rovers were founded on the principle of access to all, regardless of background or ethnicity. They have always refused to select their players by referring to any hierarchical caste system.

Among his many contributions, Tarlock was instrumental in creating a real family feel about the club. On summer evenings at Fowlers Park, upwards of sixty to eighty footballers of all ages and standards would gather together for Rovers' training nights. Although Tarlock had first-team matters dominating his attention, he would always go out of his way to make everyone welcome. In stark contrast, the atmosphere at rivals Punjab United tended to be less conducive to fraternal conviviality, indeed, it was infinitely more cliquey. Hopefully the significance of Rovers' policy of accessible football for all will not be lost on other clubs across the footballing spectrum.

In 1990 the Asian Games celebrated their Silver Jubilee. As we approach the millennium we need to ask: how long can the Asian Games survive? What evidence is there to assert that the Games, which have now become near institutions, retain the popularity and significance that have been bestowed upon them for a quarter of a century? In July 1996 the Birmingham tournament, held in the borough of Sandwell, was said to have attracted over 7000 spectators. All told, the combined annual tournament attendance (at ten to twelve different locations) has tended to range between 20 and 30,000 people. Certainly, there appears to be nothing to indicate that people are no longer willing to travel long distances to watch the tournaments. The idea of getting up at five o' clock in the morning to travel from the Midlands to London, or Kent appears to be as much in evidence today as it always has been, and those who make the long journeys continue to receive the warm welcome given to them by their hosts.

Whilst acknowledging the important contribution made to the development of British-Asian sport and culture by the Asian Games tournaments, there are recognized shortcomings. For instance, the title 'Asian Games' can be misleading because, in effect, the origin and subsequent development of the Games have been Sikh led. Despite overtures made over the years by the organizing committees to encourage the greater participation of other Asian communities, the efforts have shown disappointingly little return. Relatively few Pakistanis participate; likewise, few do from the Bangladeshi community. It is an issue that Sohan Singh Cheema acknowledges draws justifiable criticism of tournament organizers: 'The idea of changing the title from the Sikh Games to the Asian Games came from the local authorities. Because the Games were taking place in public parks and stadiums I think the councils didn't want people to think they were only supporting the Sikh community.'

Any long-term prospects for the integration of all Asian communities into the same tournaments appear to have disappeared with other Asian communities beginning to host their own events. Perhaps the notion of integrated tournaments was flawed from the beginning. After all, the rivalry between the various Asian communities has always been fairly intensive. In recent years various attempts have been made in Bradford, Wolverhampton, Birmingham and London to develop a unitary pan-Asian identity to combat racism. Unfortunately these attempts have made little headway, in part because of the inter-communal tensions in South Asia. On the other hand, here is an opportunity where migrant communities, some four thousand miles from their ancestral homes and with a great deal in common, particularly in respect of inequality and injustice, could provide a shining example of friendship and co-operation. That task may now be more difficult to achieve, but it is by no means impossible, and in many ways represents the greatest challenge ahead for tournament organizers.

A similar argument to that of non-Sikh participation could be constructed in respect of female participation. Here again there are complex factors that need to be taken into consideration, involving completely revising the social, cultural and psychological constructs that situate Asian women in subordination to Asian men. This is by no means a simple task. Centuries of naturalized understanding of gender roles, and even pseudo-religious principles, has to be radically altered to achieve a more egalitarian situation. Fundamental to this debate is, however, the need to provide far greater encouragement and support for Asian girls to participate in school sports. However, such policies will only have a meaningful impact if Asian males adopt a far more enlightened approach to this issue. Whilst an integrated male/female sporting event may currently be out of the question, in areas such as Middlesex all-girl Asian tournaments are beginning to achieve a greater degree of participation. Sports such as girls' kabbadi, hockey and athletics events are part of the Games. As yet they are in an embryonic stage and are restricted to the one specific location. However, with adequate and sustained financial backing and community support, women's/girls' Asian Games tournaments may aspire to the same levels of social, cultural and sporting importance as the men's equivalent has enjoyed for the past thirty years. The popularity of the tournaments has resisted the admonishing claims that they would not last beyond the first generation of Asian immigrants. To their credit, the tournaments have moved with the times and incorporated into their cultural sphere 'new' Western sports, particularly football, and thus ensured the captivation of newer generations of British-Asian sports fans. The fact that the Games have survived into a fourth decade is a tribute to all those involved in their inception and development, past and present. Prominent founding figures such as Sohan Singh Cheema, Labh Singh Gill and Satnam Singh Gill laid down important foundations in the early years of re-settlement in Britain for future generations to actively engage with and enjoy sporting pursuits. Shaheed Udham Singh would have been proud.

4 Rocky of Rawalpindi – British and Proud of It?

One of British football's most gifted players of recent times, Matthew Le Tissier, possesses the kind of mesmeric natural ability and innate soccer skill that not only distinguishes him as a master-craftsman amongst the hard-labouring majority but also illustrates just how majestic and spontaneously perfect football can be. Yet the inconsistency, alleged indifference and lack of ambition that have seemingly been made inherent features of his very character have shattered the international career of a sublime talent. In a lazy, epicurean world, this would be a talent that not only deserved to play at the highest level, but also, one suspects, would thrive and excel in and amongst the game's upper echelons. But Le Tissier is resigned to another indefinite period of frustration and misery; not even watching from the sidelines, he remains in international football's desolate wilderness. However, hailing from the Channel Islands, Le Tissier was offered the choice (or escape route) of playing for Scotland or one of the other home nations. Although he had represented England in a full international, he was still eligible to play for Scotland, Wales or Northern Ireland. Of these three, Scotland seemed to have the most realistic chance of receiving his talents due to their relative squad superiority and history of qualifying for major championships. Given the chance to exhibit his skills on the international stage, as a regular, indeed an imperative fixture around which the rest of the team would operate, the chance to have his talent acclaimed as truly exceptional was graciously declined by the man. His reasons? He was an Englishman, he was English and not Scottish, and so he could not represent the football team of another nation, he could not present himself in the team of another country, even if that was the only possible means by which he could play at that level. If he were to play international football it would be for England or for no one at all.

Whilst Le Tissier chose to remain loyal to his perceived national allegiance, Jawaid (Jimmy) Khan, aka Rocky of Rawalpindi, when faced by a similar treacherous dilemma, decided to allow himself the transient glory of playing football for an international team. Khan's situation was admittedly quite different to that of Le Tissier, but they both had to confront the task of selecting the country under whose flag they would ply their trade. Khan's decision was based on the fact that his ethnicity, in the British context, made it virtually impossible to reach the heights of football that he believed he could attain. A Pakistani playing for England was an absurd idea, even if this player had been born and brought up in this country; but donning the green shirt of Pakistan was a very real option and one that was laid before him. He could swear his allegiance to the flag of St George in the blind hope that maybe someday his talents would be recognized before the colour of his skin, and he could run out on to the Wembley pitch to the rapturous applause of 80,000 adoring England fans, or he could temporarily return to the land of his parents' birth, the nation of his ancestral heritage, and play full international football for Pakistan in a World Cup qualifying group that they had very little, if any, chance of reaching the finals from. To indulge oneself in the passing, ephemeral glory of an inevitably doomed World Cup qualifying campaign, or to forsake one's ambitions of greatness in the name of national belonging, national affiliation and national identity? Was he Jaiwad the son of a Pakistani immigrant in Britain, or was he Jimmy the Lancashire lad who loved playing football?

Countless numbers of British-Asians will have grown up in this country assuming two different first names. They will have their parentally ordained name, and another conferred upon them by white neighbours or friends who claim to be unable to correctly pronounce their real names. Living next door to a dear old white neighbour, Mrs Walton, resulted in the Bains children being conferred with Christian names. Mrs Walton's actions rendered futile our parents' sacred reference to the *Granth Sahib* (Sikhs' Holy Book) in selecting the names of their offspring, when all it needed was a white neighbour to give them 'proper' names. Still, at least our 'Christian' names began with the same letter as our real names, as I became John (Jaswinder), brother Reggie (Raj), sisters Susan (Surinder) and Margaret (Mohinder). For reasons unknown my younger sister, Daljinder, escaped this naming ritual and had to settle for being called Bab (Baby), a common Black Country reference to young children. Not all our friends were blessed with creative name-making neighbours, consequently Mohan became Robert, Daljit became Matthew and Jitinder was known as Derek.

Nowadays Asian youngsters are less willing to assume alternative English names. Not least because Asian names have been in circulation longer, thus making the task of pronunciation much easier. These days TV game-show hosts reel off Asian names with what appears to be consummate ease, professional competence or political correctness; either way it is one marker of modern English's expanded nominal vocabulary. Asian people are also now less willing to compromise over this aspect of their cultural identity. Contemporary developments have instead given way to a tendency to shorten first names; e.g., Baljinder is reduced to Bally, Manjit becomes Manj, Mohammed becomes Mo, and Jaswinder is abbreviated to Jas. This inclination for monosyllabic pseudonyms has since procured substantial profit for the private vehicle licence-plate industry. There's no point having a brand-new BMW without it being adorned with number plates reading A1 JAS or P3

SAN. Jawaid Khan, born in Darwen, Lancashire, on 22 September 1963 quickly became known as 'Jimmy', and the name has stuck with him ever since.

Growing up in this, almost exclusively, white Lancashire town in the mid-1960s, Jimmy remembers his family's presence there as being, initially, a bit of a novelty. Most Asian families who decided to seek work in the Lancashire cotton mills had done so in the neighbouring towns of Blackburn and Bolton. Therefore, the sight of an Asian family in Darwen made the locals curious, but not intrusive or particularly threatening. The middle child of five, Jimmy recalls that he was the only Asian child in the local primary school, St Johns: 'I think what helped me settle down very well with the other children was that I immediately took to football. I couldn't wait for breaks and lunchtimes so that I could play football. Most of my time was spent playing as a goalie. My forte was diving about. I think I was a good goalie because they selected me to play in goal for the school team. Being Asian, to be honest, wasn't the sort of thing I gave much thought to – I mean you don't when you're that age.'

For Asian children born in Britain it is not unusual to see their parents take them back to the ancestral home. This is an issue that still causes concern among school teachers, who consider prolonged absences of up to six or eight weeks in school term to be detrimental to the child's education, particularly when many Asian children are still having to come to terms with a second language. Asian parents, on the other hand, consider it very important for offspring to connect with their cultural and familial roots. Such visits can represent the first time grandparents and members of the extended family will have set eyes on the newer members of the family. The likelihood is that this occasion may well be the only time the children will see their grandparents. It was the occasion of his eldest brother's wedding that led 10-year-old Jimmy to visit Pakistan. Except, the initial stay of a few weeks eventually became a six-month sabbatical.

If Jimmy had fears about the children in Lahore (his mother's home city) playing football, they were dispelled on arrival. Within days of arriving in Pakistan the 'English' visitor was a regular in the street football matches: 'What they used to have there were football matches played across these wide streets. It was usually a case of splitting the players up into equal numbers and getting on with it. I can still remember diving about on the dusty road tracks. You had to be careful because of the passing cars and trucks, but no one ever seemed to get hurt. It was brilliant at night because passing cars would come along, stop, and use their headlights as floodlights for the football matches.'

On his return to England, Jimmy began to realize that he had a special talent for playing sport. He was selected to play for the Darwen boys' football team as well as captaining both his school's football and cricket teams. He recalls, 'At that age I began to make a name for myself. People at school, teachers and the other children used to talk about how good I was at sports. I've never been cocky, or anything like that, but I knew even then that I was a good player.' Moorland High School, like his primary school, had only a handful of Asian pupils, but as far as sport was concerned life carried on pretty much as normal for Jimmy. He again found himself to be the star player and captain of the school team. Despite this success on the playing fields his parents continued to be at best indifferent to his footballing progress. Remembering how he was greeted after arriving home from a school match: 'I used to get home and it was hardly ever a question of, "Oh, well, how did you get on today? Did you play well?" etc. My mum was just concerned that I didn't get hurt. Because they never actually stopped me from playing I think they realized how important football was to me.'

Jimmy cites his small-town upbringing as a positive factor behind his footballing development. Even into his teens, Darwen still had only a small number of Asian people resident in its vicinity. Owing to these circumstances, Jimmy did not feel the same pressure as his peers in Blackburn or Bolton to attend the mosque for prayers and to attend after-school Koran study classes. Jimmy Khan's upbringing has some broad similarities to that of Ricky Heppolate, former professional footballer. Unless they are supporters of the clubs he played for in the 1960s and 1970s – Preston, Orient and Peterborough – many people may not have heard of Ricky Heppolate. What is more likely is that they will be unaware of the fact that Heppolate is of Anglo-Asian descent and was born in Mumbhai (Bombay). He is therefore one of only a handful of Asians to have played professional football in England. In the early 1950s Heppolate and his family came to live in nearby Bolton. Growing up in a similar environment with few Asian people, Ricky Heppolate found himself, like Jimmy, influenced by the behaviour and hobbies of his white friends. The perceived 'interference' of religious worship is often cited by those in the professional game as a major obstacle to progress, in particular for the Muslim community. Jimmy acknowledges this point of ignorance: 'If professional football clubs showed a little bit more understanding towards our religion [Islam] and some Asian parents were prepared to be more flexible in their approach, then there would be very few problems.' With life revolving around playing football, and school duties and family chores being seen as minor irritants, Jimmy sought every opportunity to play the game. Some of Jimmy's white friends also played for a boys' team in Accrington and it was here that Jimmy was to get his first sample of international football, albeit representing his adopted rather than ancestral country. The tournament, involving a number of boys' teams from across Europe, was staged in Sweden. Although the team did not make the Final, it was to be a personal triumph for Jimmy, as he ended up as the tournament's best player as well as top goalscorer. Jimmy also recalls getting a real 'buzz' from representing England. What is not clear is how much of the patriotism was due to his actual loyalty to England, and how much of it was due to the influence of his white team-mates' more obvious conviction.

The rules of the Asian Games that permit the playing of two non-Asians per team were also in evidence at a much older migrant community's football club, when, at the age of 13, Jimmy went to play for a Catholic team in a local Catholic league. His real nationality was not immediately apparent to all: 'Because I am quite light skinned for an Asian a lot of people used to think that I was an Italian, what with this being a team of Catholics. While playing in this league I started to get the scouts coming to see me play. I was averaging five goals a game, and in one match I scored nine. Obviously as a prolific goalscorer they all wanted to see me play.'

For the next few months Jimmy was watched by a number of teams, including Manchester United and Tottenham Hotspur, and took part in various trials. However, when it came to making a decision about the club he would join on associate schoolboy forms, it was a matter of staying close to home. But the magnitude of his progression was not lost on Jimmy: 'The idea that clubs like Man United and Spurs were watching you still makes the hairs on the back of my neck stand up, but I am at heart a very homely person, so I decided to stick with Blackburn.'

Even though it looked as if Jimmy had a reasonable chance of playing professional football, his father continued to take little active interest in his sporting career. On the day Jimmy was due at Blackburn Rovers to sign associate schoolboy forms it was his older brother who accompanied him to Ewood Park. The hurt and disappointment felt at his father's apparent disinterest in his chosen career could not, however, temper the obvious joy and pride felt when entering the club's offices. He continues: 'There we were standing in the office of the chief scout Eddie Quigley when in walked Howard Kendall, who was the club's player-manager at the time. I'll never forget his exact words. "What's this, then? Am I witnessing the signing of the first Asian football star?"' The two years as an associate schoolboy were among the most enjoyable in Jimmy's life. Among the many people he played with and against were Mark Hughes, Paul McGrath, Simon Barker and Mark Patterson. For the most part life was enjoyable. But occasionally Jimmy would be given a painful reminder of being a black man in a white man's world, as he became the victim of vicious tackles that would send him flying through the air. This was usually accompanied by the standard 'You fucking Paki' taunt. Fortunately Jimmy had the support of his team-mates, who would tell him that the reason he was victimized was because he was a good player. He was also comforted in the knowledge that these team-mates were not necessarily saying these kind things about him out of patronizing sympathy; it was obvious to all concerned that Jimmy was developing into a very talented young player.

Jimmy's reputation as a good footballer was also preceding him in the Lancashire Asian community. When visiting friends and relatives in Blackburn he would often get called out into the streets to show off his footballing prowess. In his mind Jimmy had begun to tentatively map out his career. At 16 he would be offered an apprenticeship, and when he was 18 he would join the professional ranks. The next episode was a stark reminder of the way that life has a habit of smacking you in the face when you least expect it, or deserve it. There was to follow a temporary flicker of hope, a stay of execution, only for the dream of becoming a professional footballer to be permanently extinguished. To make matters worse, Jimmy had to second guess Blackburn's decision not to offer him a full-time apprenticeship. Eventually he managed to track down Eddie Quigley and was told that Blackburn Rovers were filling up their apprenticeship quota with boys from across the Irish Sea. This meant there was no place for Jimmy, other than to stay on as a registered but non-contract player, where he could train and play for the club. This set-up would be on an expenses basis only, and not the preferred apprenticeship arrangement. Jimmy was devastated. In the two years he had spent at the club he had performed consistently well. His performances and attitude were praised by the coaching staff and there had been no indication to suggest Jimmy would not be offered an apprenticeship. Football had become such a preoccupation that his school work had suffered. Very few school children are able to make a definitive decision about their future career; in fact most of us tend to stumble into something as opposed to pursuing a definite vocation from an early age. At least Jimmy had been decisive, and this should have saved him the sort of grief the rest of us go through during the crucial mid-teen period. It was a classic case of placing all one's eggs in a single basket. The thought of what he was going to do with the rest of his life, now that football appeared to have been vanquished, was a dark prospect that began to cast a debilitating shadow over him. The word '*izzat*' (reputation/honour) has come to play an important part in the vocabulary of British-Asians. For Jimmy, his predicament would place a strong challenge to his *izzat*. How would he confront his family, his friends and the wider community who were convinced this boy was going to play for the Rovers? He recounts the moment of epiphany, which gave an explanation for his apparent failure, with a real sense of betrayal: 'Because I lived in Darwen they [Blackburn] thought I would stay with them. I left that room feeling utterly dejected. Perhaps for the first proper time I actually opened my eyes and saw things in a different light. My friends, family and even my PE teacher said the decision may have had something to do with me being Asian. I just felt confused and hurt.'

At the end of the season a list of rejected schoolboy trainees is circulated to all the League clubs. One of the clubs who had monitored Jimmy was Bury. Jimmy was invited to a trial game, where everyone would be trying desperately to impress, in the knowledge this could be his last opportunity. The inclusion of former Liverpool and Manchester United schoolboys was going to make things even more difficult than normal. It is a testimony to his character and inner self-belief that, in spite of the Blackburn experience, Jimmy had not lost faith in his own ability. However, the game was to prove as significant for Jimmy off the field almost as much as it did on it. Up to now Jimmy's father had taken, at best, a passing interest in his football career. While Jimmy was with Blackburn Rovers his father had very occasionally come to watch him play. In respect of the trial match, the father–son relationship was to undergo a major shift in direction. On the eve of the Bury trial, it was as if his father understood that this was a last chance for his football-obsessed son. All those years of practising, travelling, playing matches, often at the expense of school work, could hinge on this one match. There was no doubt that his father's presence, sitting alone in an almost empty stand, had a positive effect on Jimmy's performance: 'Within minutes of the kick-off I scored a really good goal. I ran off towards where my father was sitting in his big sheepskin coat. I could hear him standing up and shouting at the few other parents who were in the same stand: "That's my boy! That's my boy!" It made me feel so good, because I knew my father was so proud of me.'

Although Jimmy had done well to impress the Bury coaching staff, he found himself, again, a victim of a club's over-subscribed apprentices quota, only the circumstances were different. The terms being offered to Jimmy by Bury were the same as those offered by Blackburn, a non-contract basis with out of pocket expenses being met. In making his decision Jimmy was further encouraged by his father, who offered to drive him to Bury, which was fifteen miles away, three or four times a week. During those past years Jimmy had had to fend for himself while his fellow footballers were comforted and encouraged by their parents. The occasional glance at the touchlines where the 'Come on, Johnny' shouts of encouragement were coming from, used to fleetingly remind him of a situation he had once pined for but had blanked out because it seemed the most unlikely of scenarios. He was, in effect, a footballing orphan. For the next two years Jimmy stayed with Bury as a non-contract player, mostly in the youth team, but with occasional appearances in the reserve team. On his eighteenth birthday Jimmy's football career was to receive another major jolt, only this time it was terminal. Bury FC were unwilling to offer him anything better than a continuation of non-contract terms. Recent events at the club had forced them to undergo a change of recruitment policy. Instead of looking to promote from within, Bury decided they were better disposed to recruit rejected young professional players from other clubs. This time in his heart and mind Jimmy suspected it was all over, a view that was supported by his father: 'My dad took me to one side and said, "Now look here, Jimmy, you've got to accept there is something wrong here. Either you're not as good as you think you are or the clubs don't want our Asian boys. You're eighteen now, and if you are not going to play football then it is important you sort out another career."'

But even then Jimmy clung on to that elusive dream. When you are 18, and for the last ten years your whole life has revolved around making a living out of playing football, it is difficult to come to terms with a resolute submission of those aspirations. If there was a saving grace, a silver lining, it came in the form of contacts made over the years. And it was through this route Jimmy discovered that he could eke out some sort of existence as a footballer.

The following British summer Jimmy accepted an offer to go and play in the northern state of Finland with a team called Jankoski Purkva. The road to Finland is not unfamiliar for many British footballers who find the combined prospects of playing football in a foreign country, the possibility of European competition and earning a few quid at the same time, an enriching experience. On arriving in Finland Jimmy found himself being given a notional job in a local warehouse, but actually he spent all his time either training, coaching or playing in matches. He returned the following year, and although the locals conferred on him celebrity status, he found the prospect of returning for a third season too much. The last two seasons in Finland had been a great experience, but, in reality, they had only served to prolong the inevitable. Little did he know that at the time his greatest football adventure was yet to come. It was time for a proper job. Having devoted so much of his life to football and with no particular interest in anything other than sport, it was inevitable that Jimmy should seek a career in sport and leisure. The first point of call was the local Manpower Services Commission, where he undertook some sessional coaching work in the Blackburn area. Since then Jimmy has gone on to carve out a successful and rewarding professional career working for various North West local authorities as a sports development officer. Presently, he is in charge of the Sports Development Unit at Preston Borough Council. Following his return from Finland in 1984, Jimmy continued to play football at a semi-professional level. It was not the same as playing as a full-time professional, but Jimmy had managed to overcome his earlier disappointments; in particular he was buoyed by his successful attempts to develop another career. He could now play the game for pure enjoyment, just like those early days in school and on the streets of Karachi.

It was now more than decade since Jimmy had first visited Pakistan, and, at the age of 24, he agreed with his parents that it was time to be married and settle down. So, in 1987, Jimmy returned to Pakistan to become engaged to the woman whom he would marry. Although Jimmy had been in England all his life and was fully accustomed to Western ideas and influences, he was happy to accept his parents' wish that he marry a woman chosen for him. In recent years the practice of British-Asians, both men and women, marrying someone from the Indian subcontinent has become less frequent. In part, this is due to the introduction of restrictive immigration legislative controls that have made the task of bringing over partners from abroad, particularly those from the subcontinent and parts of Africa, very difficult. The other contributory factor is that younger generations of British–Asian men and women have become more reluctant to marry partners whose cultural and social upbringing is so different from their own experiences.

Unlike his previous visit in 1973, when Jimmy had gone to his mother's home in Karachi, this time he went to Rawalpindi. Stationed there is a major army garrison, where soldiers often play football whilst idling away the hours. Jimmy's nephews had heard about his footballing exploits and were keen to get him to play. With some degree of reticence, Jimmy acceded to their wishes and went along with them to the army barracks. Jimmy states: 'I played in this match with two teams full of soldiers. It was like playing on a dirt track, with no proper markings. There were some posts, but they had no netting. The standard was basically quite bad, but I managed to score nine goals. Up in one of the stands I could see there were these uniformed colonels and generals, whom I was later told were very impressed by my performance.'

Completely unimpressed with the standard of football, Jimmy was reluctant to take up another invitation to play two days later. However, following a personal request made by one of the local army colonels, he agreed to play. Jimmy also understood that his participation would reflect well on his family, particularly his father. On this occasion the standard of play was a little better, but Jimmy still managed to score a hat-trick. In 1989 it was Jimmy's brother's turn to be married. Unfortunately, Jimmy was unable to secure the necessary time off work and did not join his brother and father in Pakistan. The visit to Pakistan coincided with the qualifying tournament for the 1990 World Cup, which was to be staged in Italy. Pakistan were not expected to qualify, but nonetheless they were in a key group with Kuwait and the United Arab Emirates, both of whom had serious qualifying ambitions. The Pakistani national squad was in training at their Rawalpindi training base. Although Jimmy may have thought little more of his footballing experiences during his last visit to Rawalpindi, his performances had created a major impression on the Pakistani footballing authorities. Evidently, when Jimmy's brother arrived in Pakistan, mis-informed word soon began to circulate around the army base that Jimmy himself was back, and in the eyes of the Pakistani team officials he was therefore eligible for national squad training. Shortly after his arrival, Jimmy's brother received a message from the German Pakistani national team coach to say he had heard about the 'boy wonder' from England. He asked whether he would agree to participate in the squad trial sessions, in preparation for the upcoming games against Kuwait and the United Arab Emirates. Having explained that the footballing brother was still in England, Jimmy's father was asked if he could persuade him to come over to Pakistan: 'When my dad called and explained the situation he didn't need to persuade me, I couldn't come out quick enough. It never entered my head that I could fail the trials and not even get to play. I was just so excited that I took the first plane out.'

It looked as if fate was to deal a cruel blow to his chances once more. Just as his plane landed on Pakistani soil Jimmy contracted the flu. He went along to the national training camp at Rawalpindi, but he was unable to do little more than a few light training sessions. Fortunately, the coach was sufficiently impressed and asked him to stay with the squad. With the away qualifiers coming up the following week, Jimmy resigned himself to not being fit to take part. Obviously bitterly disappointed at fate's cruel intervention, Jimmy was still able to console himself in a glimmer of hope that lay ahead. Following discussions with the coach, Jimmy said that he was prepared to extend his stay in Pakistan by another month. During this time he would try to get himself fully fit in preparation for the home qualifying match against the United Arab Emirates. While the national team flew out to play the qualifiers, Jimmy became the Rocky of Rawalpindi. Jimmy continues: 'I decided I would get fit by doing some road running. I don't think the locals had seen anyone running up and down the streets. Every morning I would get up, put on my Reebok trainers, shorts and T-shirt, and as I ran car drivers would beep their horns and wave.' The sight of Jimmy running up and down the streets managed to cause a little bit of a local stir in scenes that were reminiscent of Sylvester Stallone's Rocky Balboa character. It appears the locals were evenly split between those who saw him as a sporting figure and those who thought him to be a few paisa short of a rupee.

Following defeat in both away-leg qualifiers, the national squad returned to their training camp, Jinnah Stadium, Islamabad (Jinnah is regarded as the founding father of the modern state of Pakistan). The 80,000-seater stadium was built by the Chinese as a gift to Pakistan. By this time Jimmy had recovered his health and fitness, and although the German coach was impressed with him, the compliment could not be returned: 'The coach had little idea of how to coach football. For example, we never discussed tactics or practised set-pieces. He just seemed interested in how fast you could run around the pitch. Mind you, the other lads were very fit – they could leave me for dead. But when it came to playing football most of them were very average players, probably semi-professional standard back home in England.'

Prior to the break-up of the former Eastern European bloc, ties between those countries and the subcontinent were particularly strong. Much of this was to do with the strategic defence importance of the Indian subcontinental region. The build-up of military and nuclear capabilities in the region is a reflection of Pakistan's close links with China, and India's with Russia. Part of the wider 'assistance' programmes has been the provision of support to promote and develop sport. Included in these sporting packages have been football technical advisors. The problem has been the quality of some of these coaches. As Jimmy says, 'Most of these coaches have been second-rate coaches in their own countries, so it's no wonder they've failed to do anything in Pakistan.' It is interesting to compare the rise of football in the 1970s in the Middle East nations with the almost simultaneous demise of India and Pakistan as Asian footballing powers. The unlimited wealth generated by the oil-rich countries has enabled them to develop the necessary infrastructure and engage the better football coaches, whereas less economically developed nations had to rely on the goodwill of their political friends behind the Iron Curtain.

Despite his frustrations with the coach, Jimmy enjoyed the preparation to the big game. All squad members were confined to the training camp, which included live-in chalets, situated about half a mile from the stadium. With the exception of Jimmy, the squad members were nominally contracted to big employers (Pakistan International Airlines, national railways or electric companies), but as with Jimmy's experiences in Finland, training or playing matches were the predominant occupations. – A practice that is still commonplace in the subcontinent in a number of major sports, and although people may not regard it as being strictly 'professional' in the way we would in the West, it is, in effect, the same thing.

In a region renowned for conferring sporting privilege and elevated status on those belonging to the upper classes, or higher castes, it would not have surprised Jimmy to see a system of patronage in place: 'The team was selected on the basis of who you knew and how much money you had, rather than ability.' Undoubtedly, if sport could be accessed on equal terms by all the population, the subcontinent would make a far greater impact on the world sporting scene than it does at present.

Initially, Jimmy's fellow squad members were reluctant to accept him as an equal. This squad of players had been carefully chosen and had spent several months together becoming familiar with one another. The idea of introducing a stranger into the camp was always going to be difficult under normal circumstances. In Jimmy's case, circumstances were complicated by incredulous perceptions of his claims of Pakistani status. After all, Jimmy did not live in Pakistan and did not speak very good Urdu, but his worst sin was that he threatened the place of certain team members. Not only did Jimmy's linguistic difficulties cause a problem, his dietary requirements presented some novel difficulties, something he looks back with on with amusement: 'The camp's kitchen staff were unfamiliar with anything other than traditional Pakistani dishes and their only knowledge of English food was boiled chicken, chips and peas. So this became my staple diet.' Eventually, one of the fringe squad members, who not only had less to lose from Jimmy's presence but also spoke good English, began to take Jimmy under his wing. Within a few days other members of the squad also started to warm to him. Their insecurity lessened somewhat when Jimmy made it clear that he had no intention of staying in Pakistan beyond the United Arab Emirates match.

Normally the dismissal of the national team coach two days before an important game like this would not only be regarded as poor timing, but it would also create major upheaval in the dressing room. The German coach's dismissal as the head of the Pakistani team, though, did not seem to have a major disruptive effect. In fact the players appeared to rally very strongly around his Pakistani assistant, who was now acting as a caretaker head coach. One of the major difficulties with the German coach had been the language barrier. Since he spoke no Urdu, all his instructions had to be translated by his assistant. It was evident to Jimmy that because of communication problems the squad sometimes had difficulties in the execution of specific instructions. During those vital days before the game Jimmy was delighted to see the new coach seeking his assistance in training sessions. Jimmy was glad that the match was taking place in Islamabad because it would enable his family to come and watch him play. That his wife-to-be was among this group only added to what was going to be Jimmy's greatest day.

On the morning of the game the squad was gathered together for a final briefing session. The new coach announced the team, and unbeknown to Jimmy, who was expecting a traditional football cap to mark his international debut, each team member was instead awarded a green (the representative Pakistani national colour) waistcoat containing the national emblem. Even at this late stage Jimmy was showing no signs of pre-match nerves, as he admits, 'Usually I am dead nervous before every game I play, no matter what the level. But right through the day I felt really confident. Perhaps it was the high of playing in such a big match that I didn't have time for nerves.' Those nerveless moments were not to last long. Although the game was being transmitted on television, there were still 50,000 people in the crowd, making the 80,000-seater stadium almost two-thirds full. As the teams started coming out of the tunnel those nerves re-entered and momentarily that confidence disappeared: 'I thought to myself, Am I really here? What am I doing here? Both teams lined up as they do in international matches to listen to their respective national anthems. When it came to our turn I just stood there with my hand across my chest and my lips sealed, because I didn't know the words to our anthem.' (Shades of the ill-attempted lip-synchs by Jack Charlton's adopted 'Irishmen'.)

The game, which resulted in a 4–1 defeat for Pakistan, ended rather too quickly for Jimmy's liking. 'I can remember phases when I did something good, but the match seemed to last only a few minutes before we were back in the dressing room. The game had a lot hanging on it: had we won or drawn then Kuwait would have qualified instead of the United Arab Emirates. So in a way it was nice to play in a game with such a lot at stake.'

The following day the press gave Jimmy a good write-up for his performance. An offer was made by Pakistan International Airlines to combine a 'marketing' position with playing football, which would enable him to continue to play for Pakistan. However, Jimmy declined the offer for a combination of reasons: 'Although I played football for Pakistan, I saw myself as British. At the time, if Bobby Robson had called I would have played for him rather than Pakistan, but he never rang. I'm not surprised, though. England was where I lived, it was where I was brought up, where my family and friends lived. I had assumed English values and thought more like an Englishman than a Pakistani. Don't get me wrong, I love Pakistan, but it has more for my parents than it has for me. Besides which, I couldn't live out there, it's too hot for me.'

Another factor that influenced his decision was a lack of confidence about the future development of football in Pakistan. He seems almost melancholic about the fate of the game in his parental homeland: 'Everybody plays football in Pakistan. You can see the kids playing in every wasteland and in every back-street. But they don't play it in the schools. Football is simply not on the sporting agenda. There is no league structure. The only competitions are those run by the big employers. I could not see how the game was going to improve without a grand plan and government support.'

Having made his decision that England is 'home', Jimmy is keen to put his knowledge and energies at the disposal of the next generation of British-Asian footballers. 'I want to play my part in overcoming the barriers that got in my way.' For some-one of his knowledge, ability and experience it is hoped he can make a significant contribution to the development of British-Asian football as well as football in Pakistan. As the first, and as yet one of a very small number of British-Asian full professional coaching qualification badge holders, Jimmy is acknowledged by the football authorities as having a large part to play in the development of British-Asian football. Also, as a member of the Football Association's National Working Party on Asians in Football, Jimmy is seen as having a key role to play in the formulation and implementation of policies. Indeed, it should not prove beyond the wit and capability of the football authorities to engage him in a suitable capacity. Then, there is his potential contribution to football in Pakistan. Given the historical practice of foreign countries sending their coaches to developing nations, it would seem wholly appropriate, were the English football authorities to take an interest in Pakistan, that Jimmy Khan could be dispatched there to play a role in the development of the game. Of course, to do that the English footballing regimes need to reinstate the interest they once had in the subcontinent. Sadly that interest has diminished with the lure of cash from the oil-rich Middle East countries. But there is also the Middle East itself. Pakistan, as a wholly Islamic state, has much in common with its Middle East neighbours. Following the recent footballing successes of countries like Saudi Arabia, United Arab Emirates and Iran, it should not be beyond them to make a significant contribution to the development of the game in Pakistan.

It seems like a lifetime ago when Jimmy was told by Bury that his professional football career aspirations were effectively over. He understands Blackburn and Bury as being important periods in his life but he is not looking back in any self-pitying or resentful manner, and that speaks volumes for his spirit and character. Jimmy is reassuringly secure in the convoluted path his life has taken: 'I don't now regret having never played for Blackburn. Through my experiences, what I have achieved has been good enough for me. How many people can say they've represented their country at football?' Can Jaiwad 'Jimmy' Khan truly lay claims to have represented *his* country?

5 Acts of Support – TV, Terraces and Beyond

A Tribute to the Late Vijay Singh (1983–1996)

Vijay Singh was a pupil at the Stretford High School, Manchester. Aged 13, Vijay committed suicide on the 12 October 1996, seemingly no longer willing or able to endure the constant, malicious bullying that had beset his life with misery. The subsequent discovery of his meticulously kept diary revealed that the Sikh, turban-wearing Vijay, had reached a point of fearful despair from which he could see no salvation. Prolonged physical abuse and racially motivated 'bobble head' taunts from fellow pupils of his own school drove an intelligent, highly articulate and sublimely endearing child to take his own life. A staunch Manchester United fan, Vijay harboured an ambition to become the first turbaned Man United player, a dream that he constantly, and with great conviction, echoed to his parents. Ultimately, whether the football-mad youngster would have become good enough, or would have been given the opportunity to play for his Old Trafford idols, is one of the many things that we will never know. However, Vijay had one other, relatively modest, ambition: he longed to watch Manchester United 'live' at Old Trafford. Sadly, owing to his parents' justifiable fear of physical or verbal racist abuse, Vijay never managed to fulfil a dream that most people would regard as nothing extraordinary.

★   ★   ★

'The point about football in Britain is that it is not just a sport people take to, like cricket or tennis or running long distances. It is inherent in the people. It is built into the urban psyche; as much a common experience to our children as are uncles and school. It is not a phenomenon; it is an everyday matter. There is more eccentricity in deliberately disregarding it than in devoting a life to it ... Its sudden withdrawal from the people would bring deeper disconsolation than to deprive them of television. The way we play the game, organise it and reward it reflects the kind of community we are.'

Arthur Hopcraft wrote these words before the time of British football's period of sickness, during which the 'English Disease' (hooliganism) laid bare the surface of a yob-culture that had parasitically attached itself to the game. The tragic events at the Heysel Stadium in 1985, when thirty-nine Juventus fans died during the ritualistic 'taking of ends' by a group of drunken Liverpool supporters, concentrated the footballing authorities' power into highlighting and punishing the 'English tradition' that had spread the disease throughout Europe. The darker side of such yobbish anarchy was its flirtation and, at times, direct association with extreme right nationalist groups. This instilled within non-white football fans an impulsive aversion to attending live football matches; football grounds were sites of danger and the best way of avoiding danger was simply not to be there. This was not easy, considering that many clubs are located within areas of ethnic minority concentrations. But changes engendered by the Taylor Report have witnessed the emergence of some constructive developments out of unnecessary suffering: the banishment of perimeter fencing, the introduction of all-seater stadia and the promotion of the game as accessible to all levels of society, rather then being solely the preserve of the British, white working-class male. Today, live football matches are watched by many more women than ever before, and more families have been encouraged to have a day out at the match with special family packages, specifically designed to cater for the younger audience. And there has also been the middle-class adoption of the game, which is possibly a little unfair, for football does infiltrate and permeate through the lives of many diverse peoples.

But, nonetheless, in this brave new world of football for everyone, the fact remains that in a city such as Leicester, where one in four members of the population is of Asian extraction, very few Asians actually attend live games. At a League fixture between Leicester City and Wimbledon in March 1995, 190 out of a Filbert Street crowd of 15,489 were Asian: only 1.23 per cent of the total attendance figure. Whilst there has been a relative visible increase in the number of Asians attending live matches, they are still grossly under-represented as a community. The promotion of football grounds as safe, leisure-orientated environs has provided a more hospitable veneer to the surface spectacle of the game, which, in turn, has led to a decrease in the aversion to football grounds that many Asians possessed. However, amongst the many who, for a variety of reasons, elect to stay away, there are those whose devotion is as great, if not greater, than that displayed by the majority of white committed fans.

Punjabi Wolves (Jas Bains)

I first made my way on to the Molineux South Bank terracing as a 6-year-old, on April 15 1969. Although any recollection of the actual game is largely forgotten (a 1−1 draw against Coventry City) the events surrounding the match were altogether more vivid. Growing up in an Asian neighbourhood and attending a predominantly Asian school was not the ideal preparation for my initial baptism in front of 30,000 white faces. It was a situation to which I would have to get used to. Judging by the experiences of older members of the town's Asian community, electing to attend matches at Molineux was not always a sane and rational decision. Evidently the problems encountered used to be greatest in the old North Bank. For reasons of personal safety, visits to the toilets and refreshment kiosk were best taken in pairs. On leaving the ground it was not considered to be safe to walk through the notorious Molineux subway; an equally nightmarish experience for many away supporters. A close friend of my brother recalls one such occasion when he was attacked while visiting the toilets and 'advised' not to report the matter to the police. What was incredible was that any Asian still attended games. But they did. By the time I was 13, a carefully planned strategy of sustained nagging and teenage whining had succeeded in persuading my parents that they should allow me to attend matches with my friends, as opposed to the thus far exclusive 'family and friends' policy. That first season (1976) was to coincide with another memorable 'Welcome to Molineux' incident.

Standing alone outside the old Molineux Hotel awaiting the arrival of my friends I was approached by a couple of rather large Millwall fans. The conversation went something like, 'This is no fucking game for Pakis.' Fortunately, I somehow managed to escape the expected beating. Their comments were, however, to cause great personal anguish over the next few weeks. Following my aimless and futile search for Asian footballers, the grand question began to dawn upon me: Did I have a place in this white man's world? But then, as if by heavenly intervention, I managed to discover a lifeline, my salvation. One day whilst patiently and painstakingly managing to work my way through those old bubble-gum cards, I found one revealing the birthplace of the Norwich City goalkeeper Kevin Keelan as Calcutta, India. I ran up and down the street waving the evidence to anyone who was in the least bit interested. More than anything else the discovery was to help restore my faith in what soon came to be an all-consuming passion. For the next few years my association with Wolves passed relatively unspectacularly. By my mid-teens I was a regular at all home games and beginning to sneak in the odd away game. This period coincided with my first visit to Anfield. Wolves lost 1–0 in a Boxing Day fixture. My only recollection of the day was being sick all over my travelling companion Nick, and him simultaneously returning the compliment. Here was a couple of teenagers who had suffered somewhat of a reverse reaction to the four-packs which we had guzzled straight away on sitting back down on the coach. To make matters worse, on arriving at Wolverhampton coach station, the coach driver insisted that we clean up the mess. The final leg of this rather sorry experience was the sight of my angry looking parents waiting to give me a tongue lashing.

The next few years were to coincide with a period that was considered by many to be a major low point in the history of football. It was a period in which the hooligan and racist elements almost brought the game to its knees. Being an ethnic minority football fan became a dangerous occupation. The intensity with which racist abuse was directed at local rivals West Bromwich Albion's black players (Cyrille Regis, Brendan Batson and Laurie Cunningham) in the late 1970s was to provide the most sickening experiences in all my years of watching live football. Who can forget the chant, 'Pull that trigger, shoot that nigger?' The words contained appalling sentiments and images that brought to mind the violent racist history of the American southern states. Standing in amongst the Molineux masses I could only look on with a combined sense of utter humiliation and guilt. Although I considered myself to be a passive objector, it did not prevent my questioning whether or not I was in some way culpable, sort of guilty by association. Unlike the majority of my Asian friends, who took the fairly logical decision to stay away from football during the heyday of hooliganism, I, for all the irrational and emotional reasons that forge relationships between fans and their clubs, continued to attend. The turning point for my best mate and fellow Wolves fan Sukhdev was an away game at Stoke City. We arrived at Stoke train station about 2.45 p.m., accepting our prospects of arriving at the Victoria Ground in time for kick-off as being decidedly remote.

A situation that was confirmed some minutes later as we were instantly marched off to line up against a wall outside the station. It was one of those moments of innocent panic that can be temporarily overwhelming and reflexively debilitating. You know you have done nothing wrong, but sense your number may be up. One minute I happened to be chatting away to Sukhdev about the likelihood of us missing kick-off, the next minute the police had dragged him away. Immediately my mind began to work overtime: how would I explain this situation to his mother? I was a year older than he, and, to a degree, was expected to look after him. Some twenty minutes later Sukhdev reappeared, understandably more than a little shaken by the experience. The 'arrest' had taken place over a cowardly assault on a middle-aged Asian train driver, who had been hit in the face with a glass object. When the police managed to arrest the real culprit it was patently obvious that he (the assailant) bore no physical resemblance whatsoever to Sukhdev. For a start he was white. Not surprisingly, that was Sukhdev's last away game.

The purchase of Wolverhampton Wanderers in the mid 1980s by new Asian owners was surely the answer to all these problems? The intervention of the Bhatti brothers had all the hallmarks of a classic modern-day football club rescue. Three minutes before the deadline set by the receivers, in rode former Molineux legend, Derek Dougan, with a successful takeover bid of £2.3m. It was only some days later that the fans became aware that the controlling interest in Allied Properties, the company behind the takeover, lay with the Bhattis. At long last, we Asians had a genuine stake in the ownership of the club. Sadly, this was not to be the case. In fact, it was quite the reverse; it was an experience that did little to harmonize relations between the town's Asian community and some Wolverhampton Wanderers supporters. Within two years of assuming control, the notoriously elusive Bhatti brothers were incurring the wrath of disillusioned fans, as the club began its downward spiral into near oblivion. It quickly became apparent that the Bhattis had no real interest in footballing affairs. The team's fortunes plummeted as the club descended in ignominy, a proposed £22m ground redevelopment fell by the wayside and the fans, hugely dispirited at the lack of interest and non-accountability of the club's owners, began to disappear. Fortunately the Doog had the good sense to quit before his image became completely tarnished.

With the threat of bankruptcy and potential foreclosure looming, the situation became absolutely desperate for the club's supporters. On July 29 1986 – soon after the owners of the club had announced there was to be a large cash injection – Allied Properties were taken to court where the judge duly ordered Wolverhampton Wanderers to be wound up. During those next few days newspapers even carried stories that the League status of Wolves would be replaced by that of non-League Enfield. A hundred and more years of local, national and international football history were under serious threat. As a supporter, I, like others, contemplated the unthinkable. What would I do with my Saturday afternoons? Who would I go and watch instead? Under the circumstances supporters wanted something or somebody against whom they could vent their frustrations. With the continued absence of the elusive Bhattis, some of that anger began to be directed at Asian people, just because they happened to be Asian. Small sections of the diminishing Wolves following took to singing anti-Asian songs. Although the songs were targeted at the Bhattis, the circumstances made those few Asian supporters in the ground nervous about their personal safety. Once again, as if to underline just how thick-skinned I had become when it came to 'my club', I continued to remain undeterred. I did, however, make some concessions by relocating to what I considered to be a safer part of the ground. I adopted an 'out-of-sight out-of-mind' strategy and took to standing by the old hot-dog kiosk at the bottom corner of the South Bank; a point of quick departure.

The Bhattis' regime was to leave a series of unanswered questions, most notably, why did they acquire a controlling interest in the club? What was their primary agenda? Was it about resurrecting an ailing footballing giant, or it was some other agenda? Their elusiveness and inaccessibility made this task somewhat impossible to decipher. In recent times supporters of Brighton & Hove Albion have had more justification than most in decrying the ownership of their beloved club, but at least they could locate the whereabouts of the owners, and even enter into dialogue with Dick Archer, a situation which was facilitated by the Football Association. The Bhattis, however, were so elusive that neither the fans nor the media could obtain interviews with them.

More than a decade on, in which the club has survived another near fatal bankruptcy blow, I still more than occasionally survey the scene on match days, deliberately looking out for fellow Asian fans entering the ground. The findings of my rather unscientific research provide a sense of satisfaction. Having visited many League clubs in the country, I think that I can say without any real fear of contradiction that the size of the Asian support at Wolves compares favourably with that of any other professional football club. And this, in its own special way, merely adds to the reasons why I am proud to be a Wolves fan. It has to be said that this situation does not particularly reflect any specific attempts made by the club to actively encourage more Asian or black supporters to attend matches at Molineux. Admittedly, it is a club that has not always done right by way of its handling of issues relating to 'my' community. For instance, the decision to invite Bernard Manning to perform at a 'Gentleman's evening' was an insensitive move, and one which caused outrage amongst all sections of the town's community.

Manning was booked to appear at Molineux in January 1997. His proposed show brought a strong wave of protest from Wolves supporters, a similarly outraged public and the likes of David Davies and Gordon Taylor. At a local level no one person pursued the matter with more vigour than the editor of the Wolves fanzine, Charles Ross, whose actions incurred the wrath of less sympathetic forces. As far as I was concerned the club was effectively condoning the offensive and racist approach Manning uses in his acts. My immediate reaction was one of a deep sense of hurt and betrayal. The decision once again highlighted that the making of money for some, perhaps all, football clubs is far more important than any principle. What price the eradication of racism in the game when clubs are seemingly prepared to pursue almost any means to boost income? I do, however, make no apologies for my partisanship in hoping that the first British–Asian football star in this country is a Wolverhampton Wanderers player. For more than forty years Asian people have made a significant contribution to the already rich and diverse history of this famous old Midlands town, with one notable exception. That, surely, is only a matter of time?

The Boys from Bradford

'I recall that that afternoon we were playing football in the street when we started hearing this noise and screaming coming from the football ground. We started to run down to the bottom of the hill where we could see these flames shooting up from the stand. By this time everyone had come out of their houses and on to the streets. Within a few minutes people had started streaming out of the ground, many of them were obviously very distressed and were looking to make phone calls to let people know that they were safe. Outside every house with a telephone there were queues of fans waiting their turn. Although they were pushing money into my father's hands, he refused to take any because he said it was an emergency.'

Abdul Karim, then only 10 years old, was one of the many local Bangladeshi children who witnessed this tragic event. Having started as just another game of football, the afternoon's proceedings were to leave fifty-six people dead, hundreds of others injured and thousands, both in Bradford and across the nation, permanently scarred with the memories of one of the country's worst footballing tragedies. For the migrant communities who live in the rows of pre-First World War terrace dwellings, situated immediately adjacent to the (then) Valley Parade ground, this tragic occasion was also to bring about a significant change in the relationship between them and the local institution that lay on their doorstep.

Yet only two weeks before the Bradford fire, no one could have predicted a coming together of these two quite disparate groups of people. As Abdul recalls, 'Just before a match a group of thirty or so white Bradford City fans started throwing stones and bottles at some Bangladeshi youths who were hanging around by the community centre. Our youths retaliated by charging them with snooker cues and hockey sticks.'

That scene, whilst not a regular occurrence, very much reinforced the common perception held of football supporters within the local Asian community. The district of Manningham, home to Bradford City Football Club, has also been home to the city's largest Bangladeshi community for more than a quarter of a century. The prominence of the local football club on their doorsteps had been of little consequence or interest for the resident Bangladeshis. That is apart from when a home game was on. Then the potential threat posed by these marauding football fans was enough to prompt older members of the community to instruct the younger generation to remain indoors until after the masses had departed. This fortnightly ritual, although resented by the locals, had nonetheless become an accepted part of life. Whilst the football club and the local police force made many promises to intervene on behalf of the beleaguered residents, they turned out, for the most part, to be hollow reassurances. However, by the early 1980s things began to change for the better, as the submissive tendencies of first-generation migrants began to gradually give way to the less threatened disposition of the newer generation. More than ten years on, the situation on match day around the area to the west side of the recently refurbished and renamed Pulse Stadium no longer resembles that of a decade or more ago. For a start the local corner shop, once considered to be fair game to potential troublemakers, is open throughout the afternoon. Both home and opposition fans walk through the streets without a hint of trouble, only occasionally looking up at the locals – a sort of mark of mutual understanding and respect, if not exactly a touch of fraternalism. There is a wonderfully strange mix of noise coming from the club's tannoy system, bellowing out the latest chart hits at one end, while equally audible from the other end are the chants of the local Mullah reciting afternoon prayers. This somewhat incongruous theme of East meets West continues as mobile hot-dog units with their pungency of fried onions compete against the more penetrable odour of Britain's most favoured food – curry. One indelible impression remains: that of young Asian boys gathered around the street corner looking on, perhaps enviously, perhaps not, as the masses make their way towards the football ground.

Such a scene could be a throwback to the pre-fire days, only now those Bangladeshi youths confidently strut along the local streets, as if to remind the visitors of their non-negotiable territorial claims. At around three o'clock, approximately fifty or so of their peers will join the faithful on the Diamond Seal Kop – insignificant numbers compared with the 15,000 or so now regularly attending, but for the majority of the Asian youths the next two hours will be spent idly gossiping the time away. The degree of disinterest in the afternoon's proceedings at the Pulse Stadium are indicative of the general state of antipathy felt towards the football club. In fact, such are the anti-Bradford City feelings among some of the youths that, when asked about their allegiances one particular afternoon, they said they wished for Bradford City's opponents that day (Wolverhampton Wanderers) to win the game. Luckily for them, and the large contingent of Wolves fans, a palpable lack of meaningful opposition meant they were to be denied – a 2–0 scoreline somewhat flattered the visiting team.

Out of all of England's professional football clubs, it would appear that Bradford City enjoy the highest profile for their work with the local Asian community, seemingly not without good cause. The 1991 Census shows that about one in six (15.6 per cent) of the city's population consists of ethnic minorities, and, most significantly, by the year 2000 one in two pupils of school-leaving age will be of Asian origin. Bradford City Chairman, Geoffrey Richardson, has shown himself to be a very good example of how a successful businessman can deploy his economic and financial acumen into turning round the fortunes of a professional football club. His efforts to court the Asian community, or more precisely the corporate Asian community, are immediately obvious on entering the ground. Situated very prominently across almost the entire length of the advertising hoardings of the main stand is the word Mumtaz, repeated time and time again. A highly successful Bradford-based food entrepreneur, Mumtaz has, amongst others, the notable scalp of Harrods in his vast range of customers. Although less prominently displayed, Basra Solicitors is another Asian company keen to promote its association with the club. Another local solicitor, Aurangzeb Iqbal, has been very active in promoting the cause of Asian footballers and in setting up the Bradford City Asian Supporters' Club. The club could also lay claim to having the first Asian (assistant) Football in the Community Officer; a somewhat short-lived tenure, however. Shapal Rahman is highly critical of what he saw as an attempt by the club to court favourable publicity, only to deny him the time and resources to provide support and assistance to the local Asian community. He is well aware of the criticisms made against him by the local Bangladeshi community. Rahman elaborates: 'The Community Programme is expected to raise enough funds to pay for itself. The only way we could do that was to spend all our time coaching in middle-class areas where the kids could pay for the coaching sessions. This meant that I was left with no time to devote to the poorer Asian kids from Manningham.'

Rahman's argument about the almost self-defeating nature of the Football in the Community Scheme, in the way it often denies opportunities to less affluent groups, is a sentiment shared by most other such schemes.

The height of publicity surrounding Shapal Rahman's appointment coincided with the signing of one Chris Dolby. Despite having an English-sounding name Dolby was actually born of Asian parentage but was adopted as a young child by a white Yorkshire couple. Sadly, Dolby's career was troubled by persistent injury, resulting in the termination of his twelve-month contract. To the outsider it would therefore seem to suggest that the club are doing their level best to integrate the Asian community into every aspect of the club's affairs. This is not a universally shared opinion, though, particularly amongst the doorstep community. Indeed, some, like Shonu, questioned the effectiveness of the club's programme. What emerges is a measure of suspicion towards the club: 'The chairman says he is committed to getting Asians into the club. First they appointed this Asian Community Officer, but he never did any work with us. Another thing: more than eighty of us turned up for this open trial for Asians, yet on the day there was totally inadequate organization; in fact, it was a shambles. That shows commitment?'

The strength of such feelings are borne, in part, by a common perception that the club is publicly making a compelling case for its support of the Asian community, and in doing so is gaining at the expense of a section of the Asian community. Another element to this obvious show of anger is the local community's resentment at having to withstand the brunt of the tribal outpourings of the white footballing masses. This new generation of Asian fans, the new kids on the block, are seeking some form of meaningful recompense by way of a genuine dialogue and partnership with the club, and not the all-too-simple historical fobbing off. As Abdul Karim states: 'What we want is, even if it is just occasionally, the manager, or any of the top players to come over to us, a matter of a few hundred yards, and offer a few words of support and encouragement. That kind of thing shows that they are genuinely interested.'

There is no denying that central to any plans Bradford City (or for that matter any number of clubs in similar circumstances) may have for increasing the size of their Asian fan base must be the satisfying of such emotive pleas. With well above national average levels of social and economic deprivation, communities like that of Manningham may be perceived to be poor, infertile grounds for increasing the fan base, hence the emphasis on the upwardly mobile corporate sector. If this were a dispassionate footballing community, then, arguably, the club could well be justified in maintaining the status quo. However, that is quite obviously not the case.

Whilst Bradford City must be applauded for their attempts to actively encourage members of the Asian community into the club, there has to be a recognition that such measures are just the starting point. Any scheme or project that seeks to involve Asians in all aspects of a football club must be held to the same kind of scrutiny, evaluation, assessment and development as any other venture.

Research undertaken by the Sports Council and Manchester University shows the Bangladeshi community in Britain to have an interest in playing football that exceeds every other group, including white people. Also, unlike in India and Pakistan, where cricket plays an important, if not prominent, part in both nations' sporting life, there is no comparable position in Bangladesh. Indeed, such is the Bangladeshi people's fascination with football that during the 1994 World Cup finals an estimated 20,000 were said to have taken to the streets to protest against the expulsion of Diego Maradona from the tournament. Raj Patel, who is now working for an international relief agency on the subcontinent, had a recent experience at a meeting of non-governmental organizations in the capital city of Bangladesh, Dacca, which underlined the importance Bangladeshis attach to football. Raj recalls: 'We were in the middle of this meeting when the director of the women's NGO, who was actually chairing the meeting, picked up her papers and told everyone she was leaving to watch the football on the television. No one should have any doubts about football's popularity in Bangladesh. With proper financial support and assistance Bangladesh could emerge as a strong footballing nation.'

Here in Britain, and more particularly in the city of Bradford, is a community waiting impatiently for that, as yet, elusive signal, summoning them to the football threshold. A signal that would not only help to build a healthy future, but also heal the wounds of the past.

Muslim Blade

Looking distinctly conspicuous in this otherwise all-white environ (a Sheffield pub) is Ramon Mohammed, aka the Muslim Blade. With a pint (Wards best bitter) in one hand, and the deployment of the other to periodically gesticulate to all corners of this crowded pub, he could be just 'one of the lads', something he, like his fellow Asian male community, is destined never to be. For fear of stating the obvious, this is no ordinary Muslim and definitely no ordinary Blade: 'A few seasons ago I was in a pub after a game with other Sheffield United fans, who had spent half the night ridiculing Asians; somewhat semi-seriously. My response was to start singing "Muslim Blade". It was my way of saying that we, the Asian community, were also part of the Sheffield United family. I know people who think some of my actions [pointing to a pint of beer and non-halal cooked-meat sandwich] do not conform to Islamic traditions and values. However, as far as I am concerned, it's what's in the heart that counts. I have read the Koran, my father was a Pakistani, and I am proud to be a Muslim.'

Living in the shadows of their more illustrious city neighbours is a matter of great anguish for the fans of clubs like Manchester

City and Birmingham City. Only fleetingly during their long histories has either club achieved a position of some pre-eminence. However, for the most part, it has been a case of looking up with envy and hurt as the likes of Manchester United and Aston Villa parade another prestigious trophy. In fairness to the fans of Birmingham City their suffering has been that much greater than their Manchester counterparts, who can at least point to two League Championship triumphs, four FA Cup wins and two League Cup trophies. Comparatively speaking, Manchester City's success record fares well against that of most other clubs were it not for the fact that Maine Road happens to be located in the same city as Old Trafford. It would therefore seem that Birmingham City, a club with only the one major domestic triumph to speak of (the 1963 League Cup), lay claim to being the most success-starved of all the major city clubs. Fans of Sheffield United, people like Andy Pack, the club's public relations officer, dispute such a claim: 'Our only League Championship was in the last century, and of the last four FA Cup wins, the last was in 1925. Unfortunately there are not too many Blades fans still around who can remember that last win. At least Birmingham fans can point to a Wembley appearance in 1956.' (Ironically, they lost to Manchester City.)

Pack's passionate defence of his club's predicament somewhat overlooks the fact that neighbours Sheffield Wednesday's only post-war footballing victory is a League Cup victory in 1991 – although Pack argues that Wednesday have at least made two (unsuccessful) trips to Wembley during this decade. Yet despite the traumas of having to endure the perennial city under-achiever's tag, clubs like Birmingham City, Manchester City and Sheffield United continue to draw upon the passionate support of up to half of their respective cities' football following. It was a combination of where he grew up as a youngster and a fondness for the underdog that initially attracted Ramon Mohammed to Sheffield United: 'This may sound like an oversimplification but United have tended to draw their support from the working-class areas, like Darnal and Attercliffe, where I grew up. Whereas Wednesday have drawn their support from a wider cross section of the population, including middle-class areas. Secondly, as a kid, United were enjoying a bit of a heyday period, with players like Mick Jones, Trevor Hockey and Tony Currie.'

Ramon's thesis about the base of Sheffield's football support is endorsed by the report *Sheffield Divided or United?* (Sheffield Hallam University 1997): 'Sheffield Wednesday is seen as a club for the whole family, and Sheffield United as a club which appeals more to white young males.' The report, an extensive survey of fans, local residents and young people, also highlighted the extent to which racism continues to be a factor in preventing the local ethnic minority population from connecting with Sheffield United Football Club. Encouragingly, over 70 per cent of fans interviewed said that they found racist abuse to be offensive, a view most strongly expressed by female and older supporters. However, what the report also highlighted was that almost one in five fans (18 per cent), mainly young white males, did not think that racist chanting was harmful or were bothered by it. Harassment of local ethnic minority residents by football supporters was considered to contain a racial element, and the report cites these incidents as being 'commonplace' rather than 'exceptional'. Perhaps even more revealing was the finding that young ethnic minority people did not feel that, in general, attending football matches was part of their lives and saw Sheffield United as a club with an appeal to young white males rather than to them. Some of these perceptions and experiences have been founded by past clashes between football supporters, walking from the local pubs towards the ground, and local residents. On occasions the clashes were known to have been particularly violent, resulting in the hospitalization of non-white supporters.

Such ideas, however, have always been far removed from

Ramon Mohammed's mind. At primary school Ramon would spend endless hours talking about football with his teacher, Mr Howard, and, in particular, his obsession for Sheffield United. It became apparent to Howard that, unlike his fellow (white) football-loving pupils, Ramon had never seen a live match. Although a Huddersfield Town fan himself, Howard took pity and offered to take Ramon to a Sheffield United game. That game against Tottenham Hotspur in 1971 began what has become an undying love affair. The combined ingredients of being raised in a family of seven children and possessing parents who were largely disinterested in the game made the growing allure to Bramall Lane somewhat pointless, almost cruel. Circumstances were not helped by white peer group influences, who, supported by willing parents, would regularly make the two-bus-ride pilgrimage to the ground. To satisfy his newly found passion, Ramon undertook a paper round, overcoming the obstacle of the Saturday afternoon stint by subcontracting that particular round to a friend. Unbeknown to Ramon, little did he realize the magnitude of the world to which he was being exposed, memories of which haunt him to this day: 'Rather than lose what I considered to be my friends, I decided to go with the flow. These were my friends in the street, and at school, and I desperately wanted to be with them in another common interest. I am ashamed to say that I copied their actions by taking part in the racist name-calling. It was pathetic; I was looked upon as a "good" Paki, a token white man. I cannot express how low I felt.'

On leaving school Ramon found himself in a company of a notoriously petty-minded group of building-site workers, where he found there to be no escape from the discrimination and prejudice that had thus far engulfed his life. Life on the sites was difficult — at times almost intolerable — as Ramon resigned himself to accepting the standard daily racist and sexist comments of his co-workers. It was a case of either confronting someone and face the prospect of hospital and bleak future job prospects, or get your head down by being seemingly prepared to tolerate the excesses, interspersed with the odd contribution, so as not to become too isolated and alienated. He does, though, recall with some amusement his first away match, against Luton Town: 'Working on a building site meant that I had to wear these steel toe-capped boots. I had no time to change before getting on the coach to Luton. As I went through the turnstile I was told by a policeman that I could only get in if I took off my boots. You can imagine the mickey-taking I took from United fans: things like, "I forgot your lot don't wear shoes."'

Following of a period of soul searching, a process he underwent to re-examine his outlook on life, and in particular a search for his 'true' identity, Ramon took the decision to pursue a degree course at Hull University. He decided that the search for his true self was being hampered by a lack of intellectual stimulus, and the only way to overcome this situation was to acquire the necessary academic training. The three years at Hull University, notwithstanding the anguish brought about by an enforced detachment from Bramall Lane, were to bring him very close to what he had set out to find. In doing so Ramon came to the realization that he had to effectively make a choice between his 'friends' and his freshly discovered cultural and racial identity: 'I had grown up on a white working-class estate, gone to school with the same crowd, and was now working with the same people. Over the years, by not challenging racist ideologies, I had allowed myself to become sucked into almost believing something I knew to be wrong, but was previously too weak to ever do anything about.'

Having since qualified as a teacher Ramon is now able to observe racism from a more considered as well as challenging perspective. These experiences have helped him not only recognize the extent of the problem in the game, but also demonstrate his, almost foolhardy, loyalty to Sheffield United: 'Last season [1996] at Southend, one of their players was receiving medical attention when a small but very vocal group of Blades fans repeatedly chanted, "You black bastard, you black bastard." I shouted back at the morons, challenging their racism. I was joined by one, just one out of 1500 away fans. Sadly, on that night at Southend, the small but vociferous racist louts were the winners. Why? Because the majority stayed silent.'

It is precisely this type of reaction that, in 1995, saw a group of Sheffield United supporters establish a pan-European anti-racist project, 'Football Unites Racism Divides' (FURD). Across the country ordinary supporters have developed localized campaigns to remove racism from the terraces. The FURD project, driven by its dynamic and lifelong Blade-ite co-ordinator, Howard Holmes, is seen as an extension of the less intensive, but equally valuable, initiatives undertaken by other fan groups (FURD being among only a handful of national projects that have been able to secure funding to enable them to deliver their work in a dedicated fashion). By adopting a multi-agency framework, involving all relevant public, private and community partners, FURD is well placed to tackle head on the absence of Sheffield's ethnic minority community from the world of professional football.

During the first two years of the project's life, members of the local ethnic minority community have benefited from increased opportunities to participate in organized professional coaching sessions and from acquiring formally recognized coaching qualifications. With the support of Sheffield United, more than 3000 ethnic minority youngsters have also had the opportunity to sample live professional football for the first time. To their credit Sheffield United are both frank and open when it comes to explaining their reasons for being associated with the FURD initiative. Andy Pack, the club's public relations officer: 'The club is driven by both the support of a principle [anti-racism] and also commercial considerations. At the end of the day the club is run as a business, and at present we recognize a key part of the Sheffield population is an area of untapped potential.'

FURD has also lent its support to a book/film project by Irvine Welsh and Phil Vaisili about Arthur Wharton, the world's first black professional footballer, who played for Sheffield United in the season 1894–95. The project's primary funding source has been the European Commission. In 1995 the Commission agreed to support three anti-racist football projects, FURD (UK), Dortmund Fan Projekt (Germany) and the Progretta Ultra (Italy), with a view to seeking a cross-fertilization of ideas and information to the benefit of all parties.

Although the number of ethnic minority fans attending Sheffield United's home games is still very small (estimated to be around 1 per cent) there is some evidence to suggest that the Bramall Lane environment may slowly be becoming a less hostile place. In circumstances not dissimilar to that incident at Southend, only twelve months previously, Ramon detected there to be a shifting of attitudes amongst even some of the more notoriously bigoted Blades following: 'At the home game against Charlton Athletic this very large Sheffield United fan, who was standing not far behind me, was dishing out the racist abuse. Just as I was about to turn around and tell him to belt up (fingers crossed for my personal safety), I was beaten to it by other Blades fans. The amazing thing was that this big fellow apologized, saying he was "out of order". For the first time, I felt that I could truly be at one with my fellow Blades. I no longer feel like a lone voice in the wilderness.'

Singhing the Sky Blues

'We would finish our shift at 1 o'clock on Saturday afternoon, go to the local pub for a couple of pints, and then go off to Highfield Road to watch Coventry City. In those days Coventry were in the old Third Division and had players like George Curtis and Reg Matthews playing for them. City used to play in front of crowds of around 5000. Most weeks there were a hundred or so Asians at the games (sometimes a few more).

You see, in those days, we Indians had very little else to entertain ourselves, so that is probably why so many of us enjoyed going to the football matches. We would never get any trouble from the crowd. There were some who did not follow the game, so they just used to talk to each other instead of watching the football. Looking back it was funny to see some of our group with their backs turned away from the game, talking away as if they were in the market, or some other place. You see, back then there were few places where we could get together in large numbers and just talk. Over the years fewer of us carried on going to the football, but some did.'

After almost four decades of watching Coventry City, Sohan Singh Cheema is arguably one of the longest-standing Asian followers of live football in Egland (if not *the* longest-standing). As a Coventry City fan he has shared the club's highly creditworthy, if at times fortuitous, tenure in the top division. Clinching promotion to begin that stay in a memorable game against eventual runners-up Wolverhampton Wanderers (1967–68) and the 1987 Cup Final triumph against Tottenham Hotspur feature strongly in his abiding memories, as do the more recent escapologist acts. But like any other dedicated football supporter, Sohan has his own special memories, those that are unique to his circumstances. The first such memory involves trying to secure tickets for the 1987 FA Cup Final. Having watched Coventry City for almost thirty years, Sohan, now accompanied by his son at Highfield Road, was determined to cheer on the Sky Blues at Wembley. Like everyone else in the city he had been intoxicated by the enormous buzz around the place. Such was his excitement that he had made the point of telephoning relatives scattered across the country to inform them of his great news: 'It was like telling people that my first grandson had arrived. I could not have been any happier. This is my home town and I felt so proud to be part of that special feeling.'

His pursuit of a Wembley day out was to introduce him to

that peculiar British idiosyncrasy, camping for tickets. On the afternoon of the first public release of tickets, Sohan made his way to the club's ticket office only to find queues going back more than two miles. Having decided not to call into work that day he was determined to get his tickets. At around five o' clock it was obvious that he would not get them that night. As he peered in front he could see fellow fans donning their sleeping bags and getting out their flasks and sandwiches. Momentarily, he reflected on his possible course of action: 'I knew if I rang home and asked them to bring me a quilt and hot food and drinks they would tell me I was mad, and that at my age I should not be sleeping out in the cold night. But I was so desperate to go to Wembley. Within an hour my family had brought me a quilt, blanket and a pillow, as well as some curry and chapattis.'

In doing so Sohan almost certainly became the first person in this country ever to queue up overnight for Wembley Cup Final tickets armed with a traditional Indian quilt and home-made curry and chapattis. Sohan's love for football, and sport generally, has enabled him to visit many far flung places across the world. As the President of the World Kabbadi Federation, Sohan undertakes numerous international visits. On one such occasion he was in India to attend a celebration dinner. Naturally, one of the frustrations of being abroad is the inability to keep in touch with domestic football affairs. That evening Sohan, who was staying at the old colonial tennis club in Chandigargh, was making his way to his taxi when out of the corner of his eye he spotted a team playing in sky blue shirts on the television. As he approached the television screen he discovered it was his beloved Coventry City playing against Wimbledon. His dilemma took all of thirty seconds to resolve. He dispatched his driver onwards to convey a message to the would-be hosts that their chief speaker had been otherwise detained, and not to expect his arrival for another ninety minutes or so.

He also recalls with great feeling the time he took his friend, the former Indian footballing great, Jarnail Singh, to watch Coventry. In 1967, the then FIFA President Sir Stanley Rous, whilst visiting India, was said to have made the following comment when watching Jarnail Singh play in an invitational game in Calcutta: 'He [Jarnail Singh] possesses all the necessary qualities to compete at any level. I am sure that he would not look out of place in any company.' Despite receiving a number of attractive offers to play abroad, Jarnail declined all of them, preferring to remain loyal to Indian football. Following a successful domestic career playing in Calcutta, Jarnail returned to his Punjabi home to take a top sports administrative position. Remarkably, Jarnail is a descendant of the same district in the Punjab, Mahalpur (Hoshiarpur), that was the birthplace of several other fine Indian footballers, notably, Gurdev Singh and Manjit Singh, and in recent times current international and inspirational captain of India's inaugural league champions (JCT Mills), Tejinder Kumar. However, even to this day it is Jarnail Singh who is still widely regarded as the greatest ever Indian footballer. As a fellow descendant of the Punjab state and as someone passionately interested in sport, Sohan had made Jarnail's acquaintance on a number of occasions, both in India and on Jarnail's occasional visits to England. During one visit to England in the 1980s Jarnail was staying with his old friend Sohan. As Jarnail had never previously watched a live game in England, Sohan decided to take him to Highfield Road. During the game Sohan observed with real pride as his great friend and hero watched the game in the manner of a player who had done it all himself. But Sohan did have one regret: 'I looked at those players and thought that at his peak Jarnail could have been out there playing for City. Jarnail is a very nice person and not big headed in any way. He said he was from another generation, another country, and that you could never tell if he would have been able to play in English football. After the match I could not help thinking about what it would have been like if Jarnail Singh had played for City. But I was still very proud that I had taken my football hero to his first professional match in this country.'

'Boing Boing Man Utd?' (Sanjiev Johal)

At the age of around 9 I was taken to see my first live football match by a footie-mad older cousin. Being Black Country born and bred (my cousin was actually born in India, but is blue and white through and through) 'our' local team was West Bromwich Albion, the Hawthorns being only a couple of miles away from where we lived. It was a time when Albion maintained a healthy position in the top flight of the old First Division, regularly finishing in the top half; on this occasion the Baggies entertained the flamboyant, yet underachieving Red Devils of Manchester United. I can recall feeling extremely small amongst the hoard of Albion supporters shouting from the terraces of the Smethwick End. Small, because I was only about four and a half feet tall and surrounded by what seemed like bellowing giants, and also because I felt a stronger sense of affiliation to the players of the opposing team. Man United were beaten by West Brom 1–0 in that game, and from what I have been told since, were rather outplayed by the then strong Albion side. This was a team in which black players made a significant contribution; Brendan Batson, Laurie Cunningham and Cyrille Regis were key figures, but for some reason (mysticism and metaphysical intervention aside) I found the allure of Manchester United simply irresistible. I entered the Hawthorns as a hereditary Albion supporter, but departed as an affiliated Man United convert. The obligatory accusations of being a 'glory boy' and only supporting United because they win trophies are part and parcel of being a non-Mancunian Manchester United fan. My only response to such damnation is that I began supporting United when they were still struggling to escape from the glorified cesspit of mediocrity that a complacent belief in their divine right to be Champions had submerged them in.

I wouldn't say that I was especially aware of or concerned with the various pseudonyms that different clubs had, but I do feel that Albion lost out a bit when it came to boasting a vibrant, dynamic and imposing club tag. West Ham were the Hammers, Arsenal were the Gunners, Man United were the Red Devils and Albion were . . . the Baggies. It didn't exactly arouse a sense of awe-inspiring admiration within me. However, the spectacle of thousands of Albion fans bouncing up and down on the Hawthorn terraces shouting was one of the more endearing displays of team support.

Naturally, these days, I rarely have the opportunity to attend the matches of the team that I have followed for the last seventeen years. I do not purchase any of the plethora of replica shirts that seem to be in a state of frequent colour transmutation, nor do I buy any of the wonderful array of Man United merchandise that is so readily available at the club's own megastore as well as in supermarkets, sports shops, stationers, gift shops and any other retail outlet that Manchester United Plc can colonize. Yet, to this day, nine months of my year are spent religiously studying League tables, following matches on television, reading reports on games and players in the press and, of course, picking my own best eleven for the starting line-up. Then, when the season is over, hours are spent in the summer mulling over the latest release of transfer speculation, who's going where, who's signing whom? Some of my most unaffected moments of genuine emotional experience and release have been occasioned by football. Normally a reserved kind of character (especially with family) I found myself on one occasion jumping and cheering and hugging my mother in a fit of ecstasy when Mark (Sparky to his mates) Hughes equalized with a typically brilliant volley in the last minute of the 1994 FA Cup semi-final against Oldham. Whilst my mother failed to comprehend the nervous passion that exploded from me, I wallowed in the gleeful satisfaction of knowing the elusive League and Cup Double was still very much on, while refuting the envious chants of 'You're gonna win fuck all'. This is how my life is affected and infused by football, it singularly occupies a space in my being that can govern what my mood is like and alter my immediate outlook on life. How was it then that Manchester United were the team that became the custodians of my hopes, my dreams and my fears?

The multi-million pound deals between satellite and terrestrial television companies, and the governing football bodies that allow games to be shown live in homes, pubs and clubs around the world, have led to an inter-dependency which not only provides one of the financial bases for the effective operation of football, but has also given rise to a new order of football spectatorship. The armchair soccer pundit, with a satellite dish on the roof and remote control in the hand, can watch live British football matches up to three or four times a week within the familiar territory of his or her own home. For the Asian community this has been of special importance and impact. Similar to this community's mass purchase of video cassette recorders in the late seventies and early eighties (for the viewing of popular Indian films), Asians became subscribers to Sky TV *en masse*. The availability of the all-Asian super-channel Zee TV was one reason for this phenomenon, with blockbuster Bollywood films shown almost every night, along with various Asian dramas, soap operas and factual programmes, not to mention the latest news and current affairs broadcast daily from the subcontinent. For the older members of the British-Asian communities, the likes of Zee TV and AsiaNet provided much needed television entertainment that was in their own languages and beamed on to their TV screens every day of the week. Another, equally important reason for mass satellite television uptake was that young children, teenagers, adolescents and many adults, craved the consumption of the re-vamped and re-vitalized football product. Being subscribers to Sky Sports would permit their spectatorship of and engagement in hyper-real football.

Due to the specific constrictions (some self-imposed) that discouraged Asians, indeed many non-whites, from attending live matches (terrace violence, racism in grounds and personal insecurity), satellite television has given them the opportunity to follow their favourite team via TV. It has also allowed viewers to become as much a part of a particular team's fan-base as such displaced support can allow.

Television also plays a significant part in the reasons behind the widespread British-Asian support of two particular English football teams: Manchester United and Liverpool are far and away the two most widely supported, followed and recognized clubs amongst the Asian community. Liverpool's massive success through the 1970s and 1980s made them the foremost club in Britain and even Europe. All this meant that Liverpool were always on *Match of the Day*, *Star Soccer* and other regional variations; they were the team that the pundits would talk about, that TV highlights would choose to show and the newspapers and magazines cover. This widespread exposure meant that Liverpool became the team that many of the British-Asian population were most familiar with. Due to the restrictions that inhibited their attendance at football grounds, local teams were largely followed out of a sense of regional duty. If the local club was a high-flying, successful outfit that had a certain share of media exposure, then the greater the bond with and support from the surrounding Asian population. West Bromwich Albion in the 1970s were such a club and thus achieved a quite substantial Asian following during this period. Many of the current Albion fans from this community are in their late twenties or thirties, reflecting the period of time in which the Baggies had their heyday.

During the period when their arch rivals Liverpool were dominating the domestic and European football scene, Man United indulged their fanciful whims in the First Division's mid-table safe-haven. Never looking as though they had the strength of conviction to win a League title, they firmly augmented their position as the country's most glamorous club that was never really going to win the Championship. They would cruelly raise the hopes of their followers early in the season, but the club would forever struggle with the majestic Busbian legacy that hung like an albatross desperately around its neck.

United's decline coincided with the legislative curbing of the flow of immigrants into Britain, and so those second generation British-Asians who were born in this country who followed football (from the seventies onwards) knew primarily of a Man United that didn't win things but were often on television. They were part of the generation that witnessed a former United great, Dennis Law, back-heel a goal for local rivals Manchester City that would relegate the Red Devils to the old Second Division. Success was not the quintessential pre-requisite for British-Asians' support of this team. It was simply its proliferation on TV screens and in magazines, and the constant proclamations of United being the most glamorous club in the land, the richest and most widely supported that persuaded, or conditioned, young British-Asians into pledging their allegiance to Manchester United. It was this kind of club promotion that had given United a diverse fan base that was spread across the world. Young British-Asian fans have also found themselves drawn to this glamorous universalism that was inextricably linked to the psychological and emotional effects of the 1958 Munich air crash tragedy. For early Asian immigrants in Britain, this disaster was one of their first and most gripping encounters with football. It didn't matter that you were new to England, or that you knew little if anything about football. Everyone, no matter what language they speak or which culture they are from, recognizes and understands the profound grief and tragic injustice of the unnecessary loss of young lives, particularly in such extreme circumstances. United's sombre history infused many people with an endearing and enduring association with the club. People whom I knew to be fans of West Bromwich Albion at the time when Bryan Robson was still at the Hawthorns shifted their support to Man United when Robson was transferred to Manchester in 1981. Thus when United signed Robson, a great player, they also inherited an aspiring Asian collection of fans who would accompany the club along its journey to regained splendour. To this day many British-Asians in my locality cite Manchester United as their first team and West Bromwich Albion as their second; a phenomenon that also operates in the other direction.

During a televised match between Newcastle United and Queens Park Rangers at the end of the 1995–6 season, I experienced a rather poignant convergence of my footballing and ethnic allegiances. QPR had, astonishingly, taken the lead in the first half at St James' Park, at a point in the season when Newcastle were gathering speed down that slippery slide that handed Manchester United the Premier League title. I was watching the highlights of the game on *Match of the Day*, having avoided the TV and radio all day to imbue a sense of nervous tension and anticipation to my bi-weekly intake of televised football. Following the terror of going 1–0 down, Newcastle rallied to the cause and the then captain Peter Beardsley scored a stunning equalizer. At this point BBC cameras switched from a shot of Beardsley being mobbed by his fellow players to scenes of delirium in the crowd. As I cursed the Rangers keeper for allowing the ball to pass him on his near post, and nervously begrudged the Toon Army their moment of celebration, I saw an Asian man with a turban jumping up and down and hugging other jubilant Newcastle fans. I sat staring into the television screen not really able to order my reaction to such a strange sight. When the camera first showed this turbaned Asian man celebrating his beloved football team scoring a goal, I was proud, impressed and touched by the spectacle of his odd, yet quite assimilated presence within the clannish confines of the Toon Army. Then, almost immediately afterwards, the realization that he was cheering a Newcastle goal that may have a bearing on Man United winning the title quickly displaced the instinctive sense of admiration with a vocal release of expletives. This incident has endured and stands as a marker of the transcendental quality of football to create boundaries and barriers, and then collapse and overcome them. Whilst individual instances, such as the case of the Sikh Newcastle fan, support this utopian vision of football's power and presence, the dilemma of national support can shatter that optimistic myth, and indeed show that some of the boundaries that football creates are erected, policed and enforced by powers beyond the game's control.

I was born in the industrial and geographic heart of England in 1972, I have lived my life since solely on English shores – indeed, further away from the shores than most people in the country. I speak, read and write English fluently, I have had a typical English education, many of my friends are English, much of my manner is English, but am I English? The answer is quite simply no.

I have a passport which states that I am British, but my passport also displays a photograph of me looking remarkably similar to C3PO from *Star Wars*, so its credence comes under some question. My parents hail from South Asia, as did my grandparents and their parents before them, yet I was born and bred in England. But the colour of my skin and the sound of my name, as well as food I eat and the mother-tongue I speak, mark me out as being of distinctly non-English design. What then are the conditions or controls by which I can situate my national identity, or more particularly, my identification with a nation? These can be gleaned out of popular sport, and there is no sport more popular than football.

As a youngster I spent a great deal of time in the presence of football-loving uncles, elder cousins and my father, all of whom were staunch Brazil fans. They had witnessed England's 1966 World Cup victory at a time when they were only just beginning to establish a new life for themselves in this country, and when faced by conditions of complete estrangement from the dominant 'host' society, as well as a significant level of hostility in England. Due to such impositions they found it practically impossible, if not scandalous, to harbour any real affiliation with, or support for the victorious England team of '66. And England's rather more efficient, practical style of play didn't lend itself to soliciting the admiration of its new migrant residents; instead, they were drawn to the irresistible flamboyance of the free-flowing Brazilians. Some of the earlier South Asian immigrants were privileged enough to have seen, in parts, television coverage of the 1962 World Cup-winning Brazil team that boasted the likes of Garrincha, Vava and, briefly, the maturing genius of Pelé. For most of the first generation of immigrants, the love affair with Brazil became crystallized and perfected in 1970, when possibly the greatest national side of all time lifted the Jules Rimet trophy for the third time in World Cup history. Here was a football dream-team with central defenders who could effortlessly dribble the ball past lunging attackers, where each player possessed the ability to score from virtually any angle, and, most importantly, this was a team made up of players who were not afraid to show off their skills, not afraid to take on defenders, shoot from long range or attempt the outrageously spectacular. In short, Brazil were dedicated to entertainment and exhibitionism. Their players not only possessed more skill and ability than most of the players of other teams, they were also entrenched in the belief that their technical superiority assured them, indeed bestowed upon them, the greatness of World Cup glory.

Brazil played heavenly football, scored incredible goals, and won World Cups. What more reason could there be for anyone to give their support to such a team? One such reason would be that they were not English and they were not white. For the first-generation South Asian immigrants like my father, uncles and older cousins, they represented a nation that was distant to England, both geographically and culturally, and one that seemingly had no ties or commonalities with the country of their resettlement. This may sound rather antagonistic, even ungrateful – after all, this was the country that had allowed them to set up a new home, given them opportunities to earn a living, become businessmen, and the chance to manufacture a more prosperous life for their families. Yet all this could not disguise or displace the fact that they were foreigners and regarded as such by the majority of white indigenous Britons. The England football team represented traditional England, white English men playing football for England under the flag of St George, and playing against other 'foreign' teams. Since this group of immigrant residents of England were a visible and foreign 'other' within the socialized confines of the nation, they arrived at a more immediate association with the foreign 'other' teams of non-English footballing nations. In the case of Brazil, the Brazilian footballers were not only foreign in terms of them not being English, they were also visibly 'strange' in regards to their colour. Brazil comprised of players whose complexion of skin was not dissimilar to that of the South Asian men. They identified with those that looked more like them rather than with those against whom they were demarcated as being people of 'colour', as being, essentially, non-white. The likes of Carlos Alberto even looked Asian, with his tanned brown skin, while others such as Pelé and Jairzinho were black men like the ones that worked in the factories, lived in the same streets and drank in the same pubs as the South Asian immigrants. Brazil was a team that they could support because of its footballing brilliance and supremacy; it was also a nation they could support because it did not represent the people that posited them as foreign and somehow inferior, and it was a nation that had not exacted colonial oppression over their homeland for over a century.

And so this was the legacy that I inherited. Moulded into a hereditary Brazil fan, I grew up hearing about how great Pelé was, just how superb the 1970 team was, and how Brazil have always been the best football team in the world in all eras, no matter what. The indelible scar that honours the sanctity of my own relationship with the Brazilian football team was inflicted back in 1982, during a World Cup tournament that concretized my union with Brazil. This was the team that represented 'Brazil' (as the embodiment of soccer greatness) for me. Approaching my first decade of life on this earth, I recall sitting spellbound in front of our rather large television, mesmerized by the exotic sights and sounds of Spain '82. It was a similar experience to that I remembered about Argentina, four years earlier, but this time round I had my sensory and mental faculties tuned in to the sporting quest and adventure of what I had come to realize was the greatest football competition in the world. Zico was a name that had been made familiar to me through seeing the player on TV, in footie magazines, and hearing older cousins shouting it when playing football on the streets. To watch the man in all his superb glory was a thrill that is as real now as it was back then: this tanned, long-haired, slight man in the golden shirt and blue shorts, who always wore those tight gold bangles around his wrists (as did many of the Brazilian players), bangles that I thought were Karas (Sikh bangles signifying the brotherhood of the faith). He seemed to me to be a fictitious character who only existed as part of this fantastical Brazilian football paragon (an astonishingly precocious thought for a 9-year-old). He was surrounded by other players who made the whole outfit a collection of unrivalled talent: Eder was a left-winger who scored ridiculous goals by curling the ball with the outside of his foot from thirty yards, making it swerve in two directions before hitting the back of the net; Socrates was the majestic, beautifully poised midfield maestro, who passed the ball from corner to corner with grace and panache. The other members of the team could all score from virtually any range and produce moments of skilful magic that players from other teams wouldn't even attempt. These players were just as memorable for their names alone: Junior, Falcao, Cerezo, names that were joyous to shout out, or even just whisper.

Brazil reached the Word Cup second round, where they encountered a stubbornly resolute Italian team that had Paolo

Rossi, one of Europe's leading strikers, spearheading the attack. In a match that has become inscribed in the annals of football history, the cavalier men of Brazil lost the game to an Italian poacher. Rossi punished a naïve and undisciplined Brazilian defence and scored a hat-trick that effected his team's 3–2 victory over the tournament favourites. As I sat watching the TV in a state of exhausted despair, looking at Zico, Eder and the others running off the pitch looking shell-shocked, kissing the crosses they wore around their necks and crossing themselves, I too had to flee from this site of spiritual carnage. I was only 9 years old and much of what I knew about football was about Brazil. So when I saw them entertaining the world by playing the beautiful football that I had come to assume was their norm, I expected them to win all their games, score lots of goals and gloriously lift the World Cup. When they lost to Italy I had no way of handling the overriding feelings of injustice and betrayal. I had been let down by all those who had spun me fantastic yarns of Brazil's magnificence, I was aggrieved by Italy's refusal to be beaten, and I felt betrayed by who or whatever made the important decisions in life. The force that controlled the course of destiny had betrayed my innocence. Confronted by such calamitous desolation, I did what most other 9-year-olds would do in that situation, I picked up my orange plastic football and kicked the absolute living hell out of it in my back yard. Zico *did* score in the dying seconds, then Eder scored another, Socrates another, and Italy were comprehensively beaten – Brazil had reached the World Cup Final. It was only when complete exhaustion had set in that I went back inside and faced the painful truth of defeat. Football wasn't all about great goals and great players, after all, it was also about great pain and great loss.

During the '82 World Cup finals I watched only one England game: the opening match against France, in which Bryan Robson scored the fastest goal in the competition's history, finding the net after only 27 seconds. England won that game

3–1, but were held to a goalless draw in the final match of the second phase, which sent them out of the World Cup. Robson's quick goal is one of the very few memories I have of England's exploits in Spain, where they won all three of their first round matches and departed unbeaten. Yet in 1986 and in 1990 there wasn't a single World Cup game played by England that I missed, and my support for the team was every bit as ardent and passionate as that for Brazil as a child, indeed possibly more so. By the time of the World Cup finals of '86 and, especially, '90 I had become quite enmeshed into popular British youth culture. I listened to Western pop music and watched television programmes and films that were British or American, moreover white. I had friends who were English ('English' being often used euphemistically for saying that someone is white), I went to a school that had mostly white pupils and all white teachers, so I had become fully immersed in Englishness. In my teenage years, I didn't regard myself as being English *per se*, but I lived in England, surrounded by English people, and took part in the social, cultural and linguistic forms of this country. Thus when England the nation was represented in a domain conducive to pledges of allegiance, as football undoubtedly is, I found myself becoming completely drawn into the all-consuming support of the nation's representative football team.

The heroes that I held sacred as a young child, that had been impressed on to me by coercing older relatives, had been displaced by new figures of idolization. Brazil had been replaced by England, Zico and Maradona had been moved aside by Hoddle, Waddle, Robson, Barnes and Irishman Whiteside. I craved football every day, and when I wasn't playing the game I wanted to watch it on TV, where I saw players from English teams playing in the English League. Zico and Maradona were rarely seen on British television at that time, and so the likes of Waddle and Whiteside took the burden of my adoration. I even supported England against Brazil when John Barnes scored that fabulous solo goal in Rio, and also when England played

Argentina in the '86 World Cup quarter-final and Maradona revealed both sides of his flawed genius. I swore at the referee as he netted his infamous 'hand of God' goal, and sat dejected and simultaneously exhilarated at the amazing spectacle of his second, a goal that only Diego Maradona could have scored. By 1990 my passionate support of the England football team had reached its feverish zenith, a height from which it was inevitably and abruptly felled. Like many other football fans in this country, I too rejoiced and jumped around deliriously when David Platt grabbed the last-minute winner against Belgium in Italia '90. I also experienced the common acute distress that gripped the nation following England's penalty shoot-out defeat at the hands of the old enemy (West) Germany. In between these two games, however, the seeds of my forthcoming disassociation and dissatisfaction with the England team had been sown.

In the quarter-finals of Italia '90 England faced the tournament's surprise package, the Lions of Cameroon. This was a game that England were expected to win; they had players of greater experience, ability and strength than the Cameroon team, which had delighted neutral fans with the fluidity of their football in an otherwise rather austere competition. I accompanied a few friends to a local pub to watch the match on a large screen. I knew that a great atmosphere would be generated and wanted to be party to it. In my small group of friends there were only two of us who were non-white (he too was a British-Asian), indeed, once we were in the pub we realized that we were quite possibly the only two non-white people in the whole place, at least amongst those downstairs watching the football. At first we were not too dismayed by our apparent conspicuousness; we felt relatively safe for we were with other white people who were from the local vicinity of the public house.

The match started, and soon after David Platt scored to put England 1-0 ahead. We all cheered ecstatically in unison and jumped up together spilling drinks in celebration of England, the country in which we all lived, taking the lead. Then Cameroon scored. And Cameroon scored again. England were now 2–1 down and the atmosphere had changed drastically from jubilant rapture to nervous solemnity. Those watching in the pub couldn't believe that England had let their lead slip, and that they were on the brink on being eliminated from the World Cup at the feet of one of the tournament's minnows. Whether it was out of helplessness, tension or frustration, I cannot firmly say, but what proceeded left my friend and me feeling radically estranged from the rest of the worried England fans. If a Cameroon player was trying to waste time on the pitch, or deliberately fouled one of the England players, he was subjected to abuse from the crowd in the pub. The nature of the abuse was directed towards the Cameroon players' 'blackness', the fact of their being black. Terms such as 'black bastard' and 'nigger' started to become audible amongst the sporadic bouts of oohing, aahing and shouting. Since my friend and I were the only two faces of 'colour' within this collective, furtive stares were directed our way, some trying to gauge whether or not we were affected by the remarks, others signalling a xenophobic fear and distrust of any person that was not white, which had uneasily emerged from the momentary failure and ineptitude of the England football team. It wasn't simply the case that my friend and I were not willing to be party to such ignorant displays of racist bigotry, we too were made to be the targets of indirect racial taunts, the odd comment from some mindless imbecile behind us wanting to tell us that our lot were a bunch of dirty black bastards, and other remarks in a similar vein. We of course left soon after, whilst our sanity, tolerance and faces were still intact. We had entered the pub as members of the wider band of patriotic England supporters; we were forced to leave as estranged and marked foreign others. We were not white, so we could not be real England fans, not like real white English fans.

In the aftermath of Italia '90 my support of the England

football team gradually but categorically eroded away. My experience during the Cameroon match had a certain degree of influence in this, as did the reign of Graham Taylor, but the main reason for my withdrawal from the rest of the England fan base was the fact that I had begun to think about my position in British society much more deeply and analytically, analysing the effects of my ethnicity, the methods of my minoritization and the exclusion and denial of my difference. Whilst Taylor was manufacturing a team out of third-rate players, playing a dour football that was his trademark, and miserably resigning England to World Cup non-qualification and himself to the rank and file of the unemployed, I was distancing myself from a team that were becoming laughing stocks for the rest of the football world. England were indeed a bunch of 'headless chickens' who were made to look sadly inept and foolishly incompetent whenever they faced top-class teams in important matches. I did not want to be associated with such a failing England team. I, after all, was not English; I may be British but my heritage is not English and never was. The more England failed on the pitch the more I barracked them and revelled in their misery. How could I have ever associated myself, even given myself, to a football team that represented the nation which had inflicted decades of imperial rule and colonial oppression upon the country of my parents', grandparents' and great-grandparents' birth, the land in which they had lived and where many of my relatives continue to live in England's lingering shadow? I was in the same situation as that first generation of South Asian immigrants, who had found it impossible, nay damnable, to give their support to any representative of the nation under whose arrogant and self-serving rule they or their predecessors had suffered. With such memories or inherited accounts as reminders, it was little wonder that no South Asian immigrants could pledge their allegiance to the English flag, even if it was just for the sake of a football match.

For years I too could not reinstate my affiliation to England's football team. Wherever I went in this country I was reminded of my otherness, my strangeness, my foreign-ness, my non-Englishness. I found it increasingly problematic reconciling my residency in a country that had such an antagonistic past relationship with my nominal ancestral homeland. If I went to certain nightclubs or pubs where I was the only black or Asian face to be seen, my presence was immediately, and unforgivingly, conspicuous. I was not like any other person in that particular place and the inquisitive (sometimes threatening) stares that came my way pointed to the fact that I was a freak: my existence was coloured by ethnicity. Although I've endured, anticipated and even understood the prolonged looks and muffled comments made by incredulous clubbers and pub-goers, my accompanying (white) friends continue to struggle to appreciate the fact that my difference is accentuated, indeed paramount, in other people's eyes. They cannot understand why strangers view me with such curiosity. My friends know me, know my pathetic sense of humour and my personality above and beyond my ethnic membership. For those who don't know me, it is my ethnicity that blatantly marks who I am, and it remains true to say that only those who look English, who look 'white', are accepted as being English.

Nationalistic and patriotic emotions, desires and drives are difficult for me to experience or express, for I do not harbour 'true' allegiance to any nation, in fact the thought of such ritualized arse-licking of a country seems a distinctly abhorrent and ridiculous idea to me, anyhow. The fervent height (or depth, depending on your outlook) of my disdain with England was reached in the memorable European Championships semi-final clash between England and Germany at Euro '96. I felt aggrieved and dismissive of the jingoistic muscle-flexing fervour that had beset certain parts and certain inhabitants of the nation (not everywhere and everyone was caught up in the wave of the national feel-good factor that was pervaded through the media). My flat-mate at the time, although a very intelligent and perceptive man, was also adrift amongst this fervour, as was another friend of mine. They both understood my reasons for abstaining from cheering England to victory, and sympathized with the view that my ancestral heritage had a distinctly anti-thetical relationship with England's history. However, they were not of South Asian descent, my flat-mate was white and my other friend was of mixed race (black and white), and had completely immersed themselves in the patriotic celebration that Euro '96 had become. On the night of the England–Germany semi-final, they went to the local pub to watch the match amongst other suitably vehement England fans. I stayed in my flat, on my own, knowing that an England victory would cause me some distress, and a Germany win would send me into unadulterated delight. The prospect of having to disguise and deny my true affiliations amongst virulent England supporters in a pub left me quite sure that I was better off watching the match on TV in the solitude of my own home.

The end of extra-time. Southgate misses his penalty. I jump up and punch the air shouting and screaming. Then I almost immediately feel a massive sense of regret and sorrow for Gareth Southgate, even though he was an England player. I would not wish that kind of misery upon anyone. Moeller placed the ball down on the penalty spot, ran up, and scored in the top-right corner. My eyes nearly popped out of their sockets as I leapt to my feet, flailing my arms and kicking the table. I was lost in the delirium of England's defeat, defeat at the hands of their greatest footballing foe, Germany. My jubilation was not occasioned by, or in celebration of, a victory; it was for the loss. Many of my British-Asian peers (friends and relatives to whom I spoke) said that they too felt the same pleasure from seeing England beaten by Germany, but younger British-Asians had a different view. Teenagers and younger kids, who were not yet cynical enough to question their national identity, regarded England as their only feasible home. They knew of little else other than England was where they lived, where they went to school, where they watched English television programmes, listened to English music and supported English football teams. It was only natural then that they should support the English national football team as well, for this team contained the players that they knew best and most intimately. No team from any other nation could engage their mental and psychological faculties, engage their person in the way that the England team was able to. This was not simply a case of national identification, it was also about personal identification. A comparable scenario was many English people's support of the Republic of Ireland football team during the World Cup USA '94. This was an Irish team made up of players mainly from the English Premiership and Football League, players with whom many of us were very familiar.

In June 1996, as the cameras perused the carnivalesque sights and sounds of Wembley Stadium in the build-up to that epic semi-final match, we were given a hopeful vision of what Britain would truly look like as a fully operational and truly egalitarian multicultural community. England supporters, young and old, black, white, South Asian and South East Asian, men, women and children, all gathered together under the auspices of cheering on their team. South Asian families were in the crowd next to white families; kids all with their faces painted, proudly wearing their England shirts. Not a Combat 18, NF or BNP poster in sight, let alone the ugly presence of right-wing neo-Nazi thugs. Everyone singing 'Three Lions', a song that celebrates the past by looking to the present and future, acknowledging England's recent period of impotence and stagnation, but expressing the hopes for better times. Was this a momentary façade that manufactured the image of diverse unity and multi-ethnic harmony? Or was it the optimistic prophecy that attempted to illustrate the possible real achievement of a distant dream?

Today, as more and more foreign players enter the British

game, superstars such as Gianfranco Zola, Gianluca Vialli, Dennis Bergkamp and David Ginola have established ties in this country, received and locked-in the adulation of the fans of the clubs for which they play, as well as the admiration and respect of other football fans who appreciate their soccer prowess. These are players from countries such as Italy, France and Holland, all strong footballing nations. When we watch these players week in week out, plying their trade in the English Premiership, we establish a point of contact with them, a relationship with them based on familiarity and appreciation. Whenever we see a foreign player who plays for our own club representing his country in a football match, we want to see that individual do well and produce a brilliant display, so that we can say, 'He plays for us, he does. He's a Man United player, him.' In the process we are almost indirectly stating a small degree of support of the national football team that a particular player is representing. Problems arise when foreign players who play for your club side play against your national team – Zola's goal for Italy against England at Wembley in a World Cup qualifying match in February 1997 highlights this dilemma. A friend of mine who is a lifelong Chelsea fan and staunch England supporter was left with somewhat mixed feelings after the game. He was utterly dejected after England's defeat, one that put in jeopardy their chances of qualification, but he could not help but feel a little bit of pleasure and satisfaction at the fact that it was a Chelsea man who had scored what was a quite excellent goal. The club or country debate has many variations in its points of contention.

The present England football team mostly consists of players who are white, although recent times have witnessed the promising emergence of black players such as Les Ferdinand, Paul Ince and Sol Campbell – with certainly the latter two becoming established, solid linchpins in the team. Any white player playing for England is not and cannot be an accurate representation of all of England's male populace. Whilst black players can represent the minority black population of England, and embody the motifs of marginalization and racial difference that South Asians also experience in this country, they too fall way short of allowing British-Asians to feel that they are represented by England's football team, that they too are part of that team. If there was just one British-Asian, just one player of South Asian descent playing in the full England team, the level of interest and support for England would receive a massive boost, a huge injection of numbers and pride from the South Asian communities of this nation. They would be able to see a real marker of their ethnicity, of their social position and their cultural peculiarity, someone who had made it to the pinnacle of his profession.

I have recently been drawn into feelings of admiration and goodwill towards the current England team. One reason for this is that the new coach, Glenn Hoddle, was one of my childhood heroes, a man for whom I have the greatest of respect and admiration. Another factor for this resurgence of national footballing support is that many of the new crop of England players are from Manchester United, and I never want to see any United player fail. Whenever they do well and perform well amongst other internationals I feel a great sense of pride about the fact that they are 'our' players from 'our' club. But it is not just the players from Man United that I want to see achieving success on the pitch – players such as Alan Shearer and Steve McManaman are class players that enjoy showing off their abilities. And the growing influence of the black players in the England set-up is yet another reason for my burgeoning support. I want these players to do well to prove to the mindless bigots that black players can no longer be stereotyped into specific roles where it is simple to castigate and belittle them. These players can show that hard work, perseverance and talent can take you to the very top of the game, by working through and against racism and discrimination and not falling at their feet. The fact that England now play intelligent football based on passing and movement and near technical excellence endears me to the side even more.

But at the time of writing, as we approach France '98, and as the nationalistic football fervour begins to be exaggerated and manufactured once more, I find that I am yet again emotionally distancing myself and cerebrally dissociating myself from England's team of footballers. It is not the eleven men in white shirts that fuel my disdain, it is the falsifying and myopic vision of nationhood that envelops and exploits them that really gnaws at my gut. But like a certain Irish stout, I'm not bitter – desperate and forlorn, perhaps – but not bitter.

6 Celtic Cousins

Old Firm New Form

Whilst the campaign involving English-Asian footballers enjoys a relatively high profile, as well as varying degrees of institutional and governmental support, the Asian community in Scotland has, for the most part, been left to its own devices. Presently, there are over 40,000 Asian people living in Scotland, predominantly located in the big cities of Glasgow, Edinburgh and Dundee.

Scottish foundries and factories provided secure employment for many members of the various Asian communities, however, a number of Asian entrepreneurs established successful businesses in a variety of fields, such as the textile industry, wholesale foodstuff cash and carrys, retail outlets and restaurants. Scotland afforded Asians the opportunity to build the better and brighter future for their families that most Commonwealth immigrants in Britain aspired to. When, in the early seventies, manual labour in England became more and more scarce, similar vacancies and opportunities were present in Scotland. Thus there was a later surge of migration (mostly direct from the Indian subcontinent but also from England) to Scottish shores. But not everyone who went to seek their fortunes north of the border did so voluntarily. During the late seventies and early eighties good jobs, any jobs, were very hard to find, especially if you had few formal qualifications and you were black or Asian. One of my cousins, known by the family as Shinda, was in just such a predicament. With no interest in school or education, and with little regard for formal authority and a great propensity for mischief, this 15-year-old, slightly overweight school drop-out faced a bleak future of dead-end jobs, early marriage and having to rely heavily on his family for all kinds of support. But Shinda had an uncle in Scotland who had settled in Glasgow during the sixties and was now a successful businessman with his own wholesale cash and carry. This uncle had a young family who were not of an age when they could help in the running of the increasingly expanding family business, and so he sought the help of his extended family to provide him with the dynamic, dextrous and enthusiastic young partner he needed. Someone whom he could teach the practice of good business, the tricks of his trade, someone whom he could groom into a successful entrepreneur.

Shinda wasn't exactly the obvious choice, but it was agreed that he would leave Oldbury and join his uncle's family in Glasgow to begin a new life organized around the wholesale import and export of foodstuffs. On the day he was to leave, his uncle and aunt drove down from Glasgow to take him away. But Shinda was not going to go quietly. Realizing that his whole lethargic world was about to be turned on its head, he locked himself in one of the bedrooms and refused to come out. Words were exchanged, and Shinda eventually emerged from the bedroom and had to be physically 'loaded', kicking and shrieking, into his uncle's car.

The irony, though, is that the plump, mischievous and lazy teenage drop-out actually made quite a success of his re-ordered life in Scotland. Shinda recently moved back to Oldbury from Glasgow for personal reasons (the rest of the family still live or work in the Black Country) and brought with him his wife and his three Glaswegian children. Years earlier Shinda was assigned the nickname 'Jock', a pseudonym that has become his most recognized tag. Whilst he continues to speak with a broad Glaswegian accent, his kids (much to their lament) have succumbed to the distinctive droning of the Black Country brogue. Whilst their Scottish-ness is increasingly under pressure from the English cultural forces surrounding them, Jock remains fiercely Scottish. A staunch Glasgow Rangers fan, Jock has lost or dismissed his 'English heritage' from which he was taken away as a teenager. One potent signifier of this English disavowal manifests whenever he goes to watch an England international match at the local pub. You'll find him quite conspicuous amongst the lager-swigging spectators, because he'll be the one proudly wearing a Rangers shirt.

Fiaz Khan (34) and Hasib Ashgar (24) are representatives of a newer generation of Scottish-Asian football fanatics. Fiaz plays for the Scottish Asian Sports Association (SASA) and Hasib plays for Maxwell Park FC. Both are also committed supporters of the Old Firm rivals: Fiaz is a Glasgow Rangers fan and Hasib supports Glasgow's other giant, Celtic. These allegiances also provide an alternative look at issues concerning race, religion and nationalism in the context of Scottish football. According to Fiaz, the popularity of football among young Scottish-Asians is on a par with all other sections of the population: 'You go to parts of Glasgow on a Friday evening or a Sunday afternoon and the five-a-side pitches resemble Lahore. The ability of some of the lads on the ball is fantastic. The formation of full eleven-a-side teams only came about in the last two years, before that they just played the smaller five-a-side game.'

The situation in Glasgow has similarities with other parts of England, where sections of the Asian community appear to demonstrate a preference for the convenience and simplicity of the abbreviated five-a-side format. In towns like Oldham, Preston and Blackburn, members of the local Asian communities share a common appreciation of this form of football. So much so that many of them have even set up local leagues and competitions, which are not racially exclusive, but nonetheless have a tendency to attract mainly Asian players. For both Maxwell Park FC and SASA, their entry into mainstream league football has not been without incident; in fact, this experience has imbued the respective players with a penetrating sense of their multi-layered identity.

SASA have been fully pledged and competitive members of the Strathkelvin and District League for over five years. Their experiences of playing in this league and representing their community outside their immediate proximity have undoubtedly been major factors in enabling them to cope with problems of racism. Fiaz recalls: 'We were not naïve about our entry into the league and prepared ourselves for the racist abuse. But we seem to have overcome those early problems. While we still receive abuse, the situation is improving. Teams have come to terms with the fact that we are no pushovers. They look at us and say, "Hey, these guys can play, they are really skilful."'

SASA's team manager, Prem Singh, an exiled Brummie and now a member of Scotland's growing band of successful Asian entrepreneurs, does, however, recall one particular away game when SASA thought they were destined not to return home: 'We played Croys, the football team of a small mining village. I don't think they had seen an Asian before in the whole of their lives. They had five players sent off, and their supporters wanted to kick the hell out of us. It was a really violent match and one that could have turned into something tragic, but luckily we managed to escape without any major decapitation. We can look back and laugh about it now, but at the time we were scared to death.'

Compared with SASA, Glasgow's only other Asian football club is a relatively new kid on the soccer block. Maxwell Park FC was formed out of an emerging interest in playing football among young Asians living in the Glasgow Southside area. This club has had to endure a much more pronounced exposure to racism than its counterparts south of the border, and even its Glaswegian cousin. This can, in part, be attributed to the location in which Maxwell Park play their matches. Indeed, both Maxwell Park and the Scottish-Asian Sports Association cite the defining fact of location as an important feature of the antagonistic experiences they have encountered. SASA's Fiaz states: 'SASA play in a league with teams from outside Glasgow. They are mainly from the peripheral areas of Glasgow. In Glasgow, if racism manifests itself, it does so on peripheral estates because of social and economic problems.'

Hasib puts across the Maxwell Park perspective: 'With us, Maxwell Park FC, we play in the Glasgow East Sunday League, bang in the heart of Glasgow. There is a fair deal of racial tension in these inner city areas and we play teams precisely from that region. The fact that we play teams who are mostly linked to pubs, actual pub teams, probably doesn't help either. You go in for a challenge and they say "Watch out, black boy", or "you black bastard". They are clever enough to say it away from the referees so that they are not booked.'

Despite these experiences both teams are relatively pleased at the local football associations' efforts to address the problems of racism. Hasib recalls how these authorities have aided them in the past: 'The League is actually very good. On occasions when we have had to put up with heavy abuse, the League have taken quite prompt and stern action. In fact, we had one away League game rearranged because the home match had been so violent. During that game one of our players was trampled on by an opponent's studs. The League appreciated the volatility of the situation and acted accordingly.'

The faith placed in the authorities is shared by Fiaz, who thinks they are partly sympathetic because they appreciate the commitment of Asians to the game: 'Most of the teams think that we won't retaliate, we won't fight fire with fire, and most of us don't. That shows our passion for the game, that we are prepared to abide by the rules of fair play and non-violence, even though we often have to suffer the violence of other teams. Remember most of us guys work late on a Saturday night and then get up to play football early in the morning. It's not easy, but we are all very committed.'

In other parts of Britain, Asian communities are beginning to challenge their non-confrontational, passive stereotype with acts of physical retaliation. However, this is not just any part of Britain – this is Glasgow. Whilst Glasgow's Asian youths do not want to be perceived as pushovers, neither do they think they can be seen as outwardly aggressive. It would be rather easy to succumb to a superficial discussion of the archetypal Glaswegian hard-man, and so we shall. It is a widely accepted popular truism that the city of Glasgow is home to certain individuals who 'know how to look after themselves'. If a certain section of this intimidating clan displayed racially non-tolerant tendencies, then those who would be the victims of such intolerance would have to learn to 'look after themselves' as well. Fiaz elaborates on this point: 'You don't want to get a reputation for being rough in Glasgow. This is the city of hard-knocks. Perhaps, subconsciously, this is one of the reasons why it has taken us a long time to enter into mainstream leagues. What you don't want is a violent situation on the field when there are supporters around. The authorities have outlawed drinking in public parks, but the public have little regard for that aspect of the law and often just stand on the touchline swigging cans of lager. It's a violent culture up here. There is a lot of rivalry and fighting. The fact that we are Asian can aggravate matters further.'

Both Fiaz and Hasib appear to be reluctant to predict if more Glaswegian Asians will follow their clubs' example. For those who choose to pursue this route, at least they will be able to draw comfort and support from these pioneering clubs. But more immediately, what of the future for these two?

Although the SASA name unambiguously refers to itself as an Asian team, in the five years of its existence the composition of the team has become more racially mixed; something that is considered by both men to be a positive factor. Hasib: 'Maxwell Park do see SASA as a role model. The League Secretary is not placing us under any pressure, he respects our Asian identity, but he has suggested we may at some point in the future look to mix the team up. As long as we don't lose our identity we would be keen to move in this direction.'

The subject of compromise is again drawn out when discussing the question of nationality and allegiances to the adopted homeland or the ancestral homeland. Interestingly, both Fiaz and Hasib regard themselves as Pakistani-Scottish and not Pakistani-British. That is Pakistani first and Scottish second. Unlike their Asian counterparts south of the border, they refuse to have the Pakistani or Asian aspect of their identity nominally relegated as a suffix to the term 'British'; they do not call themselves British-Asians. They do, in fact, share a customary dislike of the English, an antagonizing prejudice that they acknowledge as being influenced by the native Scots. Hasib recalls: 'Everyone up here just hates the English. They all want to see England getting beat at everything. It doesn't matter who they're playing, we just want them beat.' But just how great is the extent of this alleged hatred towards the English? Where would their loyalties lie in a match between England and Pakistan's great adversaries India? Presumably indigenous Scots would be unwavering of their support of India in such circumstances. Surprisingly, for someone born in Pakistan, one would assume Fiaz to be closer to the country of his birth, but evidently that is not the case. Under the circumstances, Fiaz says that he would support India. A decision, perhaps, even more unexpected because his ancestral home, Kashmir, continues to be under Indian rule, but is also laid claim to by Pakistan. The state of Kashmir, situated on the north-west frontier that separates India and Pakistan, is an area that is predominantly inhabited by Muslims, but since 1947 the political issue of whether India or Pakistan should rule Kashmir has been a source of ongoing tension. Fiaz's Kashmiri roots do, however, explain in part his support for a Scottish Parliament, the desire for a self-governing body. Hasib takes a different stand on the England–India question. He likens the India–Pakistan rivalry to Celtic and Rangers,

142

only in his words, 'far worse'. The Celtic–Rangers debate causes major differences of opinion between the two men, but once again it emphasizes the British-Asian community is in every way as fanatical as their white counterparts in their allegiances to football clubs.

Within the realms of footballing philosophy there have been few comments to match the impact of Bill Shankly, when he spoke about football being a matter greater than life or death. Of course, Shankly was far too wise and intelligent to suggest that people should assume a literal interpretation of his famous quote; rather, what he was doing was articulating the passion which the game arouses amongst its devoted followers. It took another thirty years before Nick Hornby's *Fever Pitch* came along to put substance around Shankly's famous quote, and confirm that footballing passions are based neither on logic nor rationality, but are instead embedded in desire, emotion, culture and identity. Hasib finds it 'incredible' that a fellow Asian person could support a club, in this case Glasgow Rangers, with 'such a bigoted following'. Fiaz is somewhat uncomfortable in articulating his 'defence', but attributes his allegiance to the predominantly Protestant-supported Rangers as being akin to a situation in which love is blind: 'I simply follow the team. It's difficult to detach yourself from "your" team. Yes, a large number of the fans are very bigoted, and racist, and this rubs off on the club. Even now you can still get the British National Party distributing racist propaganda outside Ibrox. I became sucked in before learning about the bigotry and the conflict. Although on one of the first occasions I went to Ibrox, these Rangers fans shouted across the road, 'You black bastard.' I felt completely frustrated, angry and scared all at the same time. I didn't really know what to do or what their problem was. What still makes me angry, and something that surprises me, is how these so-called Rangers fans still called Mark Walters "sootie" after he scored all those goals for the club.'

In the words of John Williams of the Sir Norman Chester

Centre, football is not based on logic and rational thought channels; instead it's about emotion, space and irrationality. There is some logic, however, in Hasib's assertion that in the city of Glasgow, the Asian community's natural allegiance lies with Celtic rather than Rangers. He points to Celtic's history and their 'Bhoys Against Bigotry' campaign. Glasgow Celtic was founded in 1888 by a Marist Catholic priest, Brother Walfrid, as a charitable organization to help raise money for food, clothing and the relief of poverty among the destitute immigrant Irish population in Glasgow. Between the beginning and end of the nineteenth century, the Catholic population in Glasgow had grown more than tenfold, from 40,000 to over 450,000. It was this huge influx of migrants, against a backdrop of scarce resources, which had led to tensions between Catholics and Protestants. Brother Walfrid saw the new football club as a vehicle to bring the communities together. As an organization that grew out of the need to support the interests of migrants, it is therefore not surprising to see Celtic extend an arm out to Glasgow's latest migrant community. Feargus McCann, the club's managing director, states that: 'The founding principle of Celtic was to help integrate an immigrant [Irish] population into Scottish society, using football as the means. This was a community that was able to integrate but which was at the same time very successful in maintaining its own cultural identity. I think football is becoming elitist, and that is something we never want to see. Football is one of the largest common interests in society, almost a reference point for people. They say, "Where do we fit in?"'

Given some of the money-obsessed, autocratic chairmen running football, it is difficult to believe that these are the comments of a man who has a controlling interest in one of Britain's, arguably Europe's, biggest football clubs. Somehow it is difficult to imagine similar sentiments from the likes of Martin Edwards, Ken Bates, Doug Ellis or David Murray. There are, of course, those more cynical, who point to Celtic's motives as being altogether less than altruistic. This is an argument conceded by

Celtic, who openly admit that the club stands to gain in significant measures if it could capture a top Asian footballer. Interestingly, Celtic's alleged motives are not necessarily a particular concern among their Asian supporters. In Hasib's own words: 'Why should we be too bothered about Celtic's motives. At a time when the Scottish Football Association should have been leading on this issue they have been put to shame by Celtic's efforts. If Celtic gain in any way by their actions, then they will have done so because they rightly deserve it. Let's face it, how many other British clubs would have flown the national flags of India and Pakistan to mark the fiftieth anniversary of those countries?'

This last reference originated via a letter to the club from an Asian season ticket holder informing them of the impending half-century celebrations. Celtic's response prompted many Asians, including those based in England, to compliment the club on its actions and to forge a special place for the club in their affections. While the flag waving celebrations could be attributed to a politically correct and culturally adept public relations coup, the club has shown itself to be interested in pursuing more substantive anti-racist measures. Celtic's formulation of the 'Bhoys Against Bigotry' campaign is an attempt to demonstrate the club's stand against all forms of bigotry and ignorant intolerance. With the funds made available by Celtic, Glasgow City Council have adopted a number of measures, including the production of an ethnic minority schools' information pack, and have targeted specific monies to help the development of Asian football. The key link to the development work being undertaken is the City Council's Sports Development Officer, Kash Taank. As Kash himself acknowledges, none of the ideas being promoted and developed in Scotland may be new to England, but in Scotland it has taken a considerable period of time for clubs to even begin to move in a positive direction. Born in Coventry, but having spent the last five years of his life living and working in Scotland, Kash Taank is well equipped to offer an appropriate solution: 'Firstly, the authorities have to properly recognize that there is a genuine problem of racism in the game. Once they do that (and that is still a point of some doubt), then they have to overcome this anti-English mentality and accept that there may be valuable lessons to be drawn from the English football experience.'

Born Shopkeepers?

Mumtaz Hussain speculates that had his arrival into Britain in 1979 come much later, stricter immigration controls (a strong legislative feature of the last twenty years) may well have prevented his entry on to these shores. This is the account of someone who acknowledges that good fortune and fate have played important parts in his life. Following years of cleaning dishes and serving tables at someone else's restaurant, Mumtaz, on the advice of a close friend, decided to go it alone by buying a shop in the small village of Lesmahagow, situated almost equidistant between Glasgow and Edinburgh. In doing so Mumtaz was following a long-established tradition and pattern of employment that dates back more than eighty years.

During the early part of this century, the seaport of Glasgow, together with Southampton, Bristol, Cardiff and Liverpool, became 'home' to the first major sign of Asian entrepreneurial ingenuity in Britain. Although the majority of those who arrived subsequently moved into waged employment in major industrial cities, many, particularly those belonging to the Sikh Bhatra caste, stuck to peddling goods through self-employment. As early as the 1940s some of the more successful pedlars had moved upmarket. Some became intermediate wholesalers, acting as stockholders for their diasporic compatriots, others expanded with market stalls, whilst the most successful opened up retail shops. This trend towards business and self-employment was strongly reinforced during the severe industrial recession of the 1980s. Since then an increasing number of Asian migrants have looked towards self-employment both as a means of survival, and as the prestigious highway to continued upward mobility. They have taken to activities that required a low capital outlay, and where success depended primarily on hard work. Hence market stalls, grocery stores, newspaper and tobacco shops, restaurants, garages and small building firms were much favoured, with the most successful having now expanded into larger and more profitable enterprises, such as wholesale warehouses and supermarkets, and clothing and footwear manufacture.

As a native of the rural state of the Punjab, on the Indian–Pakistani border, Mumtaz found the idea of living and working in a small village an appealing proposition. He was also very mindful of the pitfalls of being a lone Asian in this potentially troublesome environment. At least in the main cities he could always call upon the support of the established network of fellow Asians, whereas in the village he would have to fend for himself. His mind was, however, resolutely made. The overriding concern was to establish a good standard of living for his family, and to provide opportunities for his children that were not available to him in Pakistan.

As he opened up that first morning he braced himself for the worst, anticipating an onslaught. That critical first test was not long in coming. On taking ownership of the premises it was apparent that the shop needed major investment to re-establish it as a viable business. Mumtaz remembers: 'Not long after I came to the shop, I decided to replace the shelving. I was nervous because I knew the food would need to be placed outside the shop while I was fixing the shelves. What was going through my mind was that local people would think I was unhygienic because I kept the food outside. But I shouldn't have worried because they understood why the food was outside and they still bought it. On another occasion my son was hurt in an accident and local people bought him gifts. That touched my heart quite sincerely, and from that day I made even greater efforts to take part in all community affairs.'

These two incidents formed the basis upon which the new Asian shopkeeper and the local indigenous population were to found a long and fruitful relationship. Football has come to play a very special part in this relationship. Before 1994 Mumtaz had taken no particular interest in the local team, Lesmahagow Juniors, or, for that matter, sport. He recalls: 'In the Punjab we used to play kabbadi and guli dandha [a subcontinental game involving a stick and balls or stones], but I had never really played football. One day in my shop I could hear customers talking about how the local football club was in danger of folding. What I did not realize until then was that local people, especially pensioners and the unemployed, used to watch Lesmahagow Juniors because they couldn't afford to go and see professional football. Although football was not my cup of tea I wanted to do something out of my heart to help the local community.'

That evening Mumtaz set his foot inside the club for the first time. During an open meeting, where the club's problems were shared with the local community, Mumtaz realized that he could offer the club his own business acumen: 'I listened carefully to what was being said and, first of all, it was quite difficult to follow. Fortunately I was not ashamed to ask some simple questions. Before the evening was out I understood the club's main problem. The club owned the registration of the players and every year the players are entitled to a retaining fee. If the club cannot pay this fee then the players are free to leave the club. I told the club that, in my opinion, their problem was like being a shopkeeper whose shop had empty shelves and no stock. Only in their situation the stock was the players.'

The things that were foremost in Mumtaz's mind concerned the way in which the club's affairs were managed. As for matters on the field, he surmised that if the club could be given a stable operating base, then the rest would follow automatically.

Following a great deal of anguish, when he attempted to reconcile his growing attachment to the village and its people with the prospect of losing a significant sum of money, he took the decision to help the club. However, before formally committing himself to bailing Lesmahagow Juniors out of the mire, Mumtaz sought some important safeguards: 'I agreed to lend the club £8000 on an interest-free basis. No time limit was set on the repayment period. This money ensured the club's "stock" was secured. I explained to them that though I knew little about football I did know how to run a business. By lending my expertise I could help this club avoid falling into this trap again. Maybe at first they did not like me telling them they were running their affairs badly. However, they needed to understand that they were running a club with an annual expenditure of more than £40,000, therefore it was vital they introduced some business principles.'

The injection of the £8000 staved off the immediate threat, but on the eve of a new season another fresh crisis hit the club. Most of the senior players and the coach announced that they were leaving. By now Mumtaz was beginning to become well accustomed to the inner workings and political nuances of the game. It was to leave him cynical but nonetheless realistic: 'One of the first things I learnt about football was that there is no loyalty among players, they are only after the money.' But because Lesmahagow now held the players' registration, at least the club could charge a transfer fee to any club that was interested in buying a particular player. The money realized from the sale of these players enabled the club to pay off its debts and invest in replacement players. In effect, Mumtaz had provided a bridging loan facility, only the length of the loan was considerably shorter than anyone had anticipated. Nevertheless, his money was the critical difference between sinking or swimming. Whilst the club was in its most stable financial position for many years, the last-minute exodus of players was to procure disastrous consequences on the field. Unfortunately the new players were not of the same quality as their predecessors, and the hastily prepared season was to end without the team having notched up a single victory, but at least the club remained alive and intact. Mumtaz saw this as a debt paid to his new family.

Members of the local community who had already warmed to the Hussains were once again very grateful. The shop and football club were two of the key local institutions, and within a short time the village newcomers had played a crucial role in ensuring the future of both. Jim Weir, a Scottish former professional footballer with Partick Thistle and West Bromwich Albion, and himself a local resident, spoke of the respect afforded to Mumtaz: 'This man and his family have a great respect among the Lesmahagow people. The community are grateful for everything they have done for the village. They took over the shop when it looked as if the village was going to lose their old newsagent's. All of them, his wife and wee bairns, are treated as one of the Lesmahagow family – now you can't ask for more than that.'

Weir is also involved in coaching the village's young schoolboy footballers, something he attributes to Mumtaz' influence. Together with Glasgow City Council's Kash Taank, Weir and Mumtaz have developed an innovative coaching project involving Lesmahagow and Asian youngsters. The idea behind the project is to improve mutual understanding of the youngsters' respective cultural and social backgrounds. Its pioneering spirit has, however, not always been in evidence. Weir recalls: 'There have been a few teething problems. Initially, the Lesmahagow boys refused to pair up with the Asian boys, but with the passage of time that problem has been overcome. You see the Lesmahagow kids have been brought up with the hope we all had at that age of becoming footballers. The Asians have never had the same chances available to them, so they are especially keen to jump at it.'

Owing to business commitments, Mumtaz is no longer able to play an active part in the club's committee, but he does remain a staunch supporter in many other ways. In particular he concentrates his efforts on developing new ideas for fundraising. On occasions he can still be found with his bucket at home games asking supporters to dig deep to make a contribution to club funds. Recently he has introduced a highly successful fund-raising event called the Sportsman's Dinner. It is quite remarkable to think that only a few years ago Mumtaz had no particular understanding of, or interest in, the game. Yet this chance meeting with football has, he claims, taught him a great deal more about the indigenous population than anything else could have done. 'What I have discovered is that football is part of life in this country. If you want to enter into the mainstream, then football is a good way to do it.' He claims that by failing to fully understand football's place in society, the British-Asian community is missing out on lost opportunities: 'Because I take my two sons to Ibrox and watch the football on the TV with them, they can better relate to their friends in school. You want to have seen their faces when they were sitting next to the touchline watching Brian Laudrup play. If I am going to be fair to coming generations I need to make the path clearer, otherwise I would be dishonest. If our children want to become footballers then we need to give them a helping hand. I have now truly discovered that football is such a big business, but why have we shut ourselves off from this big business? How many jobs are involved with football? When we first came to this country we weren't trained to be shopkeepers or restaurateurs, but we've just become good at it. By the same token, we can become equally impressive at many other things, football being just one of them.'

Sergeant Singh

One of the more unsavoury episodes in recent Scottish football history is the period when the black English footballer, Mark Walters, joined Graeme Souness's Glasgow Rangers from Aston

Villa. Walters' arrival at Ibrox in the 1987–88 season was, in itself, not unusual. By that time Souness had developed a fetish for signing English players; that is, white English players – Nigel Spackman, Mark Hateley, Terry Butcher, Graham Roberts. During Walters' spell playing football in Scotland he was to endure some of the worst racism experienced by a black footballer whilst playing in Britain. As if the prospect of abuse from opposition supporters by virtue of being the only black player at Scotland's most glamorized club (he was joined later by former Norwich winger, Dale Gordon) was not enough, he also incurred the wrath of many of his club's 'own' supporters. While Walters was coming to terms with his new-found terrace status, another ethnic minority representative was making his way into the fervent cauldron of Ibrox, only this man was coming to work behind the scenes and not on the grotesquely exposed pitch. In the course of his time at Rangers, he was to experience, at first hand, the extent of the outpourings of hatred and inhumane malice that were directed at Mark Walters. This is the tale told from another perspective, a slant on the rituals of football support that rarely receives widespread attention. That ulterior view is taken from inside the Ibrox Park matchday police control room.

Dilawar Singh was born in India in 1945. At 15 his family decided to up their Punjabi roots and head for Scotland. Although he was tempted to follow his friends into the teaching profession, Dilawar chose instead to pursue a career in the police force. The decision was in keeping with a family tradition that had seen generations of his family join the Indian state police or the militia. The particular dynamics that structured his relationship with a predominantly white constabulary are in stark contrast to any post he may have held in the Indian police force. For over two hundred years the Indian Army has drawn the majority of its recruits from the Punjab region. Indeed, throughout the world, a popular generic archetype used about Sikh men concentrates on their strong fighting traditions and warrior-like resolve. The contribution they made to the allied armed forces' efforts has never been particularly well documented, nor indeed told with any great vigour outside India. During both World Wars the Indian volunteer armies were to lose hundreds of thousands of men in the course of active service across Europe and the Far East.

In 1970, when Dilawar joined the police force, he became one of the first Asian recruits in the whole of Britain. Within ten years he was appointed to the rank of sergeant, his current rank. Now, in his early fifties, Dilawar has resigned himself to seeing his days out in the police force as a sergeant, although he points out with a mixture of both pride and regret that many of his superior ranking officers began their fledgling careers under his tutelage. As former police Inspector Alison Halford has recently shown in her case of alleged sexual discrimination, the police force remains a very difficult institution for both women and black people to penetrate beyond relatively junior levels. It is not therefore surprising to see the continued under-representation of ethnic minorities in the British police force. Currently only around twenty out of seven thousand police officers in Scotland are from ethnic minority backgrounds. This is a situation that intensely disappoints Dilawar: 'I think the ethnic minority community has to take some responsibility for not coming forward, but the police authorities must also do much more to help. I know down south in England they have had some success in the Metropolitan forces; maybe this is something they can learn from up here.'

The location of Ibrox Park is central to Dilawar's 'patch'. In May 1997 the national spotlight fell once more on the Govan constituency as Glasgow Rangers recorded their ninth successive League Championship, and in doing so matched the achievement of their bitter local rivals, Glasgow Celtic. However, that was not the only reason for the glaring media spotlight. Following the General Election, Govan continued to bask in the artificial light of celebrity as it made British electoral history by electing Britain's first Muslim Member of Parliament, Mohammed Sarwar, a local businessman. Owing to newspaper revelations Sarwar's initial euphoria was rather short-lived, as he became entangled in accusations of alleged bribery and electoral malpractice, leading to his temporary exclusion from the Labour Party. At the time of writing Mohammed Sarwar continues to remain suspended from the Labour Party. The district of Govan represents an interesting mix of the traditional Protestant 'Loyalist' elements, containing the zeal of Union Jack patriotism, and a significant Asian community, who have often been the 'victims' of the flag-waving British nationalists. Of course, this being Glasgow, the picture is much more complex than that. That is not to suggest Asian people are somehow immune to the excesses of the bigotry and prejudice that are all too evident in the city. It is, however, worth asking the question: is Glasgow's Asian community less vulnerable to the threats posed by racists than it may be in cities and towns in England because significant levels of anger are being exerted between Catholics and Protestants? Dilawar has his thoughts on such a poser: 'I think that is a very interesting question. You see, I cannot speak for other cities, but there is great deal of anger in Glasgow between Catholics and Protestants. That anger is out there all the time, and in all areas of life. You could say by constantly fighting amongst each other, they divert their hatred away from Asians. Then again, you could also say that because anger forms part of the make-up of people in this city, that it is then easier to transfer it to other communities.'

Shortly after being appointed a sergeant, Dilawar became involved in the investigation of a case that was to remind him of the dual evils of football hooliganism and racism. The incident occurred in a tenement block not far from Ibrox. Mirza Beg, an elderly Pakistani man, was attacked near his home by two hooligans whom the police suspected were football fans. The initial post-mortem showed the cause of death to be 'heart failure'. Understandably, the initial verdict brought outrage from the deceased's family, and general condemnation from others, including some Glasgow politicians. Owing to public pressure a fresh investigation was ordered. During the period of investigation, Dilawar came to assume the befitting guise of a reliable and understanding pillar of the local society as he helped to comfort the family and the wider Asian community. The Asian residents who lived around Ibrox were well accustomed to the nauseating and repulsive excesses of football fans. Shopkeepers would shut down by lunchtime on matchdays, and take the additional precaution of putting steel grilles around the shop fronts. This did not, however, prevent those who were hell bent on causing discomfort to the local Asian community from continuing to urinate on doorsteps, shouting racist abuse and occasionally assaulting innocent bystanders. However distressing those assaults and abuse may have been, they bore little comparison to the tragic events surrounding the death of Mr Beg. Dilawar recalls: 'It was not like as it may be today when Asian youths are more prepared to fight back against racists. Back then the whole community began to question if they should even carry on living in the area. Was it worth it? Who was going to be the next victim?'

Following the re-ordering of the investigation, an important new witness emerged. During the attack a local janitor had caught a glimpse of the alleged perpetrators and was therefore able to provide vital new information. The Asian community were further encouraged when the Procurator Fiscal undertook to personally visit Pakistan, where the body had been sent for burial, and ordered for the body to be exhumed. On his return to Scotland the new inquiry announced a revision to the cause of death. The new verdict was declared as death by 'assault'.

Although Dilawar had considerable experience of dealing with incidents of racial assault and intimidation, the four years he spent operating the Ibrox police control room were, even for him, often harshly illuminating. This experience was also to foster a penetrating process of self-examination.

Dilawar could, to an extent, empathize with the hostile conditions and effects that became 'naturally' assumed into the life of Mark Walters. He may not have had to endure the same levels of venomous racist abuse as the Rangers player, but for many years he too had been a lone black man, the solitary non-white face in a hostile environment. Dilawar continues: 'Initially, Walters suffered a hell of a lot of abuse. His early matches at Ibrox just left a trail of bananas on the pitch. Because Walters played on the wings he was in the worst position; he was left so exposed to those shouting abuse at him. Sitting in the control room I used to feel helpless, and as a fellow ethnic minority member I also felt ashamed and embarrassed. I just don't know how he stuck at it. I didn't know the lad personally, but I used to wonder how he was coping with it – he must have a strong character. In fact, a hell of a strong character, to put up with what he had to. I used to go home after the game with those scenes pictured in my mind and just get very depressed about it all. I know that because we're policemen we are supposed to be professional in dealing with these matters, but how could you not be emotionally affected, particularly if you could personally relate to what was going on out there. The whole thing was plain sick. The guy will always have a lot of respect in my heart. When we closed the cameras in on those shouting abuse at Walters you could tell from the expressions on their faces how much they hated him. Now these guys hate the Catholics, but I tell you they hated Walters as much. The problem we had was that with thousands of fans chanting abuse we were limited in what action we could take.'

The Walters experience was to place Scottish football's position on racism under close scrutiny. Previously, because very few black players had played in Scotland, the subject of racism was never considered to be a major issue, and was very rarely discussed in public. These days Scottish football has a healthier representation of black players in the various divisions. Hibernian lead the way with black footballers such as Boco, Rougier and Harper; Celtic have Larsson and Blinker, and others too are attached to various clubs. What the Walters experience did, though, was to help open up the debate on racism in football. It took the appalling abuse of one man for a whole country to stand back and engage in a moment of shameful realization. The productive initiative, however, came from a surprising source, as Dilawar outlines, 'It was one or two good journalists who decided to make a strong stand on this issue.' In 1996, Jonathan Northcroft, a reporter with the *Scotland on Sunday* newspaper, undertook a major survey of Scottish football to investigate the absence of Asian professional footballers. The major findings of Northcroft's report, in essence, mirrored those found in the *Asians Can't Play Football* report. He revealed high levels of ignorance and prejudice towards Asian footballers by many Scottish professional football clubs: 'The strength of the Scottish Football Association's efforts to prevent discrimination were also questioned. Their articles include the promise "to promote, foster and develop" football irrespective of race, religion or politics, yet the only existing anti-discrimination campaign in Scotland, the Commission for Racial Equality's Let's Kick Racism Out of Football, was refused the association's full backing at its outset.'

Although the SFA subsequently gave low-key backing to the campaign, its initial response questioned 'whether pursuing such a high-profile campaign is likely to have a counter-productive effect'. It remains quite incredible and sickeningly culpable that certain football 'authorities' can maintain such myopic reticence towards strategic procedures that will help to reduce, or prevent, the kind of abhorrent abuse and shameful ignorance that was suffered by unsung heroes such as Mark Walters.

Following the Scottish people's 'Yes, Yes' vote in the 1997 Devolution Referendum, the particular initiatives that are coming to the fore in England with respect to promoting anti-racism within football may not be granted direct transfer north of the border in Scotland. The quest for Asian recognition and breakthrough in British football must not be bifurcated into separate Scottish and English programmes. Racism, moreover, ignorance, is not bound by parliamentary specificity; it must be overcome via an informed multiculturalist policy that seeks to unite diverse peoples by promoting mutual awareness and enquiring tolerance. Whilst we must never forget that odious trail of bananas, the crucial necessity to deny racism any victory is embodied by one Jas Jutla. Who would have thought that one of Scotland's first British-Asian footballers would begin his career at the cultural hotbed of Glasgow Rangers?

Jas Jutla

In the deadly, earnest pursuit of Brazilian superstar, Ronaldo, Glasgow Rangers indicated that their ambitions match those of the more renowned 'world' club giants – Manchester United, Juventus, AC Milan and the Spanish giants, Real Madrid and Barcelona. Rangers' alleged offer of a world-record transfer fee, massive salary and 'select your matches to play in' package finally put to rest the suggestion that this is a club which chooses to thrive by bullying its smaller compatriot clubs. Chairman David Murray's bold claim that Rangers strive to be the best club in world football has to be taken seriously. The downside of this adventurous 'international' transfer policy is that first-team opportunities for home-grown Scottish talent are becoming increasingly limited. It's therefore no coincidence that in recent years the numbers of youth-team players who have broken into the first team can be counted on one hand. Despite this it would seem that the clamour among some of Scotland's finest young schoolboy footballers to join one of Britain's largest and most famous clubs remains largely intact.

Jas Jutla was born just outside Glasgow in the Bearsden district. That year, 1977, coincided with a major surge of football mania in this already football-mad country. A somewhat fortu-

itous 2–0 play-off victory over the Welsh, aided by the contro-
versial Joe Jordan 'headed' goal, had given Scotland a place in
the 1978 World Cup finals. Sadly Ally MacLeod's 'Army' was
to return home beguiled by the wizardry of those 'country
cousins' of South American football, Peru. The inability to beat
Iran and the eternal optimism of MacLeod, who claimed that
the worst the team would do was to finish third, didn't help
matters. Worse still, revelations of drug abuse by winger Willie
Johnstone had cast an even larger shadow over the sorry episode.

Fours years later, as the enthusiastic Scots hoped for greater
returns in Spain 1982, those at home, when not glued to their
screens, took to the streets to imitate their heroes. Among those
young children was a 5-year-old Indian boy. A child whose
physical appearance bore stronger comparison with the flamboyant South Americans than with his adopted compatriots. By
the age of 9 there was little doubt among the locals that this
little Indian boy was turning into a very good footballer. His
father, Kuldip, recalls, 'I used to watch him playing football
with a group of local boys. Most were older than Jas, but he held
no fear of anyone. Because I never played the game seriously, I
can't claim he inherited his talent. He just seemed to be born
into playing the game.'

Local club Bearsden Boys ran a number of junior teams,
ranging from under-11s to under-16s, and it was during Jas'
first year with the club that his talents came to the attention of
a larger and rival club, Rangers Supporters' Association Club,
which acts as a feeder club to Glasgow Rangers. Jas recalls, 'I
was playing at centre-half, where my pace and strength were
helping me to stand out, and I think it was that which impressed
Rangers Supporters' Association Club. My manager at Bearsden
was very angry when I said I was going to leave them.' Not
surprisingly the opportunity to spend two nights a week training
at Ibrox with the mighty Glasgow Rangers had proved too great
a temptation. For someone who had been associated with a
professional football club since the age of 12, it would seem

that by the time he was 15 years old his head would be full of thoughts about playing professional football. Remarkably, this was not the case with Jas. It is a situation that once again highlights the general lack of understanding of how to become a professional footballer that is still evident in some sections of the Asian community. Jas recalls, 'Neither my father nor I had any idea of the routine when it came to signing-up as a professional footballer. No one had ever told us that you could sign apprenticeship forms when you turned 16. It soon became obvious though when the 15-to-16-year-old group began to talk about who would be offered contracts'.

Even then Jas was unsure whether he had done enough to merit the offer of an apprenticeship. The club had a number of other very promising young footballers, whom in Jas' mind appeared to be ahead of him in the pecking order. The thought of a career in professional football, although desired, had never really preoccupied his mind, or, for that matter, had adversely affected his performance in the classroom. On leaving school Jas had acquired three out of four Higher qualifications and was looking to establish himself in business at the earliest opportunity. Having just lost his grandmother the thought of playing professional football was almost the furthest thing from his mind, as the family dealt with a house full of mourners who had come to pay their respects. In the middle of the commotion the telephone rang; it was the Rangers youth-team coach asking him if he would be interested in the club's offer of a two-year apprenticeship. By the end of the summer Jas was to join a group of boys with whom he would develop a strong sense of camaraderie, sharing the good times and the not so good times. Well, almost.

For the next two years, under the careful tutelage and support of coaches John MacGregor and Billy Kirkwood, the young charges were put through their paces, combining training with the more mundane aspects of football apprenticeships, which involved the performing of various chores around the club. The high jinx normally associated with professional footballers was often in evidence, as the gullible trainees were led many a merry dance by the more seasoned pros. These occasions did have their less problematic moments, though. Jas recalls, 'Once we had finished cleaning the away changing rooms sometimes we would get the chance to have a chat with the senior coaching staff and, sometimes, some of the senior players who were just returning back from injury.'

Surprisingly the curiosity of the coaches and players never once ventured into the subject of Jas' Asian identity. Jas recalls, 'Looking back I am very thankful that no one asked what it was like being an Asian player. That helped me feel as if I was not under the spotlight, and made me feel very much like one of the lads.'

Glasgow Rangers has a reputation as a club that attracts a right-wing racist following, although there is some evidence that their presence both inside and outside Ibrox may be declining. This is something that Jas has always been mindful of. 'Fortunately neither my family nor I have seen, first-hand, these people handing out racist leaflets, but I was aware that these people were around. To a large degree you, as a footballer, can not afford to get too involved. I can't imagine the club would be too happy if you did. You must remember that the club spends a lot of time trying to come across as a club that is not political.'

Much to his surprise Jas found that he received very little racial abuse from the supporters or his opponents. Although he does recall one particular incident with some bewilderment: 'We were playing against Clydebank Under-15s, I won a fifty–fifty tackle when this boy stood up and shouted: "You black bastard," straight in my face. The crowd heard it, as did the referee, who decided to turn a blind eye to the incident.'

The philosophical nature of his comments forms an impressive part of his personality. He maintains there will always be the odd racist incident and the 'cleverer' players will say things outside the earshot of referees. He also accepts that racist abuse will never be completely eradicated from the game, as it won't be from society.

Having now established the protocol, Jas and his father were well-versed with the next chapter in his fledgling career. It was make or break time for the apprentice. For the majority, that would be it, time to move on to pastures new: 'On a few occasions the coaches had said that I was doing well, but beyond that I had no inkling what the future held in store for me. Like all my team-mates, people whom I had grown to like, I knew that those five with the gaffer [Walter Smith, first-team manager] in his office would hold the key to our futures.'

During those few weeks before the 'Big Gaffer's Interview' it was difficult to concentrate on much else. Jas recalls, 'Two of my closest buddies went up before me and were given the bad news. I was shattered for them but I needed to quickly get my thoughts together, and could offer very little comfort to them at the time. Anyway, as I made my way up those stairs I bumped into youth coach, John Brown, who was grinning and shaking his head in disbelief, saying, "I can't believe we are offering you a contract." So by the time I entered into Walter Smith's office my shaking was more to do with excitement than nerves.'

The next ten minutes were to provide a major boost to Jas' hopes of developing a successful career in professional football, as Smith offered his assessment. 'The Gaffer told me that the coaches spoke highly of me, and that in the games that he had watched I had shown I could read the game well, had good pace, and that there was every chance that I could make a reasonable living out of the game.' Jas was offered a twelve-month professional contract.

The start of that first season as a 'pro' began promisingly when Jas joined another first-year professional, Barry Ferguson, for occasional training with the first-team squad. It was a sign that the club had high hopes of him. During the year Jas made regular appearances in the club's reserve team, often in front of no more than a couple of thousand people, but the company of high-profile first-teamers who were returning from injury, or simply dropped, added to the experiences. However, it wasn't long before he discovered that the club had three or four other right-backs, his preferred position, whose greater experience would prove to be an ongoing obstacle. In Alex Clelland, Craig Moore and Stephen Wright, Glasgow Rangers showed the depth and quality of their squad (Moore and Wright were also full internationals). The parting of the ways was therefore somewhat inevitable. Jas recalls, 'The club took the view that I was unlikely to challenge for a first-team place within the next few years. They recognized that I had become disillusioned after performing well in the reserves and finding that my path was blocked by more senior players. I was told there would be no shortage of clubs who were interested in me, both here and in England.'

The task of finding another club was put in the hands of Rangers' long-term employee, Kenny Moyes. Over the years Moyes had provided digs to many young Rangers footballers, his son (David) was a former professional, and he was just starting out as a football agent. Importantly, he was also someone whom Jas trusted. It proved to be a sound judgement – Moyes showed himself to be a quick operator. Within a week offers had come in from Preston North End, St Mirren and Greenock Morton. What helped to sway Jas' eventual decision was the presence at Morton of former Rangers players like Brian Read, Neil Ingles, Ross Matheson and, of course, then manager Ali McGraw, who was closely associated with Rangers. Jas was offered and accepted a two-year contract in 1997. His first game in Morton's famous blue and white hoop shirts was against none other than Glasgow Rangers, during a testimonial game for David Wylie. In front of a packed home audience Jas had a sterling game in central midfield against a Rangers team containing Theo Snelders, Tony Vidmar, Rene Gattuso, Stephen Wright and Eric Van Vossen. Within a few weeks Ali McGraw departed, only to be replaced by former Celtic men Billy Stark and Frank Connor: 'Both the Gaffer and his assistant Frank do a fair amount of leg-pulling because of my former Rangers connections. I think that I am lucky in that they will look after my interests. One of the major differences between clubs like Rangers and Morton is that the bigger the club the more difficult it is for coaches to sit you down and talk things through with you. I think those sessions are very important, particularly to the younger players.'

Although there have been relatively few Asian professional footballers, it is of concern that they have quickly slipped away from the professional game; Chris Dolby (Rotherham United and Bradford City) and Naseem Bashir (Reading) being cases in point. Can Jas Jutla go on to fulfil the expectations held by both Rangers' and Greenock Morton's coaching staffs, and more importantly attain his own playing ambitions? Those ambitions cannot be helped by his exclusive billing as 'the Asian professional footballer', a situation that brings with it a regular stream of media enquiries: 'What the media fail to appreciate is that their demands can sometimes be a real distraction. I also don't want my team-mates to think that because I do all these interviews that I have ideas above my station.' Jas' playing ambitions include international recognition, whether that be with Scotland or India: 'The English-based Jamaican footballers have shown what they can do to help promote and develop the Jamaican game. It could be that a few of us Indians could help to do something similar for the Indian game.' However, there is the small matter of a Scotland full international cap to pursue before he is prepared to switch his attentions to India.

7 From the Tearoom to the Boardroom

The opportunity to earn your living from playing professional football is a fantasy that many of our dreams are made of. Becoming a football manager has been described as the next best thing to actually playing professional football, but given the modern-day rigours and demands of the job, such claims may be a trifle overstated. If you are not good enough to play professional football then surely the next best thing is to buy the club of your dreams. Professional football clubs are becoming increasingly occupied by people whose good fortune has enabled them to return as owners of the clubs they once supported from the terraces. For the likes of Sir Jack Hayward, Sir John Hall and Jack Walker, that first entry as the new owner, through the tunnel and on to that hallowed turf, must be something approaching nirvana.

Then there are the majority, mere mortals, always seemingly looking on pitifully from the outside, trying to satisfy their insatiable appetite for any snippet of news and information about the club. They hang around the ground, phone club team-lines and studiously peruse the pages of Teletext in search of that daily fix. For this peculiar dependency they place a major reliance on newspapers, radio and television, but however valuable and interesting those informational hits may be, they can never really satisfy the lust for knowledge.

If unable to become a player, manager or director at the club, the only other route to the inside is to become a non-playing club employee. But who are these people? What exactly do they do? How do you get to become a non-playing club employee? And is the life of a club executive as interesting and glamorous as some make it out to be? One such person who can provide some of the answers to these questions, and an illuminating insight into the world of professional football executives, is Aston Villa's highly regarded, young and ambitious commercial manager. In a professional environment, where the make-up of those involved is still predominantly white and male, Abdul Rashid has struck an important blow for other ethnic minority aspirants. Rarely can anyone have had to fulfil so many different roles and responsibilities within a professional football club to achieve their current position, but in doing so Abdul has served the ideal apprenticeship.

Rashid's success at Aston Villa is, in no small part, due to his drive, energy and enthusiasm. Ex-Villa manager Ron Saunders' former secretary, Christine Lewis-Smith, knew Abdul during his first few years at Villa: 'Abdul could not have been more than about 16 or 17 when I first met him. Even then he always struck me as someone who worked very hard. He always seemed to be buzzing around the place, forever keen to help and impress. I am not at all surprised to see him occupying his current position.'

More than twenty years on from when he formally launched his career at Aston Villa, it is refreshing to see that Abdul appears to have lost none of that enthusiasm. Indeed, the very spark that started his vocational fire still illuminates his very existence: 'Football is a passion. I started playing from an early age and, like all the other kids, I wanted to play professional football. I was never going to be good enough, so I went for the next best thing. You see, everybody this side [non-playing] is a frustrated footballer. When I meet up with my mates I know I am their envy. They cannot wait for me to sit down and tell them who I have been with and what deals I have been doing, and any juicy gossip I am willing to share with them.'

It is difficult to establish how much of Rashid's enthusiasm is actually directly linked to the fact that he is employed by the club he has doted on since childhood. The daily exposure to the proud traditions of this famous football club, the impressive Villa Park environment, the regular contact with international first-team players like Dwight Yorke, Mark Bosnich, Stan Collymore and Gareth Southgate must surely all help to fuel his commitment.

The appointment of Villa fans, and those formerly with club connections, is a theme of continuity that runs consistently throughout Aston Villa Plc. At the helm is Chairman Doug Ellis. There is also Dave Ismay, former showbiz entertainer, as the special projects manager, and the former first-team managerial team of Brian Little and Allan Evans, along with Peter Withe and Ron Wylie (in charge of the club's scouting system and Football in the Community Programme respectively) are all former Villa favourites. Rashid enthuses: 'When you look around and see long-serving Villa people in the various senior positions, you realize how proud they are of what has gone on here . . . and it's not just senior staff. These are all Villa people. It's like working for your family as opposed to working for someone else. It somehow gives you an added ingredient towards your motivation.'

Having been born in Lozells, a district situated within sight of Villa Park, it is difficult to imagine Abdul Rashid being anything other than a Villa fan. His love affair with the club sprang from peer group influence rather than parental guidance. His father, who descends from Bangladesh, had no particular interest in the game. Like so many first-generation migrants, he was largely preoccupied with ensuring his family secured economic, physical and cultural survival in this foreign land. As a 9-year-old Abdul used to hang around the coat-tails of older boys who were regulars at the reserve-team, third-team and youth-team matches that were played at Villa Park. In those days, more often than not, the doors to these games were left open. For many local children this arrangement enabled them to identify with their local club at no cost and for little risk to their personal well-being. During those first few years a shortage of money prevented Abdul from attending more than a handful of first-team games; instead he had to make do with reserve and junior football. However, his relationship with the club was beginning to blossom, and his alert mind was already working overtime on how he could get to watch his first-team idols. At the age of 11, he made his first strategic move, a decision that was to serve as an important foundation for his subsequent career at Aston Villa.

As Villa Park fast became a second home for the young Abdul, he longed to become connected in some more meaningful way with the club. Abdul recalls: 'I would arrive at reserve-team games very early, which left me with plenty of time to hang about the souvenir shop. Gradually I got to know all the people who worked there. On occasions my willingness to help was appreciated; at other times they considered me to be more of a hindrance than a help. To this day Ted Small, who is the current stadium manager, continues to amuse himself by telling everyone of how he used to be the one who had to throw me out.'

Slowly, but surely, this likeable and popular young rogue had graduated from occasional helper to a sort of junior, odd job, ground-staff team member: 'Eventually I got the chance to wash some of the reserve players' cars. I remember John Deehan, Steve Hunt and Jake Findlay were among them. I would fetch sandwiches for people, sweets from the corner shop, help to cart boxes around. Basically I would do anything just to be part of Villa.'

Soon, the young Abdul faced his first major career dilemma. The 1974 FA Cup semi-final between Ipswich and West Ham was the first time ball-boys were to be used at a senior level at Villa Park. Having performed those duties at reserve-team fixtures, Abdul was selected for the semi-final. The game proved to be a success, prompting Aston Villa to make ball-boys a permanent feature at future first-team games. Abdul was burdened with the choice of being a ball-boy or continuing to work part-time at the souvenir shop. The ball-boy role had already made him the envy of his schoolmates, as well as elevating him to minor celebrity status, but his mind was made up. Even at 13 he was showing himself to be a shrewd judge of opportunities. He remembers, 'The way I saw it was that I could only be a ball-boy for a couple of more years, whereas I could work in the souvenir shop for as long as I liked.' During the next couple of years Abdul continued with his part-time position at the club, frequently switching between the main club shop and the kiosks situated inside the stands. In order to appease both teachers and parents he spoke about his intention of becoming a draughtsman on leaving school, but when it came to making a final decision both heart and mind pointed without hesitation towards Villa Park. In the summer of 1977, Abdul left school at the age of 16. He had, or so he thought, achieved his life-long dream: 'As an impressionable 16 year old I was the envy of my friends, and I simply loved going to work each day. My idols then were the likes of John Gidman and Andy Gray. The opportunity to be on the same staff and first-name terms with them was something I wanted to rush home and tell my friends about every day. To cap it all, being paid for doing this was an unbelievable bonus.'

The next eleven years saw Abdul establishing the groundwork for his eventual destination at Aston Villa by fulfilling a variety of roles and responsibilities, including a long placement with the promotions office, where he sold the club's customized lottery tickets. Part of this period saw him taking to the road alongside former first-team manager, Brian Little, whose promising career had sadly been cut short by serious injury. Neither of them then was to realize that their paths would cross again in the future, albeit in different circumstances. His next port of call was overseeing the club's own travel club operation. Remarkably, his tenure as travel club manager coincided with the club's capturing of the most prestigious domestic trophy (the League Championship in 1981) and in the next season the ultimate prize – the European Cup. Like so many thousands of other fellow Villains, he stood proudly on that balmy May night on the Rotterdam terraces, when Tony Morely's mazy run and cross was tapped into the unprotected Bayern Munich goal by a predatory Peter Withe. Since those heady glory days, Aston Villa have failed to sustain any kind of dominance in English football. However, the club has not been completely left behind in the entrepreneurial stakes. Former commercial manager Tony Stephens is regarded as the person most responsible for establishing a commercial infrastructure that is the envy of most other clubs. Since leaving Aston Villa, Stephens has continued to lend his considerable knowledge and expertise to many other football bodies and sports organizations, including playing a significant role in helping to turn around the commercial fortunes at Wembley Stadium. Within weeks of arriving at Villa Park Tony Stephens requested that Abdul Rashid be transferred from the promotions office to join him as his new assistant. The measure of Stephens' confidence in Abdul was confirmed in a somewhat clichéd analogy when he told Abdul that he saw him as a 'rough diamond'. With Stephens about to embark upon his commercial revolution, Abdul could not be better placed to begin the last leg of his commercial manager's apprenticeship. As subsequent developments have shown, Stephens was to prove an astute judge of character.

Abdul is readily forthcoming in identifying others at Villa who, over the years, have helped shape and direct his career. In his early days he was guided by club administrator Jackie Bradley, whom he regarded as a surrogate mother figure. In common with most youths of his age, Abdul had a rebellious streak and occasionally wanted to indulge his counter-cultural whims. For instance, he assumed the visual markers of the punk rock movement, but Bradley was always on hand to see he did not transgress the limits of acceptability at this grand old conservative institution. And if there is one person who, more than anyone else, epitomizes the modern-day Aston Villa it is Chairman Doug Ellis. Nicknamed 'Deadly Doug', Ellis has been instrumental in helping transform the club from proverbial sleeping giant into active contributor to the rapidly evolving Premier League. Ellis's tough reputation precedes him; Abdul, however, acknowledges Ellis to be both a tough but fair task master: 'The way that I look at it, the chairman does not suffer fools gladly, and I wouldn't be here were it not for the fact that I deliver the goods. I have no doubt that he, together with Tony Stephens, has been a major influence in my career. So much so that on occasions I come off the telephone and think to myself, Bloody hell, Abdul, you are sounding more and more like the chairman.'

It is a relationship that at one point looked as if it would never happen. In 1988 Stephens' successor, Chris Rodman, left Aston Villa and, although only 27 at the time, Abdul considered himself ready to move up from the post of assistant commercial manager to being the fully fledged commercial supremo. Having spent eleven years learning about all aspects of the club's commercial operations, Abdul made what he considered to be a strong case to the chairman. Unfortunately Ellis decided that Abdul was not quite ready for the job. This prompted Abdul to immediately tender his resignation: 'On the day that I was leaving I went into the chairman's office to say my goodbyes and to say that, should the job ever be available again, I would be the first to apply, despite having been turned down on this occasion. Having gone into the chairman's office to confirm my departure, I came out having been appointed to the job after all – the youngest commercial manager in the Football League. Rodman's successor had resigned within his first two weeks.'

That choice in 1974, between ball-boy or working part-time in the souvenir shop, had, it would seem, been perfectly vindicated. As he came out of Doug Ellis's office that afternoon, it was akin to lifting the European Cup as the Villa captain. He had come of age, an equal in the company of his colleagues. Momentarily, his mind kept wandering back to those words he had uttered in a club magazine interview as a spotty 16-year-old souvenir-shop assistant. In deadly earnest, Abdul had made it known that one day he intended to succeed the then commercial manager, Eric Woodward. However, immediately after his appointment he was under no illusions and understood that the next few weeks and months would represent a major trial period, an enormous test of his character and ability: 'I knew I had got the job on the rebound, so it was up to me to prove myself. The chairman had made it clear that I was on trial, he nonetheless made it clear that I would receive his unqualified support. But I was conscious that there were others who were less supportive, and who were looking for me to drop a major clanger, so that they could have the satisfaction of saying "I told you so". Basically it was sink or swim time.'

His task was not made easier by the temporary loss of one of his major strengths: his natural confidence. This had deserted him to such an extent that it took him three weeks before he finally plucked up the courage to move from the assistant commercial manager's desk to the commercial manager's office. Gradually that confidence began to return. The number of memos to the chairman reporting on progress became fewer and fewer. One day, some several months into the job, Abdul recalls being summoned to the chairman's office to be asked why the memos had dried up. Abdul, by now once again wholly confident and reassured in his position, enquired as to whether the chairman had any complaints about his work. Ellis' smile said it all. For the first time since his new appointment, Abdul was standing on his own two feet and was doing so as a genuine equal with all the other senior members of staff. It was another defining moment in his career.

Attempting to describe a typical day at the office is not an easy task, for Abdul: 'You can rarely sit down and plan for the day ahead. The moment you do that the chairman comes in and asks you to deputize for him at a meeting, or the manager has just signed a player and would like me to organize a press conference.'

The relatively unstructured and chaotic picture Abdul portrays is not one that he has any complaints about. How can that possibly be the case for a devoted fan? It had not been long since he was being asked to organize a press conference to announce the signing of England international Stan Collymore, for a club-record transfer fee of seven million pounds. It's a once-in-a-lifetime experience that any supporter would happily take to their grave. When not overseeing catering operations or organizing high-profile media conferences, Abdul returns to his core duty, that of maximizing commercial income – the ultimate marker of success for all commercial managers. The figures currently being brandished regarding non-footballing income run into millions of pounds every year. The combined value of the Premier League's Sky and BBC TV deals alone amounts to £743 million. In the words of Jason Tomas, the *Observer* sports writer, football clubs are 'turning their stadiums into yuppie palaces by exploiting non-football sources of income'. Aston Villa are no exception to this policy. In November 1995, on a site adjacent to the ground, spanning 3.4 acres, the club opened their own impressive merchandising complex – Villa Village. The development comprises (as well as the shop) offices, warehouse and storage units, and ample car-parking space. During Abdul's tenure, the commercial income has realized more than £50 million. Included among the more lucrative deals are those with past sponsors Asics and Müller, and the even more impressive current sponsorship deals with AST Computers and Reebok. In articulating the emotions involved during negotiations with prospective sponsors, Abdul points to the constant flow of adrenalin pumping through his system as he nears the climax of the deal. However, once it is achieved there is a momentary sense of fulfilment and triumph before it's time to weigh up the next challenge (sexual metaphors are all too easily ascribed upon such commercial, yuppie-speak). Such are the pressures to deliver results, this type of reaction is seen to be the only way to survive in the increasingly cut-throat world of professional football.

Some insurance companies, car showrooms and estate agents have been known to deploy white staff in 'white' areas, for fear of upsetting potential sales to their white customers. But according to Abdul his Asian background has never presented him with any difficulties that he or others at the club is aware of. He does, however, concede that the colour of his skin has no currency in his work when he is conversing over the telephone. But once the ethnicity or difference of his name is stated, then there is often a perceptible realignment of his correspondent's address: 'I do not know of any deal that I may have lost because I was an Asian. People whom I do business with respect me for who I am and the quality of the service we deliver to them. Much of the time when I am on the telephone, unless they know my name, clients cannot tell whether or not I am Asian because I have this Brummie accent. Actually, a few times when some of these people have asked my name, so that they can send me a fax, I've sensed some hesitation at the other end when I've said "Abdul Rashid". It's as if they cannot believe an Asian person is on the other end of the phone.'

Abdul may well be justified in his claim that people deal with him purely on the basis of what he delivers, rather than what he is. If that should be the case then he must consider himself somewhat fortunate, because his is not a universally common experience. The surprisingly obvious lack of discrimination may be, in part, explained by the fact that since leaving school people have always been able to identify Abdul with Aston Villa Football Club. Therefore, people have tended to overlook his ethnicity because his identity has become synonymous with, or subsumed into, the club. It's a point that

Abdul concurs with by acknowledging that he may have become 'shielded' from the racism other Asians may encounter: 'Ever since I started working for Aston Villa I have always been treated as part of the club family. To the staff I have always been seen as Abdul, one of the staff, and not Abdul, an Asian member of staff. Perhaps the situation would have been different, or less favourable, if I had come to the club later in my career.'

If the number of Asian individuals employed in administrative positions in the game is still relatively insignificant, there is some evidence to suggest the Asian business community may be involved to a greater extent. Fans of Wolverhampton Wanderers will need no reminding that the club almost went out of existence during the notorious Bhatti regime.

The next major high-profile experience of Asian businessmen with professional football was also to end up in receivership, only this time the circumstances were different to those at Wolverhampton. In 1990, Birmingham City was acquired by a consortium headed by the Kumar family. Unlike the Bhattis, the Kumars conducted their footballing affairs in a very open fashion, making themselves accessible to the fans. Unfortunately, though, the Kumar family, who had made their fortune through the clothing and textile industry, fell victim (along with many other Asian business folk) to the calamitous collapse of the Bank of Credit and Commerce International. Left with no alternative, the Kumars were forced to sell up their interest in the club. As if to underline their genuine feelings for the game, in 1996 the Kumars returned to football when buying out the controlling interest in Cardiff City. The contribution of Asian businesses to football clubs has, however, not been confined to professional football. Unlike their more illustrious Midlands neighbours, Wolverhampton Wanderers and Birmingham City, not many people outside the Midland non-League circuit will have heard about Bloxwich Town, members of the Inter Alliance League.

In 1993 a group of local Asian businessmen decided to bail out this ailing little club, which is situated on the outskirts of Walsall. The ground is located on the Mossley Estate, a post-war council estate. The number of ethnic minority residents has been almost negligible, and in the past right-wing groups have been known to be active in the area. Given this background one would question the wisdom of a group of ethnic minority businessmen prepared to invest a significant sum of money in the area. It is a testimony to the overall success of this venture that not only is the club free of any racist graffiti, or other acts of vandalism, but they also enjoy the support of local residents, many of who are regularly seen in the clubhouse. Since then Messrs Sanghera, Bains, Pooni and Thaper have invested more than £100,000 to pay for improved ground facilities, a new club house, fencing and training facilities. Tony Sanghera recalls how he became involved with the club: 'I gave a local Sunday league side some financial backing and seemed to catch the bug. Someone then told me there were a couple of semi-professional clubs who needed financial assistance. I came along, liked what I saw at Bloxwich, and decided to get involved.'

There are no prima donnas in the team, as is demonstrated by an egalitarian wage structure. With no stars and everyone striving for a common goal, they have managed to develop a great spirit throughout the club. Sanghera continues: 'We have invested a lot of money in the club, but will not throw silly money at team-building . . . We are in a sense a new club and are not going to run before we can walk.' A philosophy a few owners of professional football clubs could learn from. To highlight the club's goals, an ambitious application to develop a £4m stadium complex is under consideration by the National Lottery.

The general trend of increased interest in professional football by the Asian business community is also confirmed by Abdul Rashid. Aston Villa have two Asian executive box-holders, and others who take up box facilities on an *ad hoc* basis. Abdul has also noted a discernible increase in the numbers of ethnic, particularly Asian, businesses requesting the services of a star player to perform opening ceremonies. And prominently displayed on many Premier League grounds' advertising hoardings these days are the company names Joe Bloggs and Ciro Citerio. Shami Ahmed, owner of the Joe Bloggs company, is part of a new breed of very successful Asian entrepreneurs, among an increasing list of British-Asian millionaires. According to the *Sunday Times 1997 Rich List*, Ahmed, who makes his money from designer clothing and property, is worth £55 million. Ciro Citerio, owned by an Indian family, run 200 designer-clothing retail outlets across Britain, as well as acting as official clothing sponsors to Aston Villa and Leicester City. The evidence suggests the growing interest in football among Asian businesses may be linked to generational factors. A past criticism of Asian-run businesses has been that their full potential in the market-place has never been properly realized or exploited because of poor advertising and marketing policies. Evidently, this is a deficiency that the next generation appears determined not to repeat. The younger generation of British-Asian business people not only better understand the value of good advertising and marketing, but their British upbringing has enabled them to be better placed to appreciate football's place in society, and the effects of popular culture on the market-place. Pop culture has transformed Britain into a consuming arena, and association with football is being recognized as a sure-fire way of ensuring a high and visible product profile. Whilst the Asian business community represents a potentially significant market for football clubs, for the most part it remains largely untapped and mostly unrecognized. Under these circumstances it would seem to indicate that clubs like Aston Villa are actively pursuing specific measures to attract this potentially rewarding market. According to Abdul this is not the situation at Villa Park: 'The problem we would have is that if we are seen to be targeting the Asian community this may be interpreted the wrong way by other communities, like the Irish and Chinese.'

The issue of specifically targeting ethnic minority groups can, of course, be given a much wider significance than simply for the business community alone: the principle could similarly be applied to supporters, users of clubs' non-playing facilities, Football in the Community Programme participants, etc. Although Abdul's position on this issue may not necessarily be representative of all football clubs, it is a view shared by many others. At the heart of this issue is the question of perception: how would it look if we were seen to be deliberately showing favour to one section of the population? Or, more to the point, to what extent would such a policy antagonize the traditional supporter base? Under these circumstances clubs fearing the wrath of indigenous followers, who obviously make up the overwhelming majority of their support, will inevitably take the easy option. In doing so professional football remains one of the few consumer industries that, as yet, has failed to pursue advertising policies intended to woo the 'ethnic' market, *à la* supermarket chains, insurance giants and telephone companies. Abdul admits to being 'disappointed' that the local Asian community is very poorly represented among Aston Villa's sizeable following, especially given the club's location in the heavily Asian populated areas of Aston and Lozells. He points to mitigating circumstances. In recent seasons the club has enjoyed some degree of success and consequently this has reflected well in attendance figures. In 1996–97 Villa played to virtually sell out crowds of 38–40,000 every home match. Abdul's argument is that with so few seats available in the ground, the club has not felt it necessary to undertake specifically targeted measures at under-represented groups.

The successful flotation of Aston Villa Football Club, and Abdul's part in the delivery of an attractive prospectus, in many ways represents the pinnacle of his career as a commercial manager. The prospectus depicts a club whose attraction to would-be investors is made all the more alluring by the performance of its commercial activities. For Abdul, this situation represents more than a decade of long hours, sweat and toil, as well as the inevitable sacrifices to his young family. Still only in his late thirties, Abdul is fortunate in that he has a number of career possibilities. He claims that there is no other club he would consider moving to as a commercial manager because the job at Villa is among the best of its type in the country. Besides which, he has had opportunities to take up similar positions in the past. Although he is disappointed to see so few Asian people in similar positions in the game, he is acutely aware of the fact that he may be seen as a trailblazer for others to follow: 'There is a guy called Raj, who has recently started working in the commercial department at Coventry City. Raj has spoken to me a few times to seek my advice on various matters. Raj may have called me anyway, because we like to think that we are ahead of the field at Villa, but I am sure the fact that I am Asian inspired Raj with more confidence. Basically, if there is anything I can do for fellow Asians working in this area, then I will do it.'

Having seen Abdul work at close quarters, former England and Aston Villa manager Graham Taylor is only too aware of the capabilities of Asian commercial managers. His appointment of an Asian woman to the post of the commercial manager at Watford, his latest club, is a major step forward for a game that, for too long, has served as a closed shop for certain sections of the population. With an increasing number of football clubs looking to appoint chief executives and the opening up of other senior level positions within the game, the future looks bright for aspiring commercial managers, if not distinctly claret and blue for Abdul Rashid.

8 Faith and Football

In Lancashire, a region where local British Pakistanis continue to grace all levels of cricket, with the mysterious exception of county cricket, it is quite unusual to find a footballing success story from within that community. More than a quarter of a century on from when they were first formed, the story of Nelson-based Paak FC provides a refreshing account of triumph over adversity. Today, Paak FC represents more than just a football club, it stands as a local institution serving and preserving the interests of the wider community.

Accusations of unfavourable press reporting are a regular occurrence amongst professional footballers and managers. For the most part, it is not the sort of issue that causes concern among those outside the professional game, particularly for your everyday Sunday morning league players. But Paak FC's player-manager Mashuq Hussain (32) points out that the local press seem to have a way of devaluing his team's achievements. Mashuq recounts one such instance: 'We were playing in the North West Counties League against one of the best teams. We beat them well . . . no, we annihilated them. But all the papers commented on was the fact that we beat a weakened side. The season we won the Treble we hardly received a single decent or accurate write-up. Let's not forget that we were the first ever club to win this particular Treble, and yet we hardly got a mention. It may sound like sour grapes, but if we had been a white team we would have had better write-ups.'

This view would fall on some sympathetic ears in the black

sporting community. Over the years a number of prominent black sporting stars have claimed their successes have not received the same quality of press coverage as similar achievements by fellow white sportsmen or women. Paak FC's sense of injustice is not, however, just something that is confined to the local newspapers. On a particular occasion during the 1996–97 season, Paak players feared the worst when they arrived at their home ground an hour before kick-off to find about thirty opposition supporters standing on the touchline drinking beer, looking decidedly menacing. The presence of this number of away fans was very unusual, not least because it was only ten o'clock in the morning. As Mashuq recalls, 'The away team was in their changing room and we could hear them shouting things like, "We can not lose to these Pakis."' Paak's fears were confirmed at kick-off when one of the opposition's players let out a sort of rallying cry: 'Let's show the Pakis how to play,' and another shouted, 'Come on, let's break their legs.' Mashuq continues: 'I remember looking at the referee hoping he would take some action. Within the first few minutes Tariq [a Paak midfielder] went down the middle and these three opposition players – I mean three of them – all went in to tackle him. When they caught up with him we thought Tariq had broken his leg. We couldn't believe it when the ref waved play on. I ran up to the referee, and all he said was that they played the ball. How could that explain the stud marks all down Tariq's side? We knew then that the referee would be too frightened to take action against them. Eventually the ref gave us a penalty and there was a near riot on the pitch. The referee just took off and said he was going home. We persuaded him to come back on, but within ten minutes, after another tussle, he walked off again. This time he didn't return. To make matters worse we were fined for our part in the incident.'

This particular incident is one in a long line of similar experiences that have led to Paak FC being punished by the football authorities, but is it simply a case of Paak FC being innocent victims, or are they in some way culpable?

One of the common preconceptions of Asian people that pervades sections of racist ideology is that they are vulnerable because of their non-confrontational nature. The phrase 'Paki-bashing' is a by-product of this situation. It is, though, an image that is beginning to change, only it has taken a generation, two decades, for the British-Asian community to say that it is no longer prepared to turn the proverbial other cheek. This is a message that is beginning to be heard loud and clear in places like London's East End, parts of west London, Birmingham, Bradford and Wolverhampton and in Nelson. On the field, the players of Paak FC have doggedly refused to conform to this long-held popular stereotype of Asian people. Their actions indicate the new-found spirit, resolve and assured identity of the modern British-Asian community. That is not to suggest they are a 'dirty' or excessively physical side, far from it. However, what it does suggest is that they are not frightened to respond in equal kind to moments of aggression. As Mashuq testifies, 'Because of our history, everyone knows us in Nelson and Pendle as Paak, the Asian team. We're seen as good footballers and dirty so and sos. They know we won't be messed with.'

Challenging racism has many forms, some more conventional than others. Mashuq remembers one episode with some retro-spective amusement: 'We were playing in a League match at Colne. One of the opposition players kept shouting, every time one of our players went to challenge one of theirs, "Watch out there's a taxi on your back." By the umpteenth time they said this, I had become really quite wound up. They thought it was a rather funny joke. Anyway, I went into this two-footed tackle on one of their players. Admittedly it was a bad tackle, and I was deservedly booked for it. But before this injured guy had got up off the ground, I went over to him and said: "Can you give me two pound fifty, because that's the fare."'

There is a more serious side to the 'taxi debate', a subject that is a continuing cause for concern within, in particular, the Pakistani community. Mazhar Mohammed, who is in his mid-twenties, used to be a Birmingham taxi driver before embarking on a professional career as a surveyor in the construction industry. He asserts, 'Young Pakistani men wait till they are old enough to apply for their driving licences and then go to work on the cabs. Because you don't need any real qualifications most of them think they don't have to bother with exams. They just see taxis as easy money.' In Yorkshire and Lancashire many Asian taxi services started out because of an identified community need to provide transport for shift workers, working irregular hours. To the children of these migrants, the pursuit of leisure and sporting opportunities became more important than it was for their otherwise occupied parents. And it is out of these circumstances that a group of young Pakistani men got together to form a football team. Former Paak FC Chairman, Mohammed Khalid, recalls those early days for the club: 'The origins of Paak FC go back to 1969, when a group of first-generation Pakistani school boys felt they were not welcome to join with English youngsters in lunch-time and after-school kick-abouts. As a result, they were left to create their own street games which, eventually, led to slightly more organized matches in local parks between groups of Pakistani youngsters. As their knowledge and experience increased so did their desire to organize their activities on a more formal basis. Hence the birth of Paak United Football Club, registered with the Lancashire Football Association in 1972.'

For the next fourteen years Paak United progressed through the divisions of the local leagues, culminating in winning the Premier Division of the Burnley District League in 1981–82. By this time Paak United was operating and running three teams, a first and second team and a youth team. During those early days the club had to overcome some major organizational and administrative difficulties, which the chairman remembers all too well: 'At first, advice and guidance was difficult to come by because the club entered a league which was organized by people who had grown up together in the same town and had established their own conventions and methods of operation, which were not properly understood by the Pakistani youngsters. Unlike the English boys, who were able to enjoy the playing side and leave the administrative and business side to the more experienced and retired players, the young Pakistanis had to do everything for themselves. They made plenty of mistakes in those early days through not being familiar with committee procedures and through not understanding many of the unwritten conventions surrounding the game. It sometimes proved difficult to arrange meetings to get across essential information about what was involved in participating in a league. There was nowhere to hold meetings, except on street corners, where they were occasionally moved on by the police. Also, many of our parents disapproved of a sport that occasionally attracted undesirable publicity. Above all, whenever the youngsters got together, they preferred to kick a football about, rather than discuss important off-the-field matters. As a result of this, leadership from within the club emerged from a handful of players who realized that future development depended upon properly organized training sessions, regular attendance at league meetings, and assuming responsibility for all the club's affairs. It soon became apparent also that success on the field required more than enthusiastic and exuberant running around. All this was set against the background of a racial minority group attempting to enter a sport that many of the dominant community felt was "none of their business".'

For most of those fourteen years, the club's first team had changed little in terms of personnel. They had started together as a group of young men in their late teens and early twenties but had now grown into a team consisting of veterans. An inevitable consequence was the club was no longer able to maintain its once high standards. Inevitably, when the time came for overhauling the team it was a case of major rather than minor surgery. It was a task made all the more difficult by a dearth of immediate successors. This period also coincided with a state of great sadness and mourning, following the death of a key member of that squad. Whilst travelling to play in a match Mohammed Yaqoob was involved in a fatal car crash on the M65. This experience was to have a profound effect on the club and the tightly knit local community, the vast majority of whom are descendants of the Gujrat, situated in Pakistan's Punjab Province.

Asian sporting clubs are often formed by those with ancestral roots in the same villages or localities within India or Pakistan. Asian parents often urge their sons to form social contacts with those of similar backgrounds or within the same kin-group. The pattern of migration to Britain has often meant that those from similar districts in India and Pakistan have resided close to each other in Britain. Joint player-manager, Tariq Mahmood, recalls, 'Many of the good things that exist in this area are because we are all from the same district in Pakistan. Football has also played an important role in developing that sense of togetherness.' Not long after the crash, the team were on their way to Belgium to play in a tournament when some of the senior players pulled over at the site of the accident to pay respects to their friend and former team-mate; this commemorative ritual has been maintained since.

As second-generation British Muslims playing sport in a Western cultural environment, the footballers of Paak FC have accepted the need to develop a flexible approach to accommodate both their sporting and spiritual interests. According to Mashuq: 'After the match we don't go to the pub with our opponents. Perhaps if we did that may help to break down barriers. It's an issue in the league we are currently in, because most of our opponents are pub teams. Circumstances were different when Tariq and I used to play for a white Saturday league team. Then the home team would tell the away team which pub the sandwiches were in. We used to go and join them without feeling we had compromised our principles. But these leagues are not exactly your tea and sandwiches leagues.'

Experiences of Muslim cricketers show there to be an increasing level of cultural sensitivity being displayed by white host teams. In cricket, where match teas are in some ways an integral part of the sporting occasion, it is becoming commonplace for the hosts to establish the opposition's special dietary considerations. Where the hosts forget, non-Muslim colleagues have taken to removing the offending meat off the plates. While Muslim cricketers express relief at the opportunity to consume something legitimately edible, even if it is only a tomato and lettuce sandwich, their 'anything goes' guzzling colleagues fight over the extras. Senior players, like Tariq and Mashuq, are also forthcoming when it comes to assuming moral and spiritual leadership. Tariq recalls, 'As the senior players it is our job to ensure our players carry out certain disciplines – for example, no pubic hair or hair under the armpits. We also don't go into the showers unless we have our shorts on. It used to be a problem with the opposition, but I think they have just got used to us.'

If 1985 was a defining moment in the club's history, when the new guard replaced the old order, 1991 became another significant year, for two main reasons. On the field of play the club won the Treble: the League, League Cup and an open invitation Cup competition. Off the field the perception of the club among older members of the Pakistani community changed quite dramatically. As Tariq continues: 'In the past our parents have never really understood why we would kick a ball around for hours. All they thought was that it's keeping them out of trouble, so we won't stop them. When we won the Treble quite a lot of the older generation came to watch us play. Previously they would go and watch the cricket but not football. The season we won the Treble they were coming up to congratulate us.'

Whilst older members of the community warmed to the team's footballing achievements, tensions brought about by non-sporting matters have resulted in much wider divisions between younger and older generations.

Following the first mass wave of migration to Britain, most new arrivals from the subcontinent to this country arrived with little or no grasp of the English language, or indeed, an understanding of the British way of life. Interaction with the host community was very much dependent on the few who could speak the indigenous language. For the majority it was a question of getting by with a simple nod, gesture and the occasional word of two or English picked up from the shop floor. Although night classes offered a possible solution to the linguistic deficiency, shift-working patterns were hardly conducive learning conditions. Another consideration not to be overlooked was that many of these migrants descended from farming backgrounds, where time was considered better spent on maintaining crops and cattle rather than on pursuing an education. The better educated (the 'scribes') tended to double up as factory workers in the day and social workers in the evening. Their services were also in demand amongst employers and the authorities. For many of the 'scribes' their newly acquired position and status provided a way out of the unpleasant foundry conditions and into the more sedate surroundings of office life. Inevitably, as the process of cultural acclimatization has entered into its fourth decade, we have seen a major shift in the roles once fulfilled by these 'community leaders'. Today, the role of community leader is becoming increasingly redundant within a community that is becoming altogether more self-sufficient, confident and articulate. It would seem that many so-called community leaders have become too far removed from the younger elements to be considered to be genuinely representative of all their community. This process is also beginning to undermine the role of some of the more traditional institutions, once considered to be the pillars of society, and now being challenged by other less conventional institutions. Paak FC represent the emergence of such a new institution. Some of the issues around which tensions have arisen between the different generations are sensitive: for example, having relationships outside marriage, divorce and drugs, etc. In particular it is the issue of drugs that has brought to the fore tensions between younger and older elements in Nelson.

Pakistan is seen by the drug authorities to be a problematic location for the supply of narcotics. Together with Afghanistan and Iran it forms part of the Golden Crescent, a major poppy-growing region. As if to underline their growing appeal and accessibility to all sections of the population, rich and poor, hard drugs such as heroin are available in squatter areas, city streets and, even more alarmingly, rural and 'shanty town' areas. The supplies of drugs from Pakistan are known to be fed through the main European distribution channels in Spain, Germany, France and Britain. Following Pakistan's emergence as a major source of illicit narcotics, a disparaging (unfortunately, not wholly inaccurate) myth about young British Pakistanis being involved in the British drugs scene has emerged. Tariq is particularly concerned at the impact of this issue on the British Pakistani community: 'We are seen as the major pushers. I hate to say it, but we are in danger of becoming Public Enemy Number One. This sensitive issue is one that older members of the Asian community are refusing to discuss openly. Basically, the older generation do not know how to deal with the drugs problem so they pretend to ignore it. But how can they? It's a big problem that is staring them in the face, and we need to get it sorted. We have got five Pakistani councillors who, even if they wanted to, will not discuss it because it would cause offence in the community. Can you believe it? Our community is suffering, and they are worried about upsetting people's sensitivities.'

Paak have members of their squad who have had problems with drugs. The 'easy' option would have been to kick them out of the team, at least minimizing the opportunities for them to pass on their unappealing habits. Mashuq elaborates further: 'We have four younger players, all of them are under 20, who have had a problem with drugs. The way we see it is that through football we can help them get fit and take their minds off drugs. We are not soft with them and warn them that "any funny business", and they are out. You may think we are being naïve, but we feel we owe it to our youngsters.'

A strong sense of identity underlines so much of what the club stands for. Nowhere is this more in evidence than in the name Paak FC. In 1996 Paak FC entered a junior boys' team in a local club competition. It was suggested by the local headmaster, known to be sympathetic to Paak, that they consider changing their name to reflect the name of the district in which the team would be located. As Tariq recalls, the team's response was unequivocal: 'When the idea was suggested to the boys it was rejected outright. The boys wanted to maintain the club's proud tradition and call themselves Paak Juniors. Further still, they insisted on playing in the green colours of Pakistan. That's not something we have conditioned them to say, it's something they want to do.' What does the future hold for Paak FC? Will the club retain its strong Pakistani identity? Will the team become more racially mixed? Will the first British Pakistani star be a product of Paak FC? These are just some of the intriguing questions that lie in wait.

According to both Tariq and Mashuq there are grounds for optimism, something they attribute to new relationships being formed between the youth groups. Tariq: 'The Paak of old never used to see their opponents outside the football pitch. Whereas we see our opponents around town, maybe at a nightclub or something. Take Zahid [Tariq's brother], he sees white players at college. A few years ago the older Paak players never went through the college system, so they never saw those white lads, unless it was on the pitch.'

This would seem to suggest that the club should have fewer problems in recruiting non-Asian players. Intermittently since the early 1980s, Paak FC teams have contained white players. Unfortunately their stays at the club have tended to be short-lived. This is something that Tariq acknowledges with cynical realism: 'We had this really good white player join us a few seasons ago. He used to play for losing sides against us. So one year he decided to join us. But all he got was stick from other whites in the local pubs. In the end he decided that he was getting so much hassle that it was better that he left. Had he stayed others would have followed. Instead we are forced to pick our players from mainly our own community.'

If the evidence of the thirty-five young boys, aged between 7 and 14, who train with the club on Saturday mornings is anything to go by, it looks as if the future composition of the team will remain predominantly Asian. The ethnic make-up of those youngsters is such for a variety of reasons: the location of the training venue is in a predominantly 'Asian' residential area; the boys and their parents are comforted in the knowledge that they are training in a 'safe' environment; and it's the desire to identify with Paak FC that directs young Asian footballers to the club. In a similar way that Asian youngsters are reluctant to go and play in white teams, where they may feel isolated and uncomfortable, it is likely that white boys feel the same way about playing with Paak FC. Does this suggest a permanent impasse? Not if people like Mashuq have anything to do with it. He does acknowledge though that bridging the gap will not be easy: 'My lad plays for Barrowford Celtic. When I first took him down for trials I faced a lot of problems. As I went to register him everyone turned their backs on me. Out of the seventy boys that day he was the only Asian boy. Since signing on last year he has become a regular for the under-10s' side. He is getting what I didn't get as a youngster – his dad is taking him to football matches.'

Boys' football clubs are renowned for their cliquey-ness, often teams will be run by a father whose son plays in the team, and the side is likely to be made up of the son's friends. Under those circumstances it is difficult for any outsiders to break through, particularly if they are at another school, or are not members of the small network of friends.

The desire to produce a genuine Asian star player is as strong in Nelson as it is elsewhere in the country. Over the years a few players have come close to making that breakthrough. Currently on their books Paak have a talented player called Ader, who used to be an apprentice with Rochdale. Other former players used to be on the books at Preston North End and Burnley, and have gone on to play for semi-professional teams like Nelson and recent Wembley FA Trophy Cup Finalists Clitheroe. The club recognizes that if progress is to be made in this area, then they must develop closer links with the more mainstream elements in the professional game. This is a principle they have taken from the game of cricket; only the circumstances leading up to their decision were altogether less contentious than those of their cricketing counterparts. In 1990 former England and Yorkshire captain, Brian Close, commented that the failure of Asian cricketers to break through at Yorkshire had nothing to do with the county's policies, but rather more to do with inadequacies within the Asian community. Following Close's comments, both the county and Asian cricketers were forced to re-examine their relationship. Asian cricketers came to realize that they could not hope to reach the county team unless they played for clubs competing at the highest levels of league cricket, and this led to more Asian cricket players switching to play at a higher grade of club cricket. For their part, the county club has arranged ethnic minority coaching days, and the York-shire County Cricket Board has an Ethnic Minority Forum. There is an ethnic minority team, and some players have moved from this to the county's cricket academy.

To this end, Paak FC are working closely with Burnley Football Club's community programme team in delivering coaching sessions to young Asian footballers. At the same time, some Asians still seem to believe that such overtures are not entirely sincere and contain more than an element of window-dressing. According to Mashuq, clubs like Burnley will have to do much more than organize training sessions for Asian youngsters: 'Burnley are trying to encourage more ethnic minorities to come and watch, but it's all commercially driven. You see the clubs will do anything to get people in their grounds – all they are interested in is your money.'

Assuming that progress can be made and that an opportunity should arise for a local Pakistani boy from Nelson to pull on the England shirt, the queston arises: can he be relied upon to do his absolute best?

Migrant communities in Britain continue to be torn to an extent by split loyalties to their ancestral and adopted homelands. Everywhere you go around the world you see ex-patriates clinging on to their ancestral ties. In the United States of America you have people of African, Irish, Italian and Hispanic descent supporting the country of their ancestral orgin during sporting contests. The same can be said of Britain, Australia, New Zealand, Canada and South Africa. In India the Muslim community support Pakistan in sporting contests involving India and Pakistan, and in the West Indies Indo-Caribbeans cheer for India against the West Indies. As we approach the twenty-first century the effects of improved transportation systems, the reduction of space between disparate peoples via new forms of communication, and the relocation of many different peoples across the world (diasporic communities being spread globally) has had the inevitable effect of clouding what were traditional definitions of nationality. Consequently, it has become increasingly difficult for some migrant groups to conform to a singular national identity. In Nelson the dual loyalty of the Pakistani community to Britain and Pakistan needs to therefore be understood in its appropriate context. Whether a Pakistani playing for England would be as committed as a 'blue-blooded' Englishman is something Robert Henderson enquired about in the *Wisden Cricket*

Monthly in July 1995. Henderson suggested that black players in cricket and, by implication, other sports, did not try as hard as 'real' English players. Some sportswriters supported the idea that teams with a strong 'national identity' do better. Others pointed to the great performance of many 'polyglot' teams, at national and international level. Anyone with any doubts will have observed very carefully the monumental batting efforts of Indian-born England cricketers Nasser Hussain (Madras) and Min Patel (Bombay) against India in 1996 to stave off almost certain defeat against the teams representing the nations of their ancestral homeland. The scenes at the Edgbaston Test match were beautifully encapsulated by Rajan Datar, writing in the *Guardian*: 'The Indian attack of Srinath and Prasad was on fire, cylinders-a-pumping, bludgeoning England's higher order into meek submission. At the crease, the defiant Nasser Hussain remains the host's only recognized batsman. Coming out to join him, the thin, unassuming frame of debutant spinner Min Patel of Kent. Their mission: to ward off the Indian offensive and save England's blushes. Oh what a moment of delicious irony, sadly lost on the old boy network in the commentary box, but savoured by every Asian viewer; England's showcase cricket spectacle hogged by thirteen Asian players. The colonial game hijacked on its own turf by descendants of subjects of the Raj. Hussain, all grit and determination, went on to celebrate his first Test century. Patel, an unrecognized batsman, hung around to scratch together eighteen runs, and the match – the series too, probably – was won through the resistance of this partnership.'

Finally, it is often said that paradoxical adversity draws out strength and character as well as acting as a restraining force. This is certainly true of Paak FC, as Tariq states defiantly: 'Our problems bind us together. Religion does keep us together. We say a prayer before the game. Exclusion from different backgrounds, whether they are social or economic, all bind us together.' Faith and football engendering a real faith in football.

9 Forgotten Sisters

Have you ever seen an Asian woman running to catch a departing bus? Have you ever seen an Asian woman kicking a ball, going for a jog, riding a bike or taking a swim in the local baths? For many people, the answer to such questions will be a resounding no. One of the rarest sights that is scarcely beheld in this country is that of an Asian female in the throes of physical or sporting activity. Do Asian women, then, never exert themselves physically, never participate in sport or break sweat? The answer to these posers is an equally resonant no. Women's kabaddi in India is as big a spectator sport as the men's game; indeed, in certain areas (such as in west Bengal) women's kabaddi (moreover girls' kabaddi) is more popular than the men's equivalent. India also has a longer-established women's local football infrastructure, an informalized league that pre-dates the men's semi-pro Philips League. So what of the Asian women who live in Britain? What is their relationship with sport?

In Britain, sport began as a strictly male preserve for the first-generation Asian immigrant men. These men arrived in the UK committed to working hard for the good of their families, both in Britain and back in the homeland. Those who were keen sportsmen in India or Pakistan endeavoured to continue their sporting practices over here. In the main, this meant training and working out in their own homes, and then later progressing to join clubs and teams that were organized by the local immigrant communities. Volleyball matches, kabaddi matches and hockey games were arranged between teams of Asians, and, soon enough, the Shaheedi Udham Singh Games came into being, formalizing the role of sport in the lives of Britain's immigrant Asian male population, particularly the Punjabi Sikhs. For the female section of this population, these Games also formalized their specific role in the wider Asian family in Britain. While the men were at play, the women cooked.

It would be forgivable to assume that these were sporting events for the pleasures and hedonistic indulgence of Asian men (refer to Asian Games chapter). The tournaments were organized, run, played out and attended by men and boys; active female involvement was strictly prohibited. Yet out of this exclusion and out of the obsolete order of misogyny, Asian women extracted a form of social festivity that was all their own. While the menfolk staggered around a muddy field desperately clutching at sobriety, the respective kins-women enjoyed a somewhat more civil and uninebriated party in their own company. Having suitably supplied the men with their picnics (*pronthe, sabhji,* and *achaar*), the Asian women had the rest of the time to themselves. During the seventies, and into a large chunk of the eighties, there were few occasions when Asian women could congregate in one space without the imperious presence of men; and so such occasions were exploited to the maximum. They would sing and dance to traditional folk-dance songs (*gidhah*), and in the process perform their own displays of physical dexterity and prowess. They could throw off their *duputte* (head scarves) and kick off their *chappals* (sandals) and hit the dance floor like real demon *gidhah* divas; well, they sang melodic folk tunes in high-pitched voices whilst clapping their hands and shuffling around each other in a repetitive circular fashion. When the musical joviality had reached its exhausted conclusion, it was then time to catch up on all the latest gossip about what was happening in the lives of all the women and their families. Stories were swapped, future marriages were speculatively arranged, and great fun and merry making was enjoyed by all . . . and then the men came back. *Duputte* were respectfully back on heads, *chappals* back on feet and song and dance back in the annals of the day's more clandestine history. While the men were at play, the women played too; but when the men returned, the cooking beckoned once more.

There has been a relative emancipation of Asian women in the intervening years. Although the tournaments remain male preserves, women no longer dutifully make the accompanying food for their menfolk. Indeed, they are no longer expected to perform such a task, an indication of the male reappraisal of female roles. Tournaments are no more the festival events that allowed disparate extended families to socialize gregariously. Instead, they became tolerated weekend fixtures. Today, while the men play, the women do whatever else they want to do without having to work their social agenda around the men's leisure activities. By the mid-eighties sport began to assume a more central position in Asian women's lives. By wresting sport away from the protective bear-hug of the Asian males, women were also able to use sport as a form of social interaction, physical exhilaration and ethnic mobilization. The Asian sporting female had snatched the starter's pistol and shot off from the blocks.

For British-Asian girls, school is the first arena for sports participation. In multiracial schools where Asians were a significant minority, Asian girls were expected to take as full a part in PE lessons as any of the other pupils. Traditionally, physical education in schools is another 'gendered' institution, where different sports are allocated for girls and boys respectively. Boys played football, rugby, cricket and basketball; girls played netball, hockey and tennis. The injustice of this system is clearly apparent. Whilst boys had their traditional male sports, they could also participate in the games that the girls played, such as tennis, hockey and gymnastics. Of course, there was a fair deal of crossover, with both sexes taking part in athletics, volleyball, badminton and cross-country running; but football, rugby and cricket remained principally male PE sports, whilst netball and gymnastics were girl-dominated. Fortunately more and more schools are now adopting a more liberal and progressive physical education policy. Girls can do football and rugby in PE lessons, and mixed groups (up to a certain age) are not wholly uncommon in many schools; but boys playing netball are still quite rare in the educational system. So for many years, for a number of young Asian girls, netball was the main route to achieving some kind of sporting success at school. It enabled them to show their peers and their teachers that they were capable of performing at a comparatively high level in a competitive sport, contradicting and refuting the popular cultural myths about Asian women or girls being passive, submissive and ineffectual individuals. It also dispelled the belief that Asian girls weren't allowed out from their homes or schools by their parents – obviously, Asian girls who played for their school netball team were called to travel to other schools in the borough, after school hours. This is not to suggest that it was perfectly straightforward for these girls to be part of an extracurricular school activity, especially a sporting one. It was not the obligatory short gym skirts that were objectionable for Asian parents; instead, they were more concerned with their daughters being outside the 'safe' environs of the school itself, away from the institutionalized, relative security, or at least familiarity, that schools purportedly represented. The girls would also be predominantly in the company of white girls and not necessarily amongst the group of friends that they had most in common with. Parents were concerned that their daughters may be influenced by the non-Asian ways of the white girls, especially outside of school and away from their other Asian friends. In the majority of cases Asian daughters were able to convince their parents, quite rationally, that playing in the school netball team posed no real threat to their Asian identity, to their discipline or to their respectability. They conveyed the positive effects of such participation, expressing the benefits to their own standing in school, as well as pointing out that this was a chance to excel in a particular event.

As is often the case, Asian girls who were seriously into sport in their early years at school lost much of their sporting interest as they got older and discovered 'other things'. Any extra allotted time after school was spent with friends, just hanging around, talking and flirting; playing netball was a waste of the permissible 'free-time'. This was not restricted to Asian girls alone; many white girls also experienced similar indifference towards school representative sport, post-puberty. For Asian girls, however, school was *the* place for sport, where they could run, play and enjoy physical activity in a safe and recognized milieu. Once away from this environment, where would it be possible for them to practise any kind of real sport?

Hema Chauhan's parents came to Britain from the Gujerat in India in the late 1950s, settling in Belgrave, Leicester. Hema was one of five siblings, and so was part of a typical large family. Unfortunately, Hema's father passed away while she was still a teenager, and so her mother was left to bring up the family during a difficult time for immigrant communities in Britain. Hema still cites her mother as the most important and influential role model in her life.

During her school days Hema was fortunate that she was never really exposed to the kind of racial harassment that other children of Asian and West Indian immigrants suffered. Indeed, she very much enjoyed her time at school, and wanted to become an accountant or work in the financial world in some capacity when she left. Whilst still at school, Hema loved playing different sports. She was captain of the school netball team, and there was little doubt that she stood head and shoulders above the rest of the girls in terms of ability and commitment, yet she was never encouraged by any of the teachers to push her talent further, to pursue netball at higher levels outside of school: 'During all that time I was never told about the local teams that you could join, and there were a number of local teams and junior leagues. I know all this now, but I was never told when I was back at school. Maybe if I was told back then, I may have been playing at a higher level now.'

Hema's school was not too adept at informing any of the pupils as to what sort of activities lay beyond the educational domain. The white girls in the netball team were also largely uninformed about local clubs and leagues that they could become involved in. Hema believed that her teachers assumed that Asian girls weren't really very interested in sport, or willing to take it seriously outside of school. On leaving school, Hema went to work in a firm of accountants, but was soon dazzled by the intense excitement of the profession and so moved on to work in a more tempestuous cauldron of bedazzling fervour – a building society.

It was around about this time that Hema began her close association with football. She started playing indoor five-a-side games at the local sports centre with other women. They reached a very competitive standard and were regularly well placed in the local women's league. Hema had stirred an inner passion for the game, and became heavily devoted to playing the sport. She claims to have had little real interest in football before this, but did take an interest in Liverpool, largely because they were the most successful team of the time.

Since then, her work in and for Leicester (including the football club) has shifted her support over to the blue Foxes of Leicester City. Hema had attended youth clubs and community centres from the age of around 13, and after numerous trips camping, canoeing, rock climbing, and even skiing, Hema became more actively involved in the running of these clubs and centres on a voluntary basis. She would take young kids on similar adventures, and organized all-girl groups so that more girls would find it less intimidating or uncomfortable to attend the clubs. By the time she was 19 she had reached a point in her life when she had to decide whether she should continue in her financial vocation, smiling inanely at people in a building society, or pursue her passion. Hema chose the latter.

She began as a pool attendant at a local sports club and remained in this job for a year before landing the post of Leisure Manager. During this period Hema gained a broader experience of leisure management, working in the arts as well as sports recreation. Not being one to pass up broadening opportunities, especially when they were free, Hema made sure she took advantage of every different kind of training course that the local authority organized for leisure employees. She got involved in swimming, volleyball, badminton and weight-training courses.

As Hema became better qualified to run a greater array of sports and leisure schemes, so her standing in the Leicester leisure industry became much more authoritative, until she was in a position where she could make decisions as to specific forms of leisure provision. She had maintained her links with the Asian youth clubs that she was involved with as a teenager, and also had a leading role in the organization of the Belgrave Mela – a multicultural event that was held in the town every year.

Another one of Hema's initiatives was a Monday night women's sports session at Cossington Leisure Centre, in a pre-dominantly Asian part of Leicester. Here, Asian women of all ages were encouraged to attend the centre for fitness training, aerobics, Indian dance classes, badminton and swimming. Once word spread amongst the Asian women of Cossington, the sessions soon became extremely popular, fixed social dates during the working week. As Hema explains, 'We had girls from the ages of 10 upwards playing badminton, doing aerobics and taking part in the dance classes. All the sessions were, in fact, quite popular, but the ones that were most surprising were the swimming sessions. We'd have Asian *massis* [literally as 'aunties' – or older Asian women] in their swimming costumes jumping in at the deep end. It was quite an amusing sight at first, but after a while it was just a group of women enjoying a swim. Some of the women were in their fifties and sixties and so had taught themselves to swim back in India. They didn't have the best technique, but they managed to get from one side to the other quite easily.'

Information about health and fitness was also widely circulated and helped raise awareness and attendance figures at leisure centres, as did the greater number of Asian female leisure and sports workers, to hand. It seems Asian women have a desire to get involved in projects that are directly run for their benefit and run by other Asian women. They are much more comfortable when it is an Asian woman in charge of a session.

Hema's reputation and achievements in the sports recreation world received much acclaim and renown. So much so that she was appointed Sports Development Officer for the city of Leicester. In her new and much more responsible capacity, Hema, with her colleagues, was called to concentrate on a smaller number of sports. Financial and practical limitations meant that they would not be able to fully develop every sport in the city. Due to a massive demand and constant enquiries, women's football was given the greatest and most urgent priority. They were continuously being inundated by young girls and women wanting to know where they could play football, what coaching or training courses were available and what clubs they could join. Such fervent interest could not have been generated without a great deal of constructive initiative: 'If you're a good development officer, you can develop any sport. Football is another product, as far as I'm concerned, and if you gave me something else to develop then I could fully develop that as well. With women's football in Leicester, because there was a lot of demand, it meant that there was a lot of potential as well, and no one had done anything about it until recently. At first the Football Association were not all that co-operative or appreciative about women's football in Leicester. I remember going for a meeting with their representatives, who were rather old men with grey hair and blue blazers – and then in walks this Asian woman wearing a tracksuit and trainers. I think I looked quite odd to them. They had to listen to what I had to say, though, because I was a Sports Development Officer working for the council; this was my job and they would have to accept it.'

Hema soon got the people from the Football Association on her side, and they became convinced that her work was of genuine value and for the good of the game. They appointed a National Women's Development Officer and Regional Development Officers, who worked with Hema. With Leicester boasting an Asian population that amounted to 40 per cent of the city's total number of residents, the issue of Asian girls in football had to be addressed and catered for. To this end, Hema began approaching a few primary schools that had predominantly Asian pupils, and promoted the game of football within these institutions. The response was very encouraging. Schools such as Spinney Hill, attended by mostly Pakistani Muslim pupils, were very forward in welcoming and participating in the initiative. Hema believes that the teachers have much to do with this: 'There is a new era of school teachers of an Asian background, especially in primary schools. They have really forced this issue about Asian girls and sport. They have a new and more progressive way of thinking about what is expected of Asian girls today, and that they don't have to be restricted in their choice of sports activities. They are actively encouraging Asian girls into sport.'

Most of the football activities that Hema and her colleagues arrange are within school hours, so there is little difficulty for Asian girls to fully participate in them. For organized competitions, however, the weekend (usually a Saturday) is used to stage such events. Teams from all over Leicester take part in these girls' football competitions. Many are all-white teams, but there a few teams with a significant number of Asian players; again, this depends largely on which area of Leicester different teams represent. Most of the teams are accompanied by the teachers or youth workers, but parents also come along to cheer their daughters on. Hema is quite aware of the fact that most of the supporting parents are white, and that few Asian mums and dads attend the competitions. Although a few younger Asian dads sometimes turn up.

There is a great deal of women's football played in Leicester. The city, in fact, has received national acclaim for its efforts in expanding women's football. More women coaches are being trained in the essential skills of the game so that they can then coach young girls to play at the highest standards possible. More Asian women and girls are also getting involved in such coaching schemes, and so young Asian girls can have more role models and coaches to emulate. Does Hema Chauhan see herself as a role model for Asian girls? 'I suppose I've been one kind of "role model" and I've moved on to another kind now. When I first started off, obviously I was coaching and leading the sessions, so from that point of view I used to try to encourage them to play sports. Now, having moved on to a management and administration role, it's more about having a career in the field. It's something different; I'm still completely involved in sport, but without having to wear a tracksuit. It's a shame that we haven't got any more Asian women working in either aspect of sport – this is something that definitely needs working on.'

Hema Chauhan works in a white man's world, promoting a white man's game, but the race issue is not of the utmost importance – yet. It's the question of gender bias that is the major obstacle in the way of making football a universally access-ible game; ethnic and racial struggles are secondary in this spe-cific context. Unlike in the men's amateur and non-League game, in women's football there are very few incidents of racism, or racist antagonism, both on the pitch and in the organ-izational set-up. For mixed ethnic women's and girls' football teams, the problems they face concern the lack of professional or adequate coaching, funding and sponsorship. There is little attention given to which players come from which particular cultural backgrounds; instead teams concentrate on which are the best players in all the positions on the pitch. Women's and girls' teams are looking for as wide a membership as possible, in order to have enough affiliated players to put out at least one full team. Therefore they must embrace the whole of the multicultural society that exists around them – a wider pool of talent from which to choose the best players – for they can't really afford to narrow their field of selection or turn people away unnecessarily.

In Hema's opinion, Asian girls are much more involved in football now than ever before, and engage with the sport in a considerably more active way. They take a keen part in football in their schools; they play in competitions and are committed players in local teams. There are over twenty teams in the Leicester girls' football league; of these teams there are five or so teams that are predominantly made up of Asian girls, and others that have one, two or more Asian players in their sides. It is no longer a peculiar or unusual sight to see a young Asian girl walking down the street wearing a Manchester United shirt with the number eleven on her back and the name Kally proudly displayed across the top. At Leicester City's Family Nights (where families can take their kids to watch reserve-team games at reduced prices) many more Asian families with young boys and girls can be seen in attendance. This is just one way that football is trying to make itself more open and user-friendly to a more diverse audience. The game is undergoing a transition that may possibly make it more accessible for ethnic minorities to consume it with the same passion as the traditional football fan-base.

In Leicester, Hema Chauhan hasn't tried to mould football into a sport that is more attractive to Asian girls, nor has she tried to shape the girls themselves into football-appreciative fanatics. Instead, Hema and her colleagues have attempted to find a working compromise by dispelling the perceived myths and prejudices that have maintained a cautious distance between the two. The success of such a venture is apparent in the embodiment of one of the most promising under-16 players in Leicester, a footballer of outstanding quality who just happens to be a girl, and also just happens to be Asian. This player is Jaspreet Gahia, who was born in the city in 1983 to her immigrant Punjabi-Indian parents. Football came to her as a very young child, and she remembers kicking a ball about at the age of 4: 'I've always played football ever since I was a little kid. I was always out in the street or in the park kicking a ball about with friends or cousins. I haven't got any brothers, only two sisters, and so I had no boys in my family to play football with, but my cousins, the boys, were always around, so I could play football with them and other friends in my street. I mostly picked football up for myself, learning how to play myself.'

Jaspreet played football in her primary school, playing for the school team, in fact. At first she was part of a mixed-sex team then, as more girls started to take up the sport, an all-girls' team was established, which Jaspreet duly became a focal part of. Jaspreet knew that she wanted to continue playing football in her secondary school, and was lucky enough and good enough to do so. She continued to play for her secondary school girls' football team up until 1997, when for reasons beyond the control of the players, the team was disbanded. Fortunately for Jaspreet, her PE teacher was also a keen footballer who played for the Leicester City Ladies Football Club. She encouraged Jaspreet very strongly to join Leicester Ladies, where she would be able to continue improving her game and enjoying competitive football. Jaspreet soon found herself embraced as a vital member of the under-16 team too.

A keen sportsperson, Jaspreet regularly plays other sports such as netball, basketball and athletics. Due to her obvious love of sport, her parents have never denied Jaspreet the opportunity to participate in football matches at any level. They fully accepted their daughter's passion for the game and whilst they haven't pledged wholehearted support for Jaspreet's future in football, they have completely, and rightfully, refrained from the kind of active discouragement that young Asian boys encountered in previous decades when they professed their footballing ambitions. And Jaspreet's father does occasionally accompany his daughter to some of Leicester Ladies' fixtures. As the team's pivotal centre-forward, Jaspreet is the leading goalscorer at the club and consistently scores a bagful of goals. This is an admission that she states without conceit or arrogance, it is simply a matter of fact that she is the star striker, who always gets the goals and the accompanying glory.

As a keen football fan, Jaspreet tries to watch as much football as possible – usually on TV. Liverpool are the team that she supports, although she hasn't yet managed to go to Anfield or see them live. She feels no inconsistency or disloyalty in the fact that she supports Liverpool and not Leicester City, the club that she represents as a junior and as a girl: 'I do follow Leicester City, I've even been to see them at Filbert Street a couple of times, but I like Liverpool more. I don't want to see City lose all the time or get relegated, but I want Liverpool to win more, and win the Premiership and FA Cup and everything else. I used to watch Liverpool on the TV all the time, and I really liked the way they played: I liked the players and the fact that they were all really good. They used to win all their games then as well. My dad and uncles and cousins are all big Liverpool fans, and so I followed in that kind of tradition.'

Her family, including her extended family, is very positive about Jaspreet's involvement in football. Being avid football fans themselves, they are, if anything, a little in awe of the young star's achievements and maybe a little envious of the opportunities she has had. Asian boys are magnanimous in their appreciation of Jaspreet as a footballer. Apart from the obligatory mickey-taking that is very much an inherent part of boy–girl relationships during adolescence, young Asian boys often compliment Jaspreet on her soccer prowess and offer speculative invitations for her to join their male teams. Indeed one of her father's friends, the coach of a local all-Asian men's team, has invited Jaspreet to train and play with their youth team. Jaspreet's commitments, however, are firmly lodged in the Leicester Ladies camp. As the sole Asian player in the Leicester Ladies side, Jaspreet is only too well aware of the need to encourage other Asian girls into the sport: 'There aren't that many Asian girls who play football at this kind of club level. I think that one reason may be that some parents don't really encourage their daughters to play, or they stop them from playing. Some of my own friends have told me that they are not allowed to play football by their parents, and some think that there is a lot of racism in football matches. I have never ever experienced any kind of racism when I've been playing a match, not in any way. Everyone's really cool and chilled out; they take you for who you are, just another football player. If I wanted to play football at a higher level and carry it on further, then my parents would support me because they know I could be really good at what I do. I would like to play professional football, but if I don't, there are lots of other things that I want to do.'

Jaspreet has found that she has become something of a role model herself recently. Asian, black and white girls have approached her and asked for her advice on how to improve their football. They want to know whether or not they can become as good as she is if they practise hard enough. She tries her best to help them whenever she can. Once again, her remarks are devoid of any affected self-flattery.

In the summer of 1997, Leicester City Ladies under-16s took part in a girls' six-a-side football competition hosted by Leicester City Council and organized by a team which included the considerable influence of one Hema Chauhan. During a wet and windy Saturday afternoon, the sort of climatic conditions that perpetuate the myth of archetypal English football, Jaspreet and her fellow Leicester City Ladies clinically went about shattering wide-held preconceptions of girls' football being of a significantly lower standard than its male counterpart. Since the game was being played on artificial turf, the bad weather conditions did not excessively affect the quality of the football. And the girls of Leicester Ladies proved that the physicality of the game was a feature that they not only understood and effectively deployed, but actually enjoyed. There was, however, one player who stood head and shoulders above the rest. Jaspreet Gahia – a name that sounds anything but English – is a football player who resembles the classic English centre-forward. In a match in which she scored an imperious hat-trick, Jaspreet showed that traditional assets of the British game – pace, power, strength and determination – can be harnessed in conjunction with high levels of skill, tactical maturity and technical excellence. Nurtured and practised correctly this combination could produce a truly impressive footballer, who could contribute to a formidable and progressive game. As English football undergoes a period of crucial transition, acquiring and accommodating wider influences and new methods and techniques, it seems that women's/girls' football has already embraced the dominant principles of the modern game. Due to the fact that football for women and girls is a relatively recent phenomenon, it hasn't had to carry and then unload the historical baggage and myopic isolation that the men's professional game has burdened itself with. The past for Leicester Ladies is unimportant. What they have presently is a crop of talented and enthusiastic young players, players who can only get better as the English game rapidly catches up with its international cousins. Jaspreet Gahia is very much a part of this progressive and re-constituted brave new soccer world.

There is little doubt that Jaspreet is a product, and an avid consumer, of the English footballing pop-cultural machine. She has the replica kits, her bedroom wall is emblazoned with football posters, she, or rather her parents, subscribe to the satellite channels, and, of course, she plays the game itself. We know she's a talented player, and we know she's a devoted Liverpool fan; but what of her relationship with the England football team? How does she relate to them? Does she support them? 'I'm a big England fan, a very big England fan. I always want to see England win, whoever they play. I love watching the England matches on television, especially when Jamie Redknapp, Robbie Fowler and Steve McManaman are playing. I hate it when England lose, like against Germany in Euro '96 – that really hurt.'

On the face of it, Jaspreet is a staunch, traditional English patriot, but on closer investigation, the cultural and 'national' duality that she embodies begins to bravely surface. Whenever England play India in a cricket Test match she is adamant in her support for the Indian team. Her reasons? 'Well, they're Indian, aren't they? India's where my family is from.' Her support would remain loyal to India even if India played England in a football match, although much would depend on whether Messrs Fowler, Ince and McManaman were wearing the white shirts. Jaspreet's support of the England football team (however conditional) has sprung and survived the negative dissociation that her father and uncles have had with English football's first eleven. They have a very antagonistic relationship with England, cheering for their failure and defeat as much as for their opponent's victory. Their national footballing ties lie somewhat predictably on the exotic shores of South America, in Brazil. But who would Jaspreet rather play for: an England women's football team, or an Indian national side? 'That's a really difficult question. I don't really know, or I can't really give a straight answer to that. I'd love to play for the England team because this was the country that I was born in and know the most about. I would probably know the players I'd be playing with a lot better as well; they would probably be my mates, and that would be cool. But it would be great playing for India as well. That's where my parents and grandparents and whole family are from. I suppose I'm just as much Indian as I am British, maybe more so. A lot would have to depend on which was the better team and had most chance of being really good and winning the World Cup, or something. I'd probably play for the better one. In the end, I'd probably go with whoever paid me the most.'

Who said that girls don't take football as seriously as the boys? Jaspreet certainly seems to know what the modern game is all about.

10 Sporting Endeavours – An Indian Adventure

In February 1997, an all-Asian non-League football team from Coventry in the West Midlands embarked on a month-long tour of the northern Indian state of the Punjab. This was to be a footballing tour that would involve playing competitive matches (whilst not being part of any formal competition) against established football teams from various regions of the Punjab. Although football was the primary reason for the team's sojourn in India, the opportunity to visit relatives, and for the players to re-acquaint themselves with their familial and cultural roots, was just as important a part of the trip. Accompanied by one of the authors of this book, this all-Asian football team headed East; obliging the ignorant requests of unfortunate patriots of two decades previous, they were 'going back to where they came from'. For most, they were travelling to the land of their parents' birth, some for the first time, or for the first time since childhood, but for all it was a trip that held a special significance. On this occasion they took with them something more than Levi's jeans, Nike T-shirts and Gameboys as presents for rural relations. This time, they were bringing with them a world game. The game was football, the location India, and the visiting team; they were known as The Sporting Club of Coventry: Coventry Sporting.

Fortunately for this intrepid band of travellers, the task of imposing a traditional English sport upon the indigenous Indian masses had been dutifully performed by the self-ordained governors of British Imperial rule. These colonial rulers regarded sport as being a potent agent for instilling a revised, Anglicized social order in the rank and file of India's massive population. Team games in particular were seen to be invaluable and highly effective forms for teaching conformity, discipline and solidarity; thus football, cricket, hockey and rugby were rapidly established as central facets of the curriculum in schools throughout the Empire from the 1880s onwards. The first regular, organized football competition in India is said to have been the Durand Trophy, competed for by army teams in Simla in 1888. During this early period, football teams representing the resident British military were the sole soccer outfits that competed in recognized competition. These teams were made up of white soldiers who played against other all-white regiments. Around this period Indian teams began to be formed that had indigenous Indian players, who initially represented local colleges. They were closely followed by teams that played under the banner of the localized region, district or state, such as Sorabazar (1885), Mohan Bagan (1889) and Mohammedan Sporting (1891); the latter two clubs remain amongst India's strongest football outfits of today. In 1893 football in the colony received official governance and status when the Indian Football Association (IFA) was formed. The primary location for much of the early football played in India was Calcutta, a decision likely to have been influenced by the residence of a huge army garrison within its parameters. With massively superior playing and training facilities, it was of little surprise that British regiment teams enjoyed virtually unbroken success against the 'native' Indian opposition. The first defeat of a British team came in 1892, when a British regiment was beaten by Sorabazar in the Trades Cup. With the popularity of football flourishing among the local Bengali population, the British-dominated IFA permitted the entry of Indian clubs into the prestigious IFA Shield, a competition that was formerly closed to non-British (non-white) teams. The IFA Shield attracted teams, civil as well as military, from across the subcontinent and brought the season to an exciting climax. The popular significance of the Shield was keenly appreciated by Indian and British players and supporters alike, and merited extensive coverage in the national newspapers. In 1911, in what some commentators have described as a singularly momentous occasion in India's colonial history, the bare-footed Mohan Bagan team defeated the much fancied British favourites, East Yorkshire Regiment, by two goals to one in the Shield Final. This was a sporting event that both British and Indians inter-preted as having nationalistic, racial and political significance. The ignorant peasants of a culturally inferior country had beaten the educated, groomed soldiers of a divinely superior Britain. This kind of ill-informed rationale pervaded the popular interpretation of the game. The events of this game clearly injected some confidence and belief into the native people of Calcutta, and possibly influenced members of the wider popu-lation of India. It certainly effected a belief that there was nothing inherently deficient in their own make-up that set them apart as inferior to their imposed colonial masters. However, in some sections of the press, Indian journalism was forced to persist in a discourse of colonial fawning – subordinate admir-ation of the Imperial master was still very much in evidence: 'in that peculiarly English sport, football, it fills every Indian with joy and pride to know that rice-eating, malaria-ridden, barefooted Bengalis have got the better of the beef-eating, Her-culean, booted John Bull in that peculiar English sport . . . Amid the taunts and jeers of exultant youths, Englishmen, even at the bitter hour of defeat, never lost for a moment their equanimity, nay, had the generosity to express their admiration for their conquerors, to take them on their shoulders and dance with glee, so that everyone can see why the English are the rulers of India.' (*Nayak*, 30 July 1911).

This Mohan Baghan victory embodies a degree of modern ambivalence. Its great glory and great tragedy rests in its unchal-lenged position as one of the only truly momentous footballing events in India's soccer history. Indian football has failed to produce any other sporting occasion that could be reasonably placed alongside the 1911 triumph. It wasn't until 1995 that a concerted effort was made to bring Indian football up to date and up to scratch. A team of FIFA advisors (a team consisting of two individuals – Sinnathamby Subramanium and Frits Ahlstroem) was brought to India in February of that year, at the behest of the All India Football Federation (AIFF). They were required to study the structure and organization of the domestic game and to make recommendations to re-invigorate and systematically modernize Indian football in line with the rest of the world. On arriving in India FIFA's advisors found a confused and disorganized system of club and state competitions, inadequate structures, ineffective coaching and technical activities, poor financing, facilities and marketing policies. However, what they did acknowledge was that participation in football was far greater than many people outside of India understood it to be. Coupled with a determination from the AIFF, the FIFA advisors were confident that India could yet emerge from its parlous footballing position. The central plank to their proposed strategy was the setting up of a National League, a procedure that was rather aptly delineated by the official FIFA delegation: 'To build a solid house, it makes sense to start with the foundation. But in India, just now, we recommend to start with the chimney – a National League, in order to get the necessary attention and money for the whole building.'

The proposed structure suggested there be twelve teams, with clubs being owned by companies; thereby adding financial stability. Strict criteria for entry were recommended, specifying the following key principles: full-time officials running the clubs, FIFA-safety-standard stadiums, financial stability, good marketing arrangements, a paid professional coach for each club, and set basic salaries and insurance for players. This was followed by a recommendation to rationalize the domestic Cups programme; FIFA had noted the excessive demands placed on the development of the country's better players by the punishing Cup tournaments. Proposals for the international team also took a radical departure. Up until then India had hosted international competitions that were seen to be a poor use of limited funds; and the indignity of losing at home did nothing to improve the profile of Indian football. Instead, it was strongly advised that the national team participate in more touring international competitions. Within a year of the FIFA visit, India had readied itself for this major sporting revolution. India was heading for its most exciting footballing adventure ever; and a little-known football team from Britain was about to experience the burgeoning fruits of this insurgent upheaval.

Coventry Sporting had always represented something more than just a local football team. Since its inauguration in 1963, the club performed the function of a community centre, a social point of contact for young and old Asian (almost unilaterally Indian) immigrants. The central region of Foleshill in Coventry provided an adopted home for many of the first-generation Indian immigrants. Indeed, it was a group of Indian football fanatics resident in Foleshill who formed Coventry Sporting Football Club. Young Indian men were given the chance to play football in a non-hostile, all-Asian environment, where they were allowed to enjoy the pleasures of the game as well as having the opportunity to keep fit in the process. Whilst Sporting has endured volatile times of uncertainty concerning the very existence of the club in its own right, it has also enjoyed numerous moments of success. Sporting teams over the past four decades have collected trophies from across the spectrum of Asian Games tournaments, accruing in the process a devout congregation of club affiliates. As fully affiliated members of a local amateur league, Sporting operate as an organized amateur club that holds regular meetings with all members to discuss relevant issues, and approaches football with a professional outlook; obligatory attendance at all training sessions being one of the requisites for a first-team place. A structured three-tier system organizes the club into three separate teams that play under the Sporting banner. The first team, the team that the manager regards as his 'best team', occupies the top tier. The second team, a younger team, is basically the under-16 outfit, and the third team is made up of venerable die-hards who are simply known as the over-35s (a reference to their average age and not the number of pints of mild ale they can sink in one evening). It is a fluid structure that allows for the movement of players from one team into another.

Nineteen ninety-seven was a difficult year for Sporting. Off-the-pitch organizational matters required a strategic reworking and the very structure of the club and team unity was brought into question. In February of the same year, however, Coventry Sporting worked through this difficulty, assured in their identity as a distinct collective unit. They were representatives of the Indian football-playing community of Foleshill, of Coventry. The tour in India would position them as representatives of Britain as well, a charge that infused the footballing confrontations with an international dimension. The team from Coventry would have to prove themselves as Sporting by name and sporting by nature.

Few were prepared for the level of poverty, despair and deprivation that they encountered – but once they had checked in at the terminal, the team quickly forgot about the short journey from Coventry to Birmingham International Airport. Those who could get time off work, who could afford time away from family, and those who were up for a nice four-week break in India, doing a bit of sightseeing, visiting relatives and having a few relaxed games of footie, assembled at the airport anticipating the lengthy plane journey that lay ahead. Prior to Euro '96, much had been made in the media about the England football team's exploits onboard a Cathay Pacific flight to the Far East. The reputation of air-travelling British footballers had been tarnished and maligned. With their esteemed professional counterparts having assumed 'collective responsibility' for the destructive effects of riotous behaviour, it was the moral and obliging duty of the players of Coventry Sporting to restore the faith of international airlines in British footballers travelling abroad.

On boarding the plane and saying their *'merci-beaucoups'* to the staff of the French airline company, the motley crew of twenty or so Sporting affiliates proceeded to argue over seating arrangements, treat the airline's food as aerodynamic missiles and, as their *pièce de resistance*, began to consume copious amounts of complimentary alcohol. Indeed, one member of the team foolishly antagonized one of the more surly French stewardesses to such an extent that he had to make a tactical retreat to the toilets. He emerged from the cubicle having changed his clothes and put on a hat, and returned to sit in someone else's seat. Thankfully, the eight-hour flight wasn't as wanton as this account may make it sound. Most of the fellow travellers and staff enjoyed the rather boisterous and harmlessly amusing antics, and, as the alcohol wore off, the plane landed on the hallowed tarmac of Indira Gandhi International Airport in Delhi. Sporting had arrived in India.

A private bus had been hired beforehand for the leisurely road trip from Delhi up north to the Punjab. True to arrangements, there was indeed a bus awaiting the team; 'bus' here loosely used to describe a rusty tin box, furnished with an assortment of over-used seating fixtures, all propped up on seemingly under-sized tyres. The condition of the vehicle would have been largely expected, had it not been for earlier boasts by the organizing committee as to the impressive specifications of the deluxe coach that would be at the team's disposal. The decrepit state of the bus was matched only by the rather inebriated state of the driver. For at the helm of the mobile death-trap was an honest, hard-working man who was approaching the end of an amphetamine-sustained thirty-two-hour driving shift. Furthermore, the speedy driver wasn't altogether assured as to the precise route that had to be taken to get to the Punjab. It was quite obvious to everyone onboard the bus (everyone except the driver) that the best route to the Punjab from Delhi didn't involve having to do three-point turns in the middle of a stretch of woodland, or travelling a few hundred yards along a a road, only to realize that the road in question hadn't yet been fully built. If the whole situation could possibly get any worse, it did. A freak spell of dense fog settled on the main G.T. Road, the only usable passage that linked Delhi to the Punjab. The fog was so thick that we were soon resigned to spending our first night in India stuck in a less than comfortable bus, cracking jokes, and singing along (rather brokenly) to the Hindi film songs that the driver was kind enough to play. A road journey that should have been completed in eight hours came to an end after seventeen. This was an experience that was to stand everyone in good stead for the weeks to come.

The person who was responsible for facilitating the tour is a highly respected local Coventry man, one of the main players in the city's development of Asian sports. With such an esteemed reputation, and the successful completion of a tour three years earlier, it seemed as if this particular venture to the East would go swimmingly. When the tour organizer (popularly known as 'Comrade' to the Sporting team because of his political reputation back in Coventry) left the bus in a town in the south of the Punjab, where he was greeted by awaiting members of his family, the rest of the passengers were disappointed as they thought the promoter was going to devote more time to the actual tour. There was reassurance in the form of the Sporting manager and a number of the more senior players who were all part of the entourage. Fortunately, experience of the Punjab and its working practices was a commodity that was not lacking amongst this group. However, an extensive familiarity with local custom wasn't really required to arrive at the conclusion that the hotel which the organizer had booked for the team in the Punjabi town of Hoshiarpur wasn't exactly the four-star accommodation that the players had somewhat foolishly expected. There was a growing realization amonst the travelling band that there was a considerable distance between their expectations of Comrade's tour duties, and what the man himself regarded as his obligation, or what is possible in India. It was becoming obvious that he saw himself as more of a silent facilitator, a recognized figure of some repute, whose name could be used to open doors, arrange matches and access venues. Many of the players, however, assumed that Comrade would accompany them every step of their way, organize all their games personally, arrange all travel and accommodation, brush their teeth, wipe their noses and generally take care of all business. The yawning gap between the presumptions of the players and those of the organizer would become more expansive as the tour progessed.

After a brief stop for refreshments and interesting dialogues with eager beggars, we re-boarded the bus and decided to split up: everyone was to go and stay with relatives in their own home towns and villages.

Having reconvened at Jullundhar bus station forty-eight hours later, the Sporting players and staff set forth to find a reasonably priced hotel to serve as a base. They would be training at Guru Nanak College in Jullundhar, so accommodation near the college would be rather more advantageous. Indeed, a relatively plush three-star hotel, Kamal Palace, within two miles of the training venue, served as a suitable temporary home. The fact that the hotel's management were gently persuaded to place one extra bed in each room, so that three could share one room, allowed the costs of staying at such premises to be kept to a thrifty minimum. Somewhat coincidentally, the large district of Jullundhar was hosting a regional college football tournament in the very week that Sporting were staying in the vicinity. So the team felt almost duty-bound to go and watch at least one of the games. The local tournament was at its semi-finals stage when the team from Coventry arrived at the playing fields where the matches were taking place. As they jumped out of the hired vans, over-loaded to levels of obscene illegality, sporting their specially made 'Coventry Sporting Tour of India 1997' polo shirts (supplied free of charge by Carlsberg Breweries) the team were stared at with amusement by the touchline supporters. Realizing that they were the focus of a seemingly beguiled crowd, the Sporting players assumed an air of footballing superiority, almost ambassadorship; they were a soccer delegation that had come from Britain to watch over the burgeoning talent of South Asia. But it wasn't enough for them to merely stand around spectating – a few footballs were brought out from the vans and some of the players started to have a kick-about. Bearing in mind that we had only landed on Indian soil a matter of days ago, and no real physical exertion was advisable, passing a ball to one another over a few yards didn't represent any great threat of injury. But once again fate struck another unwarranted blow. One of the team's centre-backs (Jas, whose Indian nickname, Sudhiyee, suggests certain doubts about his intellectual capacity) somehow managed to strain his thigh muscle whilst kicking a ball up into the air. The watching parties took note of such a distressing display of British sporting frailty. Once the semi-finals had been resolved, we decided to head off back to the hotel to express our fears about the standard of football we had just seen.

Due to the manager (Jack) being unavoidably detained in Hoshiarpur, training began without him at the nearby Guru Nanak College. It was, indeed, the injured centre-back Jas, who took charge of the training session. He was regarded as one of the fittest members of the team, and this, combined with his martial arts background, meant that he put the rest of the players through a quite punishing first workout. Of course, such rigorous exercise called for a lengthy spell in the hotel sauna, followed by a few bottles of Kingfisher lager in the bar, and then off out into the town for more drinks and a curry. Events were transpiring in true British footballer fashion. The next morning brought with it another early start, and another bout of physical torture at the hands of Jas. Some of the players were complaining about tight muscles, some expressed doubts about pushing themselves so hard so early on. Interestingly, no such complaints had been aired the previous night, when many were up until two in the morning playing cards for forfeits that involved running up and down corridors, disturbing other guests, and the obligatory display of male genitalia. Despite all this, they all completed another extensive training session; whatever else they may have been, the Sporting players were committed, they were aware of the physical conditioning that was required. This resolute pragmatism was soon to be put to the test. The first game was only a day away. They were to face the mighty Mahalpur.

Mahalpur are one the more established Punjabi football teams. The actual town of Mahalpur isn't the biggest, but it's home to Mahalpur College, an educational establishment that is high on prestige and academic excellence, and its history is steeped in sporting success (especially footballing success). The college itself is a highly impressive edifice. Magnificent ornate architecture is combined with picturesque gardens, where the principal sat majestically in the shade, looking on at the visiting team from England as they arrived in the grounds. On speaking with him, it became patently obvious that his team regarded this match with Coventry Sporting as an opportunity to pit their talents against one of England's finest all-Asian football outfits (allegedly). It was a test as to how they would fair against a team that, in a residual context, embodied their former colonial master: the Indians from India versus the Indians from Britain.

Mahalpur College's football team was a collection of students who had their performances on the pitch assessed just as stringently as their scholarly output. With further education in rural India a privilege of the rich, or an unenviable struggle for the poor, few students could afford to waste their time at college, and thus if you represented the college at any sport it was in your best interests to perform to your optimum potential. This team trained three times a week, they had a full-time coach, and they were intelligent, articulate, successful students of various disciplines, ranging from medicine to politics. They also were acutely aware of the college's imperious footballing legacy.

The Coventry Sporting players were shown to their changing rooms, where they proceeded to prepare themselves for the ensuing battle. Thankfully, their manager Jack (a fully qualified, FA-accredited coach) had joined the team and was giving final instructions as to who would be playing and where. Jas was still not fully recovered from his thigh strain, but it was decided that there was little choice but for him to play, but there was to be the extra cover of a spare man at the back, the sweeper Ranjit. The formation would be 5–3–2: the goalkeeper (Kash) then Ranjit behind two centre-backs (Jas and Nuz), two wing-backs (Pummie and Later) supporting three midfield players (Chew, Jesus and Singhy), with the two strikers (Mo and J.R.) up front. There was sufficient cover on the bench in the form of Kully (one of the more senior players), Nutter (one of the wilder players) and Grummun (the perennial substitute who wouldn't allow the physical rigours of a game of football to disturb his hair). They were joined by Amo, the young rising star of the team, a gifted 18-year-old who was beginning to pick up some of the more cynical tricks of the soccer trade from his experienced peers. There was another substitute, Sarj, a mature, respectable, decent man, who seemed the only person able to have a sustained conversation with the mercurial Singhy.

The various names of the Sporting team members may require some explanation, especially when one player is referred to as the Son of God. The midfield battler Jesus was thus called because on his first training session with the club many years before he turned up wearing 'Jesus sandals' – not exactly suitable footwear for playing football. He did, however, impress enough to stay with the club, but the legacy of the sandals persisted, and to this day he has been known as Jesus. Front-man J.R. was so-called because of the fact that he felt it necessary to wear his 'I shot J.R.' T-shirt every time the team met up for training. Team hardman, Nutter, possessed a name that simply reflected his on-field philosophy, and Later, the left-back (and team prodigal son – a former regular whose career took him away from Coventry, but who remains loyal enough to rejoin the team whenever an exotic trip abroad is in the offing), had been known as Later for such a long time that no one actually bothered to find out his real name.

Like most top teams, Sporting had their own venerable midfield playmaking maestro, known by all as Chew. Again, Chew had become the accepted label used to address a footballer who reminded one of Glenn Hoddle, the player, but without the committed work-rate, and without the same level of sublime skill. Most of the other Sporting players had nicknames that were simple abbreviations of their full names, but each was a strong and complex character in his own right: goalkeeper Kash, a silver-haired man with agility that defied the colour of his barnet; sweeper Ranjit, a man who had the responsibility of taking the goalkicks because he was the only one who could kick the ball as far as the halfway line; centre-half Nuz, the team captain, a man of sleek dimensions that belied his mammoth food-guzzling capacity. His central-defensive partner Jas was not only a Sporting defender but also performed the role of the club secretary, a position of office that indulged his occasional cross-dressing whims. Pummie, the right-back, was Mr Dependable, a player who enjoyed playing in the team so much that he became its chief sponsor and even allowed them to stage home games in his back garden. Luckily enough his back garden was a full-size football pitch, with an adjoining leisure centre and bar. Supporting Chew and Jesus in midfield was Singhy (also known as Ray). Ray was a big man, a good footballer and a rather reserved character who only really seemed to relate to one or two of the more established Sporting stalwarts. Mo, J.R.'s striking partner, was the quiet man of the team, twin brother of Nuz, and a man who could send fear into the hearts of over-zealous beggars who asked him just once too often to appease his conscience by emptying his wallet.

These were the characters of the team who were about to face up to the challenge from Mahalpur College's first eleven. Pre-match introductions, presentations and ceremonies were duly seen through. Sporting's two strikers stood over the ball in the centre-circle. The match kicked-off.

Mahalpur, looking resplendent in their golden shirts and black shorts, stood out as an athletic, mobile and disciplined outfit. There was very little variation in the physical stature of the players, none was exceptionally tall or short, and, in somewhat of a contrast to a very small minority of the Sporting team, not one of the Mahalpurians was carrying any excess weight. A crowd of about three or four hundred spectators had gathered around the pitch to watch the match. Most were students of the college; some were locals who wanted to see the *Vileythi* (British) guys with the funny clothes and funny hairstyles tackle their town's finest. There was also a sizeable delegation of revered academics, local government officials and civic dignitaries, who imbued the occasion with a palpable degree of pomp and formality. This was no meaningless friendly, no exhibition game based on mutual appreciation and diplomatic indifference. Mahalpur College Football Club was an institution that was built on, and craved, success. It had produced outstanding football teams for over twenty years; this was a chance to show the visiting Indo-Brits, the hugely varied crowd and, most importantly, themselves just how good they really were. For Coventry Sporting, this game was the first of their tour. It was the one that would set the standard and set the morale for those to come; they were the contemporary bearers of the historic English footballing standard.

The early stages were marked by the usual struggle for any real sustained possession. Sporting, in their white shorts and blue and white diamond jerseys, mirrored the formation of the

Mahalpur team, both operating a sweeper system. Last-minute directions from the manager instructed the Sporting midfielders to get the ball forward as soon as possible, and not to aimlessly pass squarely along the centre-line. The plan was to upset the Mahalpur defenders with a direct and powerful game. The two centre-forwards, J.R. and Mo, were physically bigger and seemed stronger than Mahalpur's man-markers. At the back, the wing-backs would stay deep much of the time and push up into midfield when attacking. The two centre-halves and the sweeper were to defend as far forward as possible, closing down the space in which the opposition could play. On the face of it, this seemed like a defensive game-plan, and that's exactly what it was. The manager knew that he was without a few key players (those unable to travel to India) and that a couple of the players were still shaking off injuries, and the venerable age of one or two also contributed to the cautious strategy. Unfortunately it was obvious within minutes that Sporting were out-classed and out-gunned in most parts of the field. Players playing out of position were uncertain as to the precise requirements of their role. The left wing-back, Later, was too short of match fitness to play as an attacking winger, and thus that side was often exposed when Mahalpur had possession. This would lead to one of the central defenders running across as acting left-back leaving them short in the middle. The sweeper was not the most agile of defenders, and so two defenders would often be left facing four or even five opposition attackers. If Alan Hansen had been watching, we all know what he would have been saying. There were also problems in the midfield. Too many passes were going astray, the ball wasn't being played into the spaces where midfielders would have been expected to move into, but instead they were being forced to confine themselves to the centre-circle, pushing the ball across the line just as the manger had warned against. The two front-men were being marked out of the game. They did their best to find space, but when they received the ball to turn and run there were always at least one defender in front of them and another waiting further on. In all fairness, it wasn't simply the case that Sporting were not quite as disciplined as they should have been, or that they made too many basic errors. Mahalpur were a fast-moving, strong, dynamic team, in which each player understood his position and task, and all knew the style, principles and pattern of the team. This was an outfit that obviously trained and played together regularly, a team that was fit, athletic and tactically mature.

Sporting's sporadic attacks would break down almost on entry of the opponent's half, from whence the Mahalpur sweeper (who became respectfully known as Beckenbauer by the Sporting players) would initiate his team's offence. They passed the ball accurately to players who had the stamina to run into spaces, to run in and out of their assigned positions and, most devastatingly, they had a strike-force of outstanding pace. Normally when faced by such quality opposition, the opposing team could always employ the strong-arm tactics of 'getting stuck in'. In other words, tackle hard, be aggressive (but fair), close space and harry the opponents into making mistakes, into losing their shape and discipline. In essence, the stuff of 'traditional' English football. However, few of the Sporting players had the high level of match fitness necessary to sustain such full-on pressurizing, and, furthermore (and this came as a major shock to Sporting's footballers), amateur football in India is a semi-contact sport, which means that whilst you are allowed to tackle, you are only permitted to play the ball and not the man. Fifty-fifty challenges involving flying studs and desperate lunges are quite simply not a part of the game, and aggressive physical tackling is strictly outlawed. It was no surprise then that every time a Sporting player slid in to tackle an opponent, resulting in the opponent being felled, the referee immediately blew his whistle and gave the offender a stern reprimand for unnecessary aggression. On one such occasion, when the Sporting right-back Pummie made what would be a fair and strong tackle in any game in Britain, the Mahalpurian attacker could be heard – after picking himself up – haranguing the 'offender' in Punjabi, complaining, 'Brother, you really shouldn't go in like that, a person could very easily get injured in that way.' It seemed that it wasn't just the superiority of the Mahalpur team that was effecting Sporting's on-field difficulties; the local interpretation of soccer rules also lent considerable weight to the Coventrians' misery.

The first fifteen minutes of the match saw a number of surging attacks from Mahalpur, with their sweeper instrumental in both halves of the pitch. Kash, the Sporting keeper, had to be at his renowned best to prevent the Punjabi team from registering on the scoresheet: tipping over free-kicks from just outside the area, saving twenty-five-yard piledrivers and intercepting passes at the feet of Mahalpur strikers, passes that all too easily split the Sporting defence. Kash could not stave off the inevitable, though, and the parity the two teams shared was shattered when what looked to be a mishit cross from the left side evaded the clutching hands of the Coventry goalie. Mahalpur were ahead. The crowd shouted and applauded their team's goal – although largely indifferent to the associated passion of football supporting, the Mahalpur following made it patently clear that their real delight was in beating the *Vileythi* opposition. Mahalpur's lead was doubled minutes later when the number ten swept in a low cross from the edge of the box. Mahalpur were truly in the complete ascendancy and began to run Sporting ragged. Minutes before half-time a third goal was scored following more defensive uncertainty. As the referee blew for the half-time interval, the Sporting players looked bemused, exhausted and awe-struck. The manager had to do something.

Many of the players were feeling the effects of the afternoon heat; although it was late winter in India the temperature was still in the mid-twenties Celsius. The hard training sessions of the previous days were also affecting their performance. It was obvious that centre-back Jas was struggling with the thigh strain he picked up in Jullundhar, and he had to be replaced. The midfield also needed reinforcing and so Nutter was brought in to add some aggressive muscle. The formation was changed to a traditional 4–4–2, and along with the systematic alterations, the manager Jack also had to convey a refreshed mental approach to the players. They weren't fit enough to chase this team all over the park, they couldn't afford to make cavalier sorties forward and thus leave themselves exposed at the back. They had to play a zone-defence style of football, where the reduction and protection of particular spaces would stifle the opposition. With a change in personnel, a revised plan and the odd orange or two, Sporting took to the field for the second half.

As the second period kicked off, substitute Nutter immediately dived in on the Mahalpur central midfielder. The referee blew his whistle without hesitation and Nutter was surrounded by irate Mahalpur players. The diplomatic intervention of other Sporting players meant that the situation was cooled down and kept delicately amiable. This small incident did, however, spur Sporting on, and instilled at least some reticence into the hearts of Mahalpur. The second half proved to be a largely uneventful spectacle. Sporting were more organized and more disciplined, whilst Mahalpur had taken their foot off the accelerator pedal and were merely coasting through the remaining forty-five minutes, which was almost entirely played in the Sporting half, with Mahalpur having the lion's share of the possession. But a combination of better defending, good goalkeeping and less committed play meant that there was no addition to the score.

Sporting had few opportunities to find the back of the net themselves. Indeed, it was a point of celebration every time they managed to get out of their own half. There was no understating the superior level of application that Sporting showed after the half-time break; 3–0 down at the interval, it seemed that they were in for a hammering, but they steeled themselves and resisted the sometimes arrogant advances of

Mahalpur. As the referee blew for full-time, the scattered, lively congregations of spectators cheered and applauded both sets of players off the pitch.

After retiring to the changing rooms to freshen up, and in the case of centre-back Nuz, to have a gaping head wound stitched up with the needle and thread of a local doctor, sterility being a relative concept, the visitors took advantage of the refreshments and snacks that were courteously provided by the hosts. Then it was on to more formalities. The players of Coventry Sporting were invited to step up to the presentation stage and individually receive fine, boxed, cotton shirts from the college principal. It is an accepted Punjabi custom that shirts are given as presents at special occasions, such as weddings and birthdays. A large, impressive trophy was also presented to Sporting's captain as a gesture to show the college's appreciation for giving them a game. The Mahalpur players were next up to be rewarded by their principal. There was obviously a great deal of formal respect for the head of the college from the student-players. In turn they approached the principal, showed their respect via the traditional cultural practice of touching his feet, and moved away to the applause of watching female students and the entourage of dignitaries. As a gesture of goodwill, Sporting made the collective decision to hand their presents over to the Mahalpur players. Although much appreciated, Mahalpur insisted that Sporting should leave their college with some token of their hosts' appreciation. And so Coventry Sporting left with the shirts. They had played, and had been comprehensively beaten by a superior Indian football team. Was this a taste of things to come?

The team returned to their hotel base in Jullundhar, where they had a few days to recover from their opening game. This welcome leisure time was spent enjoying the hotel's complimentary facilities and sampling the culinary delights of the local Wimpy burger bar. It was, and is, testament to the unity and collective team spirit of Coventry Sporting that such an early setback hadn't severely dented their common morale. There had to be a period of reflection and projection, and differences of opinion were quickly and diplomatically resolved. It may have been the fact that they were all five thousand miles from home, away on a footballers' holiday, that could have resulted in their unified decision to forget troubles on the pitch, and all have a good time while they could. Nevertheless, the next match was only around the corner, and the initial loss had to be put behind them.

The next fixture was supposed to have been against a much vaunted team from Chabewa, but on arriving there the team were told that the match had been cancelled and that the tour organizer had already been notified. Naturally, the said organizer, Comrade, turned up a few minutes later to tell everyone that the game had been called off. Suffice to say that the players weren't overly chuffed at the way in which news of the cancellation had reached them.

Well, what were they to do now? No game to play, no real organization to be relied upon, and not the keenest of desires to spend another few days being paraded around home villages by proud relatives. One of the players was aware of a football tournament that was being held at a town near to his own. Maybe there was a chance that Sporting would be allowed to enter the competition and play a few competitive matches. Once more everyone crammed themselves back into the hired vans and jeeps, whose drivers were the only ones who seemed quite pleased with the way events were unfolding (they were getting paid by the mile). The tournament's venue was a town by the peculiar-sounding name (even in Punjabi) of Bunga. As they approached the vicinity, Sporting's spirits were lifted by banners that were strewn across the town's roads, promoting the competition. This was real, this was happening and they were there. Unfortunately, their impetuous optimism was misplaced. The tournament was taking place in Bunga, but it had been under way for a week, and they were at the semi-final phase. Late entrants, even those boasting some of the finest

English footballing talents, would not be admitted at such a stage in the competition. Alas, it seemed as though the gods were firmly against Sporting's quest for football challenges. It would have been very easy to have given up on the whole tour itself; a helpless sense of disillusionment, of betrayal and of apathy was beginning to envelop individual members of the team and starting to spread over the team as a whole. What was the point in continuing with a tour that was not exactly proving to be a great success? Since each player had spent so much money on air-fares and travel expenses, would it not be more beneficial to abandon the remainder of the tour and go sightseeing and have a leisurely time? This was a very real option and one that was seriously addressed. However, to walk away now would simply be a cowardly reaction to a few minor setbacks. Sporting were made of sterner stuff than that; they would carry on as planned and make the best of an unbecoming situation.

Football is a popular sport in the northern regions of the Punjab, and many schools and (especially) colleges have representative teams that play and train on grass pitches which are of a decent standard. With this in mind, a delegation of the senior Sporting players ventured into Bunga College to enquire as to whether they could train on their pitch that day. While the respected elders were embroiled in diplomatic negotiations inside the college, the younger players (and therefore those less likely to possess the persuasive qualities of their venerable counterparts), stood around outside talking things over. Unsurprisingly, the main topic of conversation remained the option of abandoning a sinking ship and doing a runner to the idyllic sandy lap of Goa. Unfortunately, integrity prevailed once more.

When the others returned from within the college, they brought with them some unexpected news. The college had agreed to allow Sporting to train on their pitch, but on one condition. As a token of appreciation for the use of their pitch, Bunga College would be most grateful for the opportunity to pit their soccer wits against those of their British guests. Now, the free use of a full-size pitch for training purposes was generous enough; the eager request for a proper game of football was an opportunity to get the whole tour back on track. And so it was agreed, Coventry Sporting would play Bunga College of the Punjab in two days' time.

Training at the college went without any major disasters. There were still one or two players who were as yet unable to shake off niggling injuries, and the extensive travelling and constant upheaval had left many of the players somewhat tired and not as full of zest as their manager would have liked. Come the day of the match, everyone seemed to be reasonably confident as to their chances of success. After all, this team was no Mahalpur. Yes, they might have younger, fitter players, keen to impress their coach and teachers, keen to show off their talents in front of a considerable crowd of fellow students (and the girls watching from high up in the classrooms), and perhaps they were most keen to stick it to the *Vileythi bandhar* (British monkeys – the English translation losing a degree of the intended ridicule), to beat them at their own game, literally.

Sporting were once more without the direction of their manager. Although he represented a focal point of guidance and instruction, they were experienced enough as players to be able to take control of the game themselves. In Jack's absence, the most experienced players – Chew, Kully and Kash – took charge. They picked the team and decided on the formation and tactics – Chew, being unable to play through injury, oversaw the team's performance from the sidelines. As the two sides posed for commemorative photographs, more and more students, pupils and locals began to gather around the pitch. Word had spread around of the big match in town, this had now become a major civic sporting occasion.

Bunga kicked off and immediately took possession of the ball. They played it around in midfield and then sprayed it wide to the wings, where they had exceptional pace on both flanks. Sporting were once again being shown to be collectively below match fitness, the absent players who couldn't make the trip were beginning to be missed and, although the senior players acquitted themselves admirably, there were always going to be occasions when speed and stamina would find them a little wanting. Any football team at a competitive level requires the use of a full squad to be adequately equipped for the rigours of a series of matches, especially an overseas tour. The first half saw wave upon wave of Bunga attacks. They seemed to be able to pierce the Sporting defence at will, and it was only the miraculous heroics of goalkeeper Kash that saw the teams coming in level at the end of the first half. Caretaker manager Chew would have to rally his troops.

Chew, by nature, was a laid-back type of character who wasn't the sort to tear into players, ranting and raving and reading the riot act. Renowned more for his Herculean alcohol threshold and piss-taking qualities rather than his managerial credentials, responsibility for the team was a charge that didn't necessarily correlate with his personal attributes. Yet in his own quiet and assured way he encouraged the players, saying that they were still very much in the game and that the midfield had to start taking greater control of things. The ball was being humped upfield too often, the midfielders had to get hold of the ball and pass it along the ground and wait for movement up front. Ironically enough, it was Chew himself who was just the type of player who could perform such a function, as the nominal midfield playmaker. The overcast, humid conditions were dehydrating, and so plenty of water was taken on. As the match resumed for the second half, Chew's instructions to the midfield seemed to have been heeded. Sporting began passing the ball around much more assuredly. They got to grips with the job in hand and looked to threaten the opposition's goal for the first time. Bunga, to their credit, were not overawed by Sporting's revitalized performance. In fact they matched them for attacking prowess and there were few signs of soccer naïveté amongst their players. They all seemed to know the tricks of the trade – pulling shirts, professional fouls, knowing how to win free-kicks – and once more it was the experience and technical expertise of Sporting's goalkeeper that prevented them from scoring. The large crowd were adding that vital sonic element by shouting and cheering and taking the mickey out of some of the Sporting players. One of the follicly challenged players had to endure continuous chants of '*Gunjoo. Gunjoo.*' ('Baldy. Baldy.') Grummun, who could only play with the support of a hairband, was mocked continuously for his flowing locks. It was very difficult for him to give his best while being constantly subjected to taunts that questioned his gender.

It seems that football supporters universally have to pick on the overweight, the hairless, the hair-stylists, the inept and the arrogant. But what separated these Punjabi-Indian footie fans from others was their generosity of spirit to support, cheer and deify one of the opposition's players. Bunga College supporters seemed to have become besotted by the breathtaking saves of Sporting's goalie Kash. At first they made comical remarks about his apparent age, commenting on the whiteness of his hair. Then they were lost in admiration of his goalkeeping exploits, and wildly cheered his every save. The colour of his hair remained a source of great amusement, however. They were not familiar with his name so they began to chant the name of the then Indian Prime Minister Dev Gaura instead – the Right Honourable Mr Gaura was another man of a certain age who had grey hair, although very little of it remained. A scything, satirical bunch, the Bunga students. So much so in fact that the sharpness of their wit was unleashed in the direction of the entire Sporting team as a whole. This was done behind the backs of those members of Sporting who were watching from the touchline. Comments about Sporting's footballing deficiencies were water off a duck's back for the team, but when the crowd's abuse began to assume a degree of personal vilification, something had to be done. Shouts of '*Eh Vileythi bandharanoo kithe khelnah ondha ya*' pierced the thickest of Sporting skins. On hearing 'these English monkeys don't know how to play this game' one of the English monkeys turned around and said, '*Sahnoo be Punjabi dhe vech makhol kudna ondha ya*' ('We know how to take the piss in Punjabi as well'). This retort was met with howls of laughter and cheers of mocking derision.

Although Sporting had a greater share of possession in the second half, they were unable to convert it into shots on goal. But as the half wore on, the Bunga players became more and more frustrated by their inability to find the back of the net. Just as it seemed that Sporting were going to hold on for a somewhat undeserved goalless draw, the Bunga left-winger crossed the ball into the box, it was flicked on by the centre-forward straight into the path of Singhy, who could do nothing but deflect the ball into his own net. And with only a few minutes of the match remaining, Sporting could do little to fight their way back into the game.

It wasn't all doom and gloom at the final whistle. As the two sets of players shook hands and expressed their mutual appreciation for a good game of football, undisputed man-of-the-match Kash was carried off the pitch on the shoulders of the Bunga supporters. This was truly a novel and exceptional football occurrence. These were shades of 1966, when the late Bobby Moore was paraded around Wembley by his fellow England players with the Jules Rimet Trophy held aloft. But here was a losing, although brilliant, goalkeeper perched not on the shoulders of his team-mates but on those of the opposing team's fans, who carried Kash all the way to the changing rooms. Some things were more important than winning or losing; the human spirit was capable of appreciating brilliance in many forms and from many sources. The unhealthy tribalism of foot-balling support was vanquished by a common human desire to rejoice in the majesty of a perfect, exhilarating moment. But would they have reacted in the same fashion if Kash had superbly saved a last-minute Bunga penalty that would have resulted in the home team's defeat?

Following the Bunga match, the Sporting team gathered outside the college to discuss the arrangements for the next game. This was to be played against a select eleven representing the village of Langheri, and there was a full five days before it was scheduled to take place. The Sporting players decided that they would split up and all do their own thing. Some returned to their home villages to spend more time with family, others made the decision to travel to the more cosmopolitan reaches of northern India to indulge their urbane Western decadence, but a small group of them chose to take a brief departure from the playing side of football, and elected instead to go and watch an exhibition match that was being staged in the Punjabi industrial district of Phagwara.

Coventry Sporting's footballing trip to India coincided with the inaugural year of the country's first semi-professional football league. Sponsored by Dutch electronics giant Philips, the Philips League represented the first real organized soccer structure that professionalized competitive football across the whole of India. The Punjab boasted one of the new league's most accomplished and most established clubs, JCT Mills. This team were sponsored by, owned by and bore the name of Phagwara's premier industrial exponent, Jagjit Cotton Textiles Mills. JCT Mills represented a massive source of revenue for the region, providing employment for thousands of locals as well as serving as a benefactor to many local institutions such as schools, temples and charities. The football team was another by-product of the mill's magnitude and power. It could be regarded as a toy of the rich, a permissible hobby for those who could afford it. In fact, it is much more serious than such flippancy might suggest.

The JCT Mills team employs professionals to play football to the highest level possible under the guidance of a full-time coach and associated staff. JCT were not an exception in the Philips League. The team they would be facing in this exhibition match hailed from Bombay, and went under the nominal banner of Mahindra Jeeps, one of India's largest automobile manufacturers, based in Bombay, and sponsors of a football team that contained many local players. All professional teams sport the names of their club sponsors on the fronts of their football shirts – Manchester United have Sharp, Glasgow Rangers have McEwan's and Juventus have Sony – but how many teams actually embody and operate under the very name of the sponsoring bodies themselves? Not many come to mind. It's like Rupert Murdoch starting his own professional football club and calling it News Group International.

JCT Mills were the home team in this match, and so the game was to be played at their home ground, situated, conveniently enough, at the rear of the mill complex. There was a full-size football pitch with a main grandstand to one side and tiered concrete blocks on another side, where spectators could sit and watch the game. The two ends were left open, although there were still facilities for supporters to sit or stand there during the match. One of the Sporting players was quite familiar with the JCT Mills coach, so much so in fact that the Sporting lads who went to watch the game were given free tickets and a prime vantage point from which to spectate. The ground had an unofficial capacity of around twenty thousand, but on this occasion the estimated attendance was in the region of around eight or nine thousand people. The Mahindra team was made up entirely of Indian players. JCT, however, had players of Indian descent alongside two Gurkhas from the northern most climbs of India, and three Nigerian footballers, who plied their trade in the Philips League whilst awaiting interest from European or Japanese clubs. The average weekly wage for these players was approximately £150–£200, which may not sound like an awful lot in comparison to the colossal salaries of European footballers, but in India £150 a week means that a person can live a life of relative luxury.

The stakes in the exhibition match were high. The winning team would receive the staggering amount of £17,000 with

£2000 to the scorer of each goal. Players from both teams were aware of the possible bounty that awaited them, and so one would assume that they were going to approach the game with great verve and disciplined application. As is often the case with exhibition or testimonial matches, though, the match was more of an opportunity for players to show off their skills and perform tricks that would not be possible in a full competitive confrontation.

The game was played at a rather leisurely pace, with the home team almost totally dominating possession. Their players were taking on three or four Mahindra defenders at a time, dribbling their way through with a great deal of skill and flair. One of the Nigerian JCT forwards beat three defenders before outrageously outwitting the keeper by flicking the ball over his own head, over the stranded goalie, and then juggling the ball into the net on his knee. That was two thousand quid in the bank for him. The few thousand spectators made the event into a festive occasion. Most of the crowd weren't necessarily ardent JCT Mills fans, but they were football enthusiasts who enjoyed the game being played with a sense of creative flair and impudent spontaneity. The watching Sporting players were treated to a footballing spectacle that was high on entertainment, but low on competitive vigour. It ended 5–1 to JCT, and the climactic award ceremony saw the outstanding Nigerian JCT striker, Stephen Abarowei, receive the Man-of-the-Match prize. After the match, the Sporting players were invited to meet up with JCT's coach, Sukhvinder Singh.

Sukhvinder, an amiable thirtysomething, spent the first hour quizzing his British guests on the latest developments in the English game. He professed his allegiances to be with Manchester United, but not untypically spoke of having relations in Wolverhampton, and therefore harboured a distant, almost forced affinity with Wolves. His awareness and knowledge of English football did somewhat surprise the Sporting players. He welcomed the National League as a long overdue but essential ingredient in the successful future development of the Indian game. A view expressed in some quarters of Indian football is that the influx of foreign players would ultimately be to the detriment of homegrown talent, a familiar argument across a number of footballing nations. JCT Mills, however, have the reputation of being India's most prolific acquirers of non-Indian playing staff. Although coach Sukhvinder acceded to the benefits of greater encouragement of homegrown players: 'I would not be against the idea of putting a cap on the numbers of foreigners. There are a few teams, like Salgaocar and Air India, who keep faith with only Indian players. Another thing you have to remember is that not all foreign players are better than our own players. As Indian players' standards improve then the standard of the foreign players coming into our football will also need to be higher, otherwise we will not sign them.'

But overall Sukhvinder was convinced that India was preparing itself for a healthier footballing future. He then wished the visiting players all the best for their forthcoming matches, and proceeded to join the rest of the JCT Mills team for their victory celebrations.

The sublime extravagance of this game would be in stark contrast to the harsh reality of Sporting's next challenge against a hand-picked team from the town of Langheri.

Langheri isn't renowned for its footballing pedigree, and so this fixture could have been regarded as the least difficult match on the tour. But true to Coventry Sporting's misfortunes, the odds for achieving some sort of success, even in this game, were drastically reduced when it became clear that the five-day interlude between matches had resulted in a number of players deserting the team. The sights and soccer of Langheri were not appealing enough for certain Sporting players to interrupt their hedonistic excursions to more exotic destinations.

Another major obstacle in the way of a much needed Sporting victory was the line-up of the Langheri team itself. The town's mayor (the *sarpanch*) was a personal friend of Comrade and so had requested that Sporting should play against a select eleven that would represent his town. Comrade wasn't one to refuse the requests of close associates, especially those in positions of political influence. The eleven players who were selected to play for Langheri were a blend of former Langheri greats, current favourites and up-and-coming young superstars. This was the naïve, lightweight, rural football team that Sporting would be facing. The pitch that was to be used for the game was at the rear of the local primary school, so the arrival of the *Vileythi* brigade was a cause of great excitement and amusement for the young children. Having arrived early, the players had the opportunity to sit in the small grandstand in the shade and chat to the eager youngsters who had gathered around them. The light-hearted banter that the players exchanged with the friendly Langheri juniors belied the worrying fact that they had only eleven players to use in the forthcoming football match. This eleven consisted of three reserve players approaching the age of 40, three players with injuries that would normally prevent them from taking part even in light training and the manager Jack, who hadn't donned his boots in earnest for more years than he would care to remember. Even one S. Johal was called upon to be a substitute.

The game started in a tentative mode with both teams playing cautiously, trying to suss out the opposition's formation, strengths and weaknesses, and the best way of unlocking defences. Within the first five minutes, Langheri had discovered the key to break Sporting open. What was this intricate, highly specialized tactical advance they deployed? Well, they pumped the ball forward to the right flank, where the flying winger would cross the ball into the box through the flapping arms of the Sporting goalkeeper, and perfectly on to the head of the completely unmarked centre-forward. This was a game-plan straight out of the Graham Taylor school of football. The match was but ten minutes gone when Sporting found themselves 2–0 down, both goals scored in identical fashion. Super-keeper

Kash had gone from hero to villain, from the sublime to the embarrassingly ridiculous. Worse was to follow. Ten minutes later, another Langheri raid, this time through the middle, sliced through the Sporting defence. The move culminated with the man-mountain that was the Langheri sweeper (a giant of a man with great technical ability for a guy of his size) rounding the keeper to slot the ball calmly into the back of the net. This gave rise to great applause from the flattering crowd of schoolkids and the obligatory local dignitaries. The third goal induced a greater intensity of joyous approval because the scorer, the sturdy sweeper, was the son of the mayor. Three down and we were only halfway through the first half; the Mahalpur nightmare was visiting the Sporting subconscious once more. A rout was most definitely on the cards.

But on this tour Coventry Sporting were a team that were only stirred when confronted by a desperate situation. This was just such an occasion. Somehow, and not without a great deal of hard work, luck and polite indifference on the part of their opponents, Sporting managed to see the remainder of the game through without conceding any more goals – they didn't score any goals themselves, but that was a forgivable deficiency in light of their extenuating circumstances. The now customary post-match award ceremony proved to be somewhat of a farcical event for all concerned. The Langheri fixture was one of the better-organized matches. Their officials had been given a full list of Sporting's first-team players who would almost definitely take part. The names on this list were then inscribed on to specially designed trophies that were to be presented to the teams. The mayor began to call out the name on the trophy, and the Sporting players would look at each other thinking, Well, that player isn't actually here, so which one of us is going forward to claim the prize? There was a rather frightening lack of hesitation or apologetic regret in the eager acceptance of trophies with other people's names on them. But this had been the greatest test of their beleaguered squad. Stripped to the bare minimum, they were forced to field a team that they normally wouldn't put out in the local park against 9-year-olds. At least they had fulfilled their obligation to play the match; now they had only one game left to go.

The players missing at Langheri would be back for the last fixture in Barnala, but would they be willingly accepted back into the fold? Did the Sporting spirit possess enough substance to provide its team with the will and desire to complete the tour successfully? With a few days to prepare for their final challenge, some of the players decided to indulge in a rather novel form of big-match preparation. A jeep and driver were booked for the following morning's journey south to Delhi.

In keeping with the salient theme of the India tour to date, the excursion to Delhi not only proved the old adage that 'if it can go wrong it will go wrong', but illustrated another, somewhat more obscure axiom: 'no matter how bad things get, they can always get far worse'. This was evident before the trip to Delhi even began. Having realized the extent of the financial expenditure involved in such a sojourn, most of the players refused the tempting break and headed back to the lap of their families. This left a small party of three Sporting players and myself brave enough to embark upon an adventure that defied all known laws of probability. On arriving in Delhi, we were taken to a hotel by our driver. The driver had brought us to this establishment without any error and without any consultation with his passengers. He assured us that it was a place of great repute, great value and mostly reliable. What he failed to divulge, something that we deduced for ourselves, was that he was paid a commission for every guest that he could bring to the hotel. We had been done once again, but by now we were beginning to accept it as a vacational hazard.

We decided that we would lock up our bags in our rooms (keeping money, passports and tickets with us) and then proceed to sample the nocturnal pleasures of one of the world's most famous cities. Having found a taxi, we asked the driver where we could go to enjoy ourselves. Were there any bars or clubs that we could go to, somewhere we could have a good time? Somewhat confused by his passengers' strange Punjabi brogue, the driver asked for clearer direction as to the desired destination. One of the eager players responded rather candidly in English, 'We want to go to a nightclub. You know, club. Music, dancing, girls, drink. You know?' From his amused shrieks of 'Oh, yes, yes' it seemed that the driver had understood the broken, back-seat instructions. So when he dropped the five of us off at a brightly lit establishment, set somewhat back from the main road, we thought that we were in for a good night. We paid our entrance fee outside the club, and sat on the covered terrace, where other people were also waiting to go in. Then we noticed a discreet sign that had 'show-times' posted up on it, indicating that the next and final 'show' was only a matter of minutes away. It also became apparent that we were amongst a lot of other men ... in fact, only men, of various ages but of similar, flawed rectitude. If the other obvious signs hadn't made it quite apparent that the Sporting players and I were not at the sort of nightclub that we expected, then the name of the establishment confirmed all our worst fears, and it has to be said (as Freud would insist) our unspoken, subconscious desires. We were at a sleazy, backstreet strip joint. The taxi driver had mistaken our meaning of a club that involved dancing, music and members of the opposite sex. It was too late to leave and we found ourselves entering into the main hall. All the 'guests' were searched by stern-looking security officials. Just before the Sporting party approached the door, a group of smart-suited, slick men walked straight to the front of the queue and stood squarely in front of the doormen. Thinking that a major brawl was about to commence, we brave Brits stepped back. Our fears were unfounded, for the doormen bowed in front of the well-attired guests, and touched their feet as a mark of respect. These guys were the local mob.

Sitting in the club, gangsters to one side, drunken perverts to another, we considered leaving before the start of the 'show'. However, once inside the iniquitous hall of undress, no guest was allowed to leave. Everything was seemingly done behind closed, and firmly locked, doors. We then sat through a procession of erotic dancers, some old, others young, but all made to suffer the indignity of drunken individuals shouting and jeering and de-humanizing the women who were obviously part of a profession that circumstances had forced them into. All of us felt ashamed and uneasy. When we were finally allowed to leave, we were the first to walk out and be swamped by eager taxi drivers, all hell-bent on securing our fare. We chose to travel in an 'auto', a moped-like three-wheeled vehicle designed to carry four passengers and the driver, and a much more economical way to get around town. But this particular auto already had one other passenger in the front, which meant that all five of us had to cram ourselves into the back.

Having assured his newly procured passengers that he knew precisely where the hotel was, the driver proceeded in getting everyone quite lost. As he circled the same block for the seventh time in a vehicle that was carrying twice its own weight, he foolishly pulled up at a police kiosk, where he approached the two officers who sat awaiting some kind of action. Generally speaking, of course, officers of the law are necessary and mostly welcome figures of authority that imbue people (particularly those alien to any given environment) with a sense of assurance and confidence. So the sight of Delhi's local constabulary eased the growing diffidence that we were all experiencing. The two officers saw that the auto was carrying an excessive load, and moved towards its passengers. They quizzed the driver as to his professional credentials, wanting proof of his official status. Before he could respond, he was smacked on the legs with a cane by one of the officers. The others then began to ask us questions as to where we had come from, who we were and where we were going. It was a very tense and intimidating situation. It was obvious that these particular police officers were purely in search of monetary appeasement. They were going to question, harass and even beat us if we didn't catch their illicit drift and grease their palms. Thankfully this degenerate duo were not wholly typical of the Indian police force. (It only takes a tiny minority of dishonourable individuals to sully the name of an entire organization.) As one officer repeatedly beat the driver with his cane, the other asked us to get out of the vehicle. Knowing that we could be taken for every rupee we had, or suffer a beating, we decided to make a break for it, and did a runner. We ran like we've never run before, not knowing where we were going and not even daring to look back. Miraculously the frantic, panic-driven fleeing had brought us to the vicinity of our hotel. Once inside we refused to sleep for fear that the police may have tracked us down. The next morning we took the first train back to the Punjab. Delhi was a misadventure that could have devastated the whole trip; but it was football that reinstated our faith in the people of India.

The 1997 Coventry Sporting tour of the Punjab had reached its concluding leg. The team were off to the town of Barnala. Barnala was in fact eight hours away by van, and so Sporting left their base in Phagwara the day before the match, leaving them enough time to adequately prepare for the game. Cramped into the space of two vans, the players arrived in the host town just as evening began to fall. Getting to the town was the easy part, actually finding the college where they were staying proved to be more challenging. One after the other, team members claimed to know the precise route to the college, and one after the other they all proceeded to confuse the van drivers into states of near hysteria. Eventually, after visiting almost every other place in the town, we reached Barnala College. If the players had previously experienced a sense of detachment from the home teams they played against, not being familiar with the areas or the people or the local history, then this last stop on the tour would prove to be the most rewarding on many accounts.

Sporting were greeted by a whole welcoming committee of college representatives, and after being shown to the dormitory where they would be spending the night, they were taken on a guided tour of the campus and all its facilities. This was followed by a personally guided tour of the town of Barnala itself, taking in the wonderfully colourful bazaars, the local temples and the rural splendour of the region – a great treat, made all the more surreal by the mysticism of the twilight hour.

If the players were gratified by the hospitality shown to them thus far by the Barnalians, they hadn't yet seen the half of it. When they got back to the dorms, they found, laid out before them, a magnificent feast fit for a medieval banquet. The quality and variety of the food was obligingly supplemented by a plentiful supply of cold beer and malt whisky. It was extremely generous of the consummate hosts to lay on such a splendid spread, but Sporting had a football match to play in the morning, a very important football match, the final game of their hitherto unsuccessful tour. Being a team with a strict professional outlook, the Sporting players thanked their hosts most earnestly for the trouble they had gone to in order to make them feel welcome, but had to point out that they would be partaking of a rather strenuous game of soccer in the morning, and therefore would have to limit themselves to no more than seven or eight litre-bottles of lager each, just to wash down the tender pieces of tandoori chicken, followed by the odd bottle or two or three of fine malt whisky. Then the next surprise of the evening was presented before them. A group of college professors and students were the resident designated bards, using poetry and song to impart the folk traditions, myths and moments in local history that distinguished Barnala on the Punjabi map. As the bards and accompanying minstrels informatively entertained their guests, the guests themselves were taking full advantage of the free food, and even fuller advantage of the free alcohol. Indeed, one of the Sporting entourage, Tari, felt comfortable enough to stand up and join in with the singing professors, with his own version of a classic folk song that became somewhat confused in a barely comprehensible rendition. Cheered on by his equally intoxicated team-mates, the Sporting songster continued with his cacophonous verse until the point when his glass became empty and a refill was in order. This was a fantastic way to round off the tour. After the troubles and disorganization that had disrupted the projected smooth course of the trip, a night of great food, song, music, mutual appreciation and free-flowing liquor more than made up for previous misadventures.

After the singing and drinking was over and the players were left in the dorm to get a good night's sleep, the fun and games began once more. The early hours of the morning were spent dragging unsuspecting individuals (it's always the ones who want to get to sleep, who try to stay out of the fooling around and pretend to be deep in rest) out of bed and throwing them on the floor with most of the team jumping on their backs. Such foolishness eventually wound to a predictably antagonistic conclusion, but not before the Sporting collective spirit had been restored.

The bright and early morning brought with it a collective hangover: quick washes, numerous cups of tea, and the repeated request, 'Who's got the paracetamol?' Amazingly enough, the players seemed remarkably fresh and alive for a group of drunken, over-fed, sleepless louts. The pitch where the game was to be played was right next to the dorm where Sporting had spent the night, and so they could get kitted up and virtually walk straight out on to the playing field. As they strode out on to the pitch they were confronted by the biggest crowd of any game they had played on the tour to date. Obviously this fixture had been very effectively organized and promoted. There were students, professors, town officials, parents, kids and interested local folk who had gathered around the pitch, closing it off, giving the illusion of an enclosed tiny green space.

Barnala College were a very respectable football team, with talented players who could all last the full ninety minutes. What's more, they had the reputation of being very difficult to beat, with opponents finding it difficult to score against them. But even with such a pedigree, Barnala were not in the same class as Mahalpur, and Sporting had kept them to a mere three-goal haul. Before the kick-off, the Sporting players were given a final team talk. Their manager assembled his troops, huddled them together and emphasized his desire for the team to play as a united whole. Each player was to play for his fellow team-mates, all differences were to be put aside – those missing from the last match were just as much a part of Coventry Sporting as others – and this was the last chance for Sporting to show just what they were capable of. They were to go out there and enjoy themselves; they may not get the opportunity to play competitive football on another continent again. With that, Sporting took to the field.

Straight from kick-off they went on the attack. The team were full of a new vigour and intensity that was missing in all the previous matches. They passed the ball around sharply and accurately, moving into space, running effectively off the ball and playing with controlled skill and pace. The first quarter of an hour was all Sporting. In this period, they created a number of scoring chances, but were unable to convert them. Half-time was approaching and Jack was shouting from the touchline for his players to remain focused, to keep their shape and to be patient. For once his instructions were heeded. A thrilling move from one end of the pitch to the other ended with the striker Mo smashing a right-foot volley high into the Baranala net. Sporting were in the lead for the first time on the tour.

The score remained 1–0 up to the half-time interval. During the break, Sporting's manager made two substitutions, just so the other players could have their final experience of Indian football. The second half began where the first had left off, with Sporting very much in the ascendancy. Barnala seemed to be carrying their gracious hospitality on to the pitch; this wasn't the team that were reputed to be mean and tough to break down. They were scarcely getting a touch of the ball. Sporting were playing the game at a leisurely pace, seemingly well within themselves. The only fear with games such as this was the onset of complacency, and in time-honoured tradition Sporting fell foul of that very affliction. They were in cruise mode when the ball was carelessly given away in midfield. With the defence unprepared for an attack at that point, Sporting were caught short at the back – the full-backs had pushed up too far forward too early, and so left the central defenders exposed. An incisive pass from the right edge of the box was neatly controlled and slotted home by the unmarked Barnala centre-forward. The one match that Sporting had looked as though they were in charge of had been turned right around.

Barnala now came streaming forward, sensing an air of dejection in the hearts of the Coventry players. Every one of Sporting's outfield players was in his own half, desperately defending their goal. There was no doubting the commitment of the team, to a man they tackled and chased back and harried the Barnala players, throwing themselves into the path of threatening goalbound shots. Kash was forced back to his brilliant best to maintain Sporting's parity with their insurgent opponents. With two minutes left before full-time, Barnala's centre-back unleashed an almighty shot from fully twenty-five yards out. The ball had beaten Kash, who could only watch as it sailed over his head. For those brief nanoseconds, from the point the ball left the boot of Barnala's stopper, to the moment when it passed the helpless Kash, time seemed to elapse in slow motion. The Sporting bench watched as the ball, having beaten the keeper, smacked the top side of the crossbar and flew behind for a goalkick. Sporting could breathe again. Straight from the goalkick the ball was pumped forward into the Barnala box, one of the very few occasions in the previous twenty minutes when Sporting had made an excursion into the opposition's penalty area. As he attempted to clear the ball from the danger zone, the same Barnala defender wildly hacked at the ball and sliced it over the byline for a last-minute corner to Sporting. This was the ultimate throw of the Sporting dice, and so Kash was ordered to join his team-mates in the Barnala box in an all-out attempt to achieve that elusive victory on Indian soil.

As the ball was swung in, Kash rose to head it but he jumped too early, and the ball flew over his head. It landed, though, at the feet of Nuz, the team skipper. He hit the ball low and hard into the penalty area. It seemed to pass through the flailing legs of a hundred players before injured centre-back Jas stuck out his right foot to deflect the ball into the goal. Sporting had scored. The final whistle blew. In a game that would be befitting of a Hollywood movie, Coventry Sporting had escaped to victory in the most dramatic fashion. After all they had endured, the long journeys, the crazed coach drivers, the superior football teams, this victory tasted of the sweetest juice of the rarest sugar cane.

Sitting in the airport lounge awaiting the long haul back home, the Sporting party observed with more than a passing interest the football headlines showing that JCT Mills were the inaugural winners of the National League. News of the triumph prompted a cause for celebration, for an affinity with the Punjabi team had been superficially formed. The celebrations were somewhat tempered, however, on discovery that JCT Mills' prospects for the following season would be adversely affected by a likely exodus of star players. Among those pledging loyalties elsewhere were Baichung Bhutia, the current young star of Indian football, and Tejinder Kumar, the inspirational playmaker and team captain. Nigerian striker Abarowei was also rumoured to be dissatisfied with the restricted social life of Indian football and the non-decadent ways of Indian culture.

The Sporting players themselves were beginning to be consumed by a sorrowful regret at having to leave their meandering adventure behind. It wasn't just the separation from family members who remained in the idyllic rural villages; it wasn't just the fact that they had a wonderful time playing football and enjoying the thrills and challenges that they encountered; what they had on this trip was a common unity, a shared experience of India that was special to them all. It was an experience that would live in the hearts, minds and souls of these players beyond their secular lives, an elusive sensation that could not be replicated back home in England. The sound of a certain song, the mention of a certain place, or the telling of a particular joke would invoke the sacred memory of a month-long footballing tour of the Punjab. A tour that had become inscribed upon the hearts of those fortunate enough to have been part of the whole escapade.

Britain's Asians had taken the most British of games back to their ancestral homeland and attempted to use it as a means of expelling distances or differences between themselves and their Indian national peers. For them, football was an everyday component of their very existence, a cultural phenomenon that they were mostly born into and conditioned into treating as one of the major markers of the social order in which they operated. For the indigenous Indians of the Punjab, football was an acquired skill, a learned form of social and physical activity, and an assumed passion. They may not have spent hours screaming from the terraces of Highfield Road, or crying in front of the television screen at their team's defeat, but their appreciation and aptitude for the sport were the equal or the better of their British counterparts. Mahalpur College weren't the winners; Bunga College or Langheri weren't the winners; Coventry Sporting weren't even the winners. It wasn't about winners or losers. The whole tour was about winning the respect of those you played against – whether they were indigenous Indians or British-Asians – the gaining of mutual understanding and appreciation. The only losers in this event were ignorance and prejudice.

Coventry Sporting: British–Asian ambassadors for an English game in India. When points of difference seemed to override the obvious point of commonality, football was the common currency that united the distant cousins. Somewhere here, there's a valuable lesson that the world may be wise to learn.